THE SINS OF BROTHER CURTIS

A STORY OF BETRAYAL, CONVICTION,
AND THE MORMON CHURCH

LISA DAVIS

Scribner

New York London Toronto Sydney

Scribner
A Division of Simon & Schuster, Inc.
1230 Avenue of the Americas
New York, NY 10020

First Scribner hardcover edition March 2011

SCRIBNER and design are registered trademarks of The Gale Group, Inc.,
used under license by Simon & Schuster, Inc., the publisher of this work.

For information about special discounts for bulk purchases, please contact
Simon & Schuster Special Sales at 1-866-506-1949 or business@simonandschuster.com.

The Simon & Schuster Speakers Bureau can bring authors to your live event.
For more information or to book an event contact the Simon & Schuster Speakers
Bureau at 1-866-248-3049 or visit our website at www.simonspeakers.com.

Designed by Daniel Lagin

Manufactured in the United States of America

1   3   5   7   9   10   8   6   4   2

ISBN 978-1-4165-9103-0
ISBN 978-1-4516-1285-1 (ebook)

PHOTOGRAPH CREDITS:
Images 1–3 and 4: Photos courtesy of the Michigan State Archives
Images 5, 11, and 16: Photos courtesy of Keith Webb
Images 6 and 17: Photos courtesy of Stanley Saban, Jr.
Images 7, 8, 10, and 12: Photos by Lisa Davis
Image 9: Photo by Brad Dosland; yarn dog courtesy of Keith Webb
Image 14: Photo by Ellen M. Banner/*The Seattle Times*
Image 18: Photo by Leah Hogsten/*The Salt Lake Tribune*

For the survivors. It wasn't your fault.

AUTHOR'S NOTE

The account that follows is a true story. The names and identifying characteristics of the Johnson, Penrose, and Carter families have been changed. Their stories and all quotes are factual, however.

Wherever possible, I have relied on recorded transcripts and documents to depict events accurately. To the extent possible, I confirmed firsthand accounts of events with others who were present. All quotes that are not part of the historical record are taken from my interviews.

I am not, nor have I ever been, a member of the Church of Jesus Christ of Latter-day Saints. All information on the Mormon religion comes from my research and interviews.

Child sexual abuse is a horrible crime that can have devastating long-term psychological and emotional effects. There are many ways to get help. If you or someone you know is the victim of abuse, please contact your local police. Assistance in dealing with past abuse is also readily available. Several national organizations provide resources and referrals, among them Childhelp USA: National Child Abuse Hotline, 800-422-4453, www.childhelpusa.org; Stop It Now!

888-773-8368, www.stopitnow.org; Rape, Abuse & Incest National Network (RAINN), 800–656-4673, www.rainn.org; Adult Survivors of Child Abuse, www.ascasupport.org.

PRIMARY CHARACTERS

Franklyn R. Curtis—Perpetrator

Jeremiah Scott—Victim, plaintiff

Sandra Scott—Mother of Jeremiah Scott, briefly both a plaintiff and defendant

Gregory Foster—Former bishop of Jeremiah Scott and family, defendant

Church of Jesus Christ of Latter-day Saints—Defendant

ATTORNEYS FOR THE PLAINTIFF

Timothy Kosnoff (Bellevue, WA)

Joel Salmi (Bellevue, WA)

Gary Rhoades (Dunn, Carney, Allen, Higgins & Tongue, Portland)

James Hillas (Dunn, Carney, Allen, Higgins & Tongue)

David Slader (Portland)

Jeffrey Anderson (Minneapolis)

Dayna Christian (Law Offices of David Slader, Portland)

OTHER PLANTIFF TEAM MEMBERS

Linda Walker—Researcher, founder of Child Protection Project

Lisa Thomas—Paralegal at Dunn, Carney, Allen, Higgins & Tongue

Dawn Krantz-Watts—Paralegal at Law Offices of David Slader

Bill Anton—Private investigator for the plaintiffs

Ginger Goforth Simmons—Private investigator for the plaintiffs, employee of Bill Anton

ATTORNEYS FOR DEFENDANT, CHURCH OF JESUS CHRIST OF LATTER-DAY SAINTS

Stephen English (Bullivant, Houser, Bailey, Portland)

David Ernst (Bullivant, Houser, Bailey)

Randy Austin (Kirton & McConkie, Salt Lake City)

Von Keetch (Kirton & McConkie)

Scott Brooksby (Bullivant, Houser, Bailey)

ATTORNEYS FOR DEFENDANT GREGORY FOSTER

Jeffrey Kilmer (Kilmer, Voorhees & Laurick, Portland)

Janet Knauss (Kilmer, Voorhees & Laurick)

Pamela Stendahl (Kilmer, Voorhees & Laurick)

JUDGES

Hon. Ann Aiken, U.S. District Court, Oregon, 1998; also served as mediator (with Hon. Lyle Velure) in Multnomah County, Oregon, Superior Court, 2001

Hon. Joseph Ceniceros, Multnomah County, Oregon, Superior Court (until March 2000)

Hon. Ellen Rosenblum, Multnomah County, Oregon, Superior Court (after March 2000)

Hon. Lyle Velure, mediator (with Hon. Ann Aiken) in Multnomah County, Oregon, Superior Court, 2001

Hon. Emmanuel Vuvunas, Racine County, Wisconsin, Circuit Court

THE SINS OF BROTHER CURTIS

PROLOGUE
PHOENIX, ARIZONA

———

1999

Tim Kosnoff stepped off a plane in Phoenix on a summer after-noon in 1999 and was immediately hit with blast-furnace-like heat, followed by the chill of an over-air-conditioned terminal, and then the furnace again outside. The temperature had climbed well over 100 degrees. He'd come from the cool, misty green of Seattle, where he made his living as a lawyer. He might as well have landed on another planet. And he was already sweating by the time he found his way to a rental car, adequate but affordable, and settled in for the drive north. Traffic thinned as Kosnoff navigated through the massive tangle of freeways around Phoenix and headed toward Prescott. He passed settlements of beige and pink stucco homes, a sea of tiled roofs interspersed with more and more desert landscape until there was only giant cactus and red rock, truck stops and gas stations. He stared out the windshield and thought about what lay ahead. If things went well, the man he'd come to see could make a big difference in Kosnoff's case, and he badly needed a break.

Tim Kosnoff was the man on the ground in this project. He worked the phones, following one clue after another, painstakingly unwinding the details of each mystery that presented itself, sometimes to ridiculous lengths. He hunted witnesses relentlessly. He was the curator of a collection of detailed facts that spanned a century. These were the sorts of jobs generally handed off to investigators or associates in the legal business. But staff was a luxury. He'd already given up his office and begun working from home to save money. Besides, Tim Kosnoff liked being in the trenches. He liked knowing things firsthand. He had always made a point of looking a witness in the eye before he got into the courtroom.

The beige desert was increasingly interrupted with green. Prescott Valley runs through the central part of the state, home to mountainous terrain, pine trees, and snow in the winter. Economically, the area was booming, a recent target of Californians who could sell their homes and build small mansions in Arizona with money left over. The development had brought with it uninspired malls, colossal grocery stores, and near-constant controversy as builders encroached farther into the desert with each passing month.

Manny Saban, the man Kosnoff was on his way to visit, had benefited from the real estate boom. He worked for contractors as a house painter and lived in an outpost called Humboldt, a few miles off the main highway that heads into Prescott. There, he shared a trailer with his girlfriend and their baby son. Kosnoff had spoken to Manny on the phone a few times before embarking on this journey, and they were scheduled to convene with other lawyers the following day in order to memorialize the man's story in a deposition. But Kosnoff wanted to meet with his witness first, to get a better feel for who the guy was and what he was likely to say.

Their conversation had been a long time coming. The first time Kosnoff called, Manny hung up on him, something that was getting to be a regular occurrence with people attached to this case. The lawyer's monologue and the response it elicited were always variations on the same theme.

"Is this Manny Saban?" Kosnoff had said back in that first call.

"Yeah."

"Hi, Manny. You don't know me. My name is Tim Kosnoff, and I'm a lawyer in Seattle."

"What do you want?"

"Well, I don't quite know how to tell you this, but I represent a guy named Jeremiah Scott who is suing the Mormon church . . ."

Silence.

"Do you remember a man named Frank Curtis?" Kosnoff continued.

"Yes, I do," Manny said.

Kosnoff had gotten out another couple of questions before Manny ended the conversation.

"I don't have anything to say. Good-bye."

Manny hadn't been ready for a yank back to the old neighborhood—the friends, the apartments, the church, all the things he'd left behind a very long time ago in another state. This unspoken piece of his past, this thing Manny had shared with only a handful of people, was tossed through the phone at him by a stranger, a lawyer.

Ultimately, curiosity had gotten the better of Manny and he'd called Kosnoff back. And now here they were. Kosnoff left the highway and made his way to the address written in his notes. He stepped out into the dust kicked up by the car. Manny was at the door and ushered him into the small trailer, thick with cigarette smoke. At thirty-two, Manny was a short, beefy man with a tough-looking exterior. Kosnoff was aware of the outstanding warrants from Oregon that highlighted Manny's lengthy career of largely alcohol-fueled crime, the most felonious of which was stealing a car.

Manny was like so many others involved in this thing. Pieces of a puzzle of human wreckage that Kosnoff had committed countless hours and borrowed money to solving. He was determined to see how it ended, though he sometimes thought it never would. Regardless, there was no stopping now. He was in too far. Somewhere along the way his pursuit had ceased to be about winning a lawsuit. It had become an epic crusade for justice.

PORTLAND, OREGON

1976

I

The basketball hoop in front of Billy Loyd's house was the epicenter of the southeast Portland neighborhood where Billy and Manny Saban and Bobby Goodall and their various siblings spent much of the second half of the 1970s. No one remembers how it came to be there, but it remains there today, like a monument to lost boyhood, its chain-metal net hanging scrappily from the hoop on a pole stuck firmly into the concrete.

Manny lived around the corner, toward the Dairy Queen on Duke Street. Bobby lived a block or so from there. His backyard was connected to Billy's by an unpaved alleyway underneath two big trees that conspired to create an umbrella of foliage, which is how they came to be best friends just before second grade. Kids gravitated toward each other in the neighborhood without need for formal structure or organizing. Play was instinctual. If there was a ball, it was tossed. When enough boys arrived, a game started.

On most days, the boys gathered at the hoop to shoot baskets or toss footballs across the street in the field that was technically a park, though the weeds had long ago swallowed up everything except an aging metal roundabout and the skeleton of a swing set. Things were like that here, where Portland meets a suburb called Milwaukie. Officially, this was the edge of the Lents neighborhood, a disregarded part of Portland that the city hadn't annexed yet. Unofficially, and as far as anyone around here was concerned, the neighborhood was Felony Flats, a name bestowed by police officers some years earlier because of the concentration of criminals among the citizenry.

To the boys growing up around Duke Street, the world existed mainly west of 82nd Avenue and north of Johnson Creek Boulevard. They attended Joseph Lane Elementary School, an old brick building dating back to the 1920s that sat adjacent to the lush acreage of Brentwood Park—even in the poorest neighborhoods in the Pacific Northwest, street-level decay is decorated with evergreens and rhododendrons. Families lived in small houses, what real estate agents might call cottages or bungalows somewhere else, with weather-beaten exteriors ringed by short cyclone fences, or in apartments with rusting barbeques on the porches. They shopped at small corner markets where shelves were crammed with one or two of everything and negotiated deals with neighborhood mechanics who fixed cars and motorcycles in their garages. Especially in the summertime, kids were gone all day, engaged in one or another adventure involving varying levels of criminal mischief or moneymaking schemes to fund the purchase of candy, cigarettes, admission to movies, or arcade games at the mall.

Few of the mothers worked regularly or more than part-time. Most were overwhelmed by too many children, a lifetime of disappointment, and, in many cases, bad men. They dulled the pain of broken promises and routine domestic violence with alcohol and drugs. Husbands and boyfriends came and went. Fathers were significantly absent. Sometimes it was better for a kid to be gone than get caught up in whatever was going on inside the house.

Word in the neighborhood was that Billy's father had died on the job some years earlier. None of the kids really knew the details of the story, other than he'd been killed at work, which involved doing something on a bridge. The late Mr. Loyd had also left behind a mess of kids, three boys and three girls, more than could be easily managed by their mother. Added to that were some cousins who stayed periodically while their family reorganized. The Loyd house was considered among the best in the neighborhood, mostly because, despite the usual lack of adult supervision—the oldest teenage girl was, by default, in charge—there was always food. A kid could find loaves of bread, big bags of potato chips, and crates of bottled soda pop in the Loyd kitchen.

Bobby shared a house across the alley with his older brother, older and younger sisters, their mother, her boyfriend, and sometimes his son, who was a few years younger and thus often the unwitting victim of an array of pranks. (Bobby and Billy regularly dangled Bobby's younger siblings by the ankles from the big tree that leaned over the alley.) Bobby's brother, Jimmy, older by about three years, often stayed with their father in Yakima, Washington, but he was well known in the neighborhood. Jimmy enjoyed a certain status as one of the oldest boys in the immediate vicinity and therefore the first to get into significant trouble, his palpable anger having landed him in juvenile detention before he became a teenager. Plus, his sisters and, to some extent, Billy couldn't seem to keep their mouths shut, so Jimmy had plenty of opportunities to fight.

Manny was the most recent addition to the boys in Felony Flats. His family had arrived in much the same way as most of their neighbors, having lost everything somewhere else. Manny's given name was Stanley Jr., after the father who had left for another life in another state, but everyone called him Manny. He was ten years old when he moved into the small blue house with his mother, Raquel, his brother, Jeff, who was two years younger and Manny's best friend, and their baby sister, Roseanna. For practical reasons, Manny's father had taken their twelve-year-old sister, Janice, with him when he moved to Las Vegas. Stanley Sr. had managed to reach middle age without having learned to read or write well enough to function on his own without difficulty. He'd grown up in rural outposts and spent most of his youth working on farms. That wasn't to say he couldn't earn a living. When he worked, Stanley often made good money painting big structures like bridges. When he didn't work, he drank, which generally got him in trouble. Stanley Sr. had spent time in prisons up and down the West Coast before he met Raquel, who already had three older children from a previous husband.

The Saban family had come to Portland from Grants Pass, Oregon, about 240 miles south. Grants Pass was still dominated by the timber industry then, and Raquel had worked at a cabinet manufacturer there to add to the income from Manny's father's painting business. They'd lived relatively well in a double-wide trailer on five or so acres they shared with a few cows, pigs, and a roving band of peacocks. Manny had liked their life in Grants Pass, but it ended when his parents split up. For a while, the kids had lived with Manny's father in north Portland, which wasn't too bad. But then he'd found opportunity in Las Vegas and passed them back to Raquel, which is how they all landed in the house on Duke Street. Financially, it marked a new low. Whatever other problems Manny's father might have had, he'd managed to bring enough money into the house to buy clothes and shoes and groceries. In Grants Pass, the boys had BMX bicycles, nice clothes, and new sneakers. But there were no extras in Felony Flats. There wasn't much of the fried chicken or meat loaf Manny liked. These days, Raquel served up rice and beans and tortillas, a staple of her Mexican heritage. She'd grown up in eastern Oregon, where her father had worked on the railroad, and had a lifelong relationship with poverty, interrupted by the brief periods of something resembling lower middle class that came along with each husband. Raquel was skilled at making something from nothing. Soon after she'd secured the house on Duke Street, and perhaps bolstered by the accomplishment, she had signed up for nursing classes at the nearby community college. The rest of the time she worked in one or another care home, feeding and cleaning up after the elderly and disabled. At home, she retreated into her bedroom and read books from the library or from school. And she cleaned the house. Regardless of what kind of chaos rained down on Manny's family, they lived in what was widely regarded as the cleanest house in Felony Flats.

For a boy, no single possession was as important as a bicycle, perpetually tinkered with in yards and garages. A bike was freedom, the means to exploration, the passage to adventure. A bike could take a kid fishing in the creek beds and to buy candy at the corner store. A bike broke up the emptiness of long, warm days where there was no summer camp or vacation or trips to amusement parks.

Bikes also brought religion to Felony Flats. Young Mormon men wearing suits and ties and crisp white shirts glided through the neighborhood on ten-speeds, inviting people to church. Raquel listened to what they had to say about the Bible and God and a wonderful Mormon community where everyone helped everyone else. It was hard to argue the appeal when you had your hands full of kids and low-paying jobs. Raquel had been raised a Catholic and had taken her children to Mass earlier in their lives, but churchgoing had turned from sporadic to non-existent here. Raquel was eager for spiritual comfort, though, and she invited the young Mormons inside.

Both of the missionaries, one short and one tall, had blond hair and blue eyes. They were young, clean-cut men who called each other "elder." Manny was enraptured by the yarns they told, which he considered on the order of adventure tales. There were stories of how Mormon pioneer Joseph Smith, guided by an angel, had found the tablets that ultimately became the Book of Mormon, and read them using his special glasses.

They talked about Boy Scouts and other activities going on at the church, and how there were lots of other kids there. They were selling religion, to be sure, but the truth was that these young men brought more in the door than anything else going on in the neighborhood.

Manny didn't just want to go to church, he secretly wanted to become a missionary, to wear a suit and ride a ten-speed through the city, saving citizens and slaying sin.

After a few visits, Raquel packed her kids into their beat-up green Pontiac Bonneville with the white rag top and drove them the mile or two to the Linwood Ward of the Church of Jesus Christ of Latter-day Saints for a Sunday service. The church couldn't have been mistaken for anything else. It was housed in a redbrick building with a steeple on top, all surrounded by lawn with a wide cement path and two short sets of stairs leading into the building, where lots of people were milling around. Manny was glad to see that the young missionary men from the adventure stories were there. A man named Brother Hunt, whom Raquel had met earlier through a neighbor, greeted the family as they walked up the steps toward the building. Everyone seemed exceedingly friendly and wore nice clothes.

Shortly after that first Sunday, the missionaries, or Brother Hunt, or someone persuaded Raquel to bring her children to a baptism service at a larger Mormon building known as a "stake" house. Several Mormon wards comprise a stake, like a district. The ceremony featured men in robes reading from the Bible and the Book of Mormon. A large older man in a robe launched into prayer with a booming voice that began, "Oh God . . ." This startled Manny and Jeff and sent them into uncontrollable snickers, immune to their mother's nudges and swats. When the service concluded, a flow of people smiling and shaking hands carried them out of the chapel. Brother Hunt had brought the loud man over to where Manny and Jeff were standing with their mother. His robe now gone, the man was dressed in a corny-looking outfit of gray polyester slacks and a baby blue jacket with white stitching. The ensemble reminded Manny of something the father on *The Brady Bunch* might wear, except that this man was considerably older. Manny's eyes locked on the man's large hands, the left one missing part of three fingers. Brother Hunt introduced him as Brother Curtis and then explained that Manny's mother was having a hard time "controlling her boys." Manny quickly put together that they were in trouble; the snickering in church, he figured, had sealed their fate. Fear slowly climbed up his insides. The large man was there, it seemed, as part of some plan for their future. "Bring them over," he was telling Raquel. There was some talk about other boys and going places, and then Manny heard the words "straighten them out" and "get them out of your hair" and knew he was in a mess.

In the months and years that followed, the Mormon church became a semipermanent part of life in Felony Flats. Not long after Manny and his family had connected with the church, some of the other boys in the neighborhood began tagging along. The missionaries were enthusiastic visitors, and curiosity mixed with the simple desire to join the crowd swept down this part of Duke Street.

On Sunday mornings, some collection of Manny and his siblings, Billy, Bobby, and, when he was around, Bobby's older brother Jimmy went to church in Raquel Saban's Pontiac or in an old yellow school bus that the church sometimes used as a kind of shuttle. Brother Curtis was always there, and he periodically brought along one or two boys who lived near him. Brother Curtis didn't drive, so they'd come on the city bus or catch a ride with another churchgoer.

Everyone in the Mormon church, regardless of age, attends Sunday school before going into the chapel for a religious service, known as a Sacrament Meeting. The boys were corralled into a room the size of a large office, furnished with a table, metal chairs with plastic seats and backs, and a chalkboard, all of which contributed to making the place smell like school. Books, games, and toys were scattered around. After Sunday school, the boys played tag in the hallways and then sat with Raquel in the sanctuary, where they engaged in a competition to see who could smack the other the hardest without getting caught. Brother Curtis was usually up in front playing some role in the service, which inevitably begat snickers from the boys. Religious lessons, lacking the appeal of the missionaries' adventure tales, were quickly forgotten. Mostly, Manny and his friends went to church for the social aspect, the promise of something more than the stretch of Duke Street between their homes. Mormonism emphasizes the idea of a religious community, and church doesn't stop on Sunday. There are activities scheduled for women, men, children, and teens throughout the week.

Manny and one or more of the others would go with Brother Curtis to the church building during the week for Boy Scouts and jump on a trampoline in the back. The boys didn't get uniforms or badges, but they called it Boy Scouts, anyway, and Brother Curtis was their leader. He taught the boys how to cook and camp, and occasionally took them to movies or hockey games. In the winter of 1977, the famed Harlem Globetrotters came to Portland for an exhibition game, and Brother Curtis managed to get enough tickets to take a handful of boys from the church and the neighborhood, including Bobby, Billy, and Manny. Bursting with excitement, they rode the bus downtown to Memorial Coliseum and made their way through the throng of fans to their seats. The coliseum was also home to the Portland Trailblazers, but none of the boys had ever seen them or any other professional sports team play. It was enormous and loud. The lights dimmed. And for nearly two hours they were mesmerized watching Meadowlark Lemon and his teammates perform amazing stunts with a basketball, stunts that would be discussed and reenacted by young boys for weeks to come.

2

Frank Curtis was seventy-three years old and lived in an apartment in the back of the Southgate Animal Clinic on King Road, about three miles from the Duke Street neighborhood. He held some sort of caretaker job at the clinic, and the apartment came with the deal. Occasionally, the veterinarian who owned the clinic, a Mormon bishop in another ward, came out of his office to talk to Brother Curtis about one thing or another, but the boys didn't see him much. The clinic consisted of two buildings—Frank's apartment was in the back of the larger one—with a wide asphalt parking lot between them, where someone had erected a basketball hoop. There were empty cages stacked up near the door to Frank's apartment, and it smelled like animals. Manny and his brother met two other boys who lived near the clinic and were about the same age, give or take a couple of years (no one had broken into the teens, and many of them weren't even ten yet), and spent time there. Brother Curtis sometimes brought one of them to church with him, but they mainly hung out around his place.

When the boys weren't playing basketball or riding skateboards in the parking lot of the clinic, they hunted for treasures in the city dump next door. When the weather was too wet to endure, they lay on the floor in the apartment, in front of the secondhand television. Brother Curtis made snacks, lunch, sometimes even dinner. He liked to brag about how he made the best chocolate cookies around, and kept premade logs of cookie dough, wrapped in aluminum foil, in his small freezer, ready to be sliced into discs and baked for his young guests. A small glass bowl filled with gooey orange-slice candies sat near the television.

Brother Curtis also became the boys' connection to contraband, as they grew closer to adolescence. He'd walk to a store on 82nd Avenue, a major thoroughfare through southeast Portland, and buy cheap beer. He allowed the boys to drink at his apartment in defiance of both the law and the Mormon religion, which forbids alcohol consumption. Occasionally Brother Curtis produced a small pile of "girly magazines," like *Playboy*, and left them on the floor for the boys to look at. Manny leafed through the pages, curious at the content, only briefly. He figured that sooner or later it would land him in trouble. The older boys perused the magazines more seriously.

Bobby and Billy came to the veterinary clinic too. Sometimes they helped Brother Curtis clean cages, or tagged along while he fed the animals. Bobby, in particular, liked that chore. One day Brother Curtis let him watch while he anesthetized a cat with a shot and then smeared ointment in its eyes. Bobby tickled the cat's paw and then became terrified when he found it lifeless. He was not more than eight years old at the time, and he began to sob, convinced that Brother Curtis had killed the cat. Later, the old man pointed out that the cat was up and around again, but Bobby was traumatized nonetheless.

Manny tended to follow the lead of the older, bolder kids. One boy in particular, a kid who lived in the trailer park behind the clinic, had established himself as the leader of the group. He seemed more worldly, a self-appointed expert on numerous subjects, including making out with girls and procuring just about anything. One summer afternoon while they were all shooting baskets, the topic turned to the boy's skateboard, envied by Manny and his brother. Before long, they'd devised a plan by which each of the boys would shoplift a skateboard from the Fred Meyer supermarket nearby.

At the store, the boys headed directly into the sporting goods department and inspected the merchandise. Manny eyed a brand-new fiberglass board that was rainbow colored with the silhouette of a seagull in the center. He put it under his arm, while the other boys each grabbed one too. They all took off through one of the grocery aisles, heading toward the front door. The plan's success seemed to hinge on the confidence of the players, which also may well have been where it fell apart. Manny and his brother had never done anything like this and didn't lose their nerve as much as they'd never really had it in the first place. The group was busted within sight of the door and hustled into a back room. Terrified, Manny tried unsuccessfully to fight back tears. The more savvy boys named Brother Curtis as their guardian and gave his phone number to their captors. Before long, the big man appeared at the store, conferring privately with the manager. In the end, the boys were released to the custody of Brother Curtis, who seemed to be mostly angry at them for getting caught. Much to Manny's surprise, Brother Curtis didn't tell any of their parents what had happened, nor did he really say much more on the subject at all. The entire incident remained their secret.

Brother Curtis sometimes hosted boys from the church and the neighborhood for a sleepover in his apartment. During one such evening, the atmosphere inevitably turned to horseplay, and a water fight broke out during which the boys used large syringes from the veterinary clinic as water guns. In short order, everyone, including Brother Curtis, was soaked.

"Take them wet clothes off," he ordered.

Soon they were all in their underwear, but that didn't stop the game. They continued to chase each other, and ran from the old man, who moved significantly slower, though the apartment was too small to get very far away. There was no chance of someone running outside, since the doors were secured with dead-bolt locks to which Brother Curtis held the key.

Afterward, the boys took turns showering in the tiny bathroom attached to the bedroom and then settled onto blankets arranged across the living room floor for a sort of camp-in. Manny was the last boy into the shower. Brother Curtis wrapped him up in a yellow robe and then closed the door behind them. The other boys were already lying down watching television. Manny emerged from the bathroom and suddenly decided that he wanted to go home. Tearfully, he called his mother and asked her to come pick them up, without explanation. Raquel Saban would have none of it and instructed Manny to stay with Brother Curtis. The next morning, the neighborhood boys walked home and Raquel picked up Manny and his brother.

Manny's sister Janice, back from Las Vegas, sat in the backseat. As they had gotten older, it seemed that Manny and Janice couldn't be within close proximity of each other without an outbreak of verbal sparring or minor violence. Now Manny couldn't get in the car fast enough. His mother chatted with Brother Curtis and waved as she backed the car out of the driveway. But they weren't more than a few blocks down King Street when things got crazy. Manny blurted out that Brother Curtis was a pervert. He couldn't stop his need to testify, to purge the experience. He ignored his mother's admonition about language, about saying things like that, and kept going, wound up. He was talking nonstop now, spraying words across the car like a fire hose: Brother Curtis had kissed him on the lips . . . his penis . . . sex . . . jacking off.

"He tried to do it with me," Manny said.

Janice immediately called Manny "faggot" and the situation escalated until Raquel pulled the car to the side of the road, in front of the old dump, reached into the backseat, and slapped Manny for saying those awful things about Brother Curtis. "Don't you lie to me," she told him. The ride home remained silent.

Bobby was the quietest of the boys in the neighborhood. On the smaller side and shy under his mop of brown wavy hair, he preferred to follow Billy, a significant talker, or Bobby's older brother, Jimmy, whose bravado could hardly be contained.

Felony Flats had brought Bobby a better arrangement than some of his family's previous homes. His mother's last husband had been in the military, and they'd all lived in a high-rise apartment building in Germany while he was stationed there. The boys had entertained themselves by stealing beer delivered to their German neighbors and spitting wads of saliva down the stairwell onto unsuspecting passersby. Their stepfather drank until he got mean and beat on their mother and, eventually, one or more of the kids. Finally, Bobby's mother left both her husband and Germany. They arrived back in Oregon with nothing. Jimmy went to his father's house in Yakima and the rest of the kids stayed in their grandmother's small apartment above a bar until their mother hooked up with her current boyfriend, and they all moved into the house off Duke Street. Gale, the boyfriend, was a decent guy, a Vietnam vet who'd worked his way into middle management at a bank in Portland. He taught Bobby how to fish, and they'd sit by the water on the rare weekends when Gale wasn't working. Billy regularly came along on the fishing trips; they did most everything together. But Gale worked a lot, and as things started to come apart between him and Bobby's mother, he was around less and less.

Bobby's love of the outdoors didn't fade. Brother Curtis scrounged up cheap fishing poles from somewhere and sold Bobby's mother on the idea that her son would surely benefit from joining in the church scout adventures that he was leading. In truth, these expeditions amounted to nothing more than Billy and Bobby going to a fishing hole with Brother

Curtis, who wasn't exactly an outdoorsman, having spent much of his own early life in and around big cities in the Midwest.

Bobby was the most skilled in the fine art of catching fish. He'd punch a hole in the top of a can of corn and let it sink to the bottom while they dropped the fishing lines into the creek. The corn attracted the fish and they nearly always left with crappie, or sometimes even trout. Bobby baited hooks for Brother Curtis, who, missing most of those three fingers, couldn't manage such intricate tasks.

No one really knew how he'd lost the fingers, but Brother Curtis liked to tell tales about his past, involving gangsters and Al Capone. The boys were generally under the impression that Brother Curtis had been involved in a shadowy underworld of men in overcoats making Mafia-style hits in faraway cities. And that, despite all evidence to the contrary in his current physical state, the man might at any moment receive a phone call and have to drop everything and resume his former life of crime.

Bobby showed Brother Curtis his favorite place to fish under the Hawthorne Bridge, an ancient tress that crosses the Willamette River into downtown, and some less-populated spots along Johnson Creek and Eagle Creek in neighboring Clackamas County. Johnson Creek dominated much of the landscape around Felony Flats. Its polluted, greenish water wound through Milwaukie and the southeast end of Portland, zigzagging back and forth between Multnomah and Clacka-mas counties until it emptied, finally, into the Willamette River. For most of the way, the mossy creek bed was lined with tangles of over-grown blackberry bushes and oaks whose scraggly branches poked out over the mucky water. The creek had provided a backdrop for both recreation and mischief to generations of kids.

Navigating the trails to a fishing hole could be difficult for Brother Curtis. The old man was a bit unsteady on his feet, a situation made worse by the fact that he usually wore dress shoes or something equally unsuited to the terrain, but he managed to keep up with the two youngsters well enough. Whatever fish the boys caught, Brother Curtis cooked into a meal with vegetables and other trimmings. He could boil crawdads and fry up breaded trout. Regardless of the menu, it was regularly better than what Bobby had at home, where there were more mouths to feed and less culinary interest. Brother Curtis always set a proper table in his small kitchen and insisted that the boys use at least basic table manners. Sometimes, instead of the cookies, he produced desserts, which were a big hit; Bobby burned his mouth on a pie that he couldn't wait to let cool.

Brother Curtis saw that the boys brushed their teeth with toothbrushes he kept in the bathroom for them to use, and that they cleaned up after playing or before going out. The man was a stickler for hygiene and cleanliness. The apartment was small, but it was spotless and uncluttered. The few clothes that Brother Curtis possessed were either hung neatly in the closet or institutionally folded in drawers. He taught Bobby, in particular, the importance of taking proper care of himself. And given the functional absence of other adults in his young life, Bobby became increasingly attached to Brother Curtis.

Manny was convinced that Brother Curtis was up to no good. He stopped going to the veterinary clinic after the slumber party incident. Manny and Jeff had been baptized into the church, and their mother was studying with Brother Hunt in anticipation of her own conversion into Mormonism. Brother Curtis went out of his way to talk to Manny's mother, Raquel, and people noticed that she was friendly to him. Raquel treated everyone in the church with respect, but there was something more with Brother Curtis. They lingered after church events and talked. She saw him at the veterinary clinic too, when she took her Chihuahuas there. Sometimes Brother Curtis came to visit with Raquel at home and the two of them would sit and talk for hours. And then, with little warning, Brother Curtis became an even bigger part of Manny's life.

Everything in the Mormon religion, including missionary work, is designed to prepare men for their role as leaders of church and family, and women as supporting players and homemakers. The Mormon church operates with a lay ministry of members, mostly men, who are called into service by church leaders thought to have been guided by God in their selection. Mormon men are considered to hold the priesthood after adolescence, and Mormon women must be attached to a husband in order to gain entry into the Celestial Kingdom that is the Mormon version of the afterlife. Men and women are expected to marry and raise families. A single Mormon is a Mormon searching for a spouse.

It was, therefore, relatively unsurprising in the ward that Raquel Saban married Frank Curtis, despite their nearly three-decade age difference.

One technical hitch had to be overcome, however. In the early 1970s, the state of Oregon had significantly changed the laws governing divorce, allowing the entire process to be completed within ninety days of filing. Frank and Raquel were confused about this and thought that earlier laws, which required a waiting period, were still in effect. Though they'd separated earlier, Raquel had not legally completed her divorce from Manny's father within that period. So, with little fanfare, she and Brother Curtis were married by a justice of the peace in Vancouver, Washington, across the Columbia River from Portland, on March 20, 1978. The bride wore a light blue dress with a veil, and the groom a secondhand suit. A small reception with punch and cake followed, attended by some members of the church, neighbors, and Raquel's family. Bobby, Billy, and Jimmy were there too.

Brother Curtis left the veterinary clinic and moved with Raquel and her children into another rented house about a block away from their Duke Street place. He also maintained a small caretaker's apartment attached to a junkyard about a mile away, where he sometimes stayed for no particular reason. Manny liked the idea of Brother Curtis having his own place. None of the Saban kids got along well with him. Things were more relaxed when he wasn't around, and Manny felt freer to come and go as he pleased. An endless sound track of Kansas, ABBA, and the Eagles blared from a suitcase-style record player they had. Neighborhood kids regularly filled the house, dropping their bikes on the weedy front yard.

Around the time that Frank Curtis married Raquel Saban, he was hospitalized for something that remained a mystery to the kids around him. They were allowed to visit, though, and one day Bobby and Billy took the bus up to the hospital on the hill toward the freeway out of town. They figured that since Brother Curtis must be sick, they should go see him. Manny wasn't going anywhere to see Brother Curtis.

The hospital was sort of ominous, but the old man seemed okay and was sitting up in bed. Eventually, curiosity got the better of Bobby, and he asked Brother Curtis why he was in the hospital. The man raised the sheet and gestured down toward his penis and said he was there "to get this fixed," and that he was doing it for his wife. At nine years old, Bobby did not possess any knowledge that would allow him to make sense of a penile implant, but he came away with the impression that Brother Curtis's penis somehow didn't work properly, that it involved sex, and that he wasn't supposed to know about it. This was confirmed when, after Bobby mentioned it to his mother, who wondered how he knew about such things, Brother Curtis seemed pretty upset that he'd run off at the mouth. Bobby had never been in trouble with Brother Curtis and felt bad that he'd disappointed the man by telling some secret that made people talk.

It wasn't long, however, until Brother Curtis's routine resumed. Bobby thought the man had an uncanny ability to show up whenever Bobby was available. Then again, Bobby didn't have many conflicting activities except for school, which, given the opportunity, he gladly skipped. As with the fishing trips, Brother Curtis would call or come to the door and talk quietly to Bobby's mother, explaining that he was leading some church activity and thought it would be good for Bobby to come along. Billy usually was involved as well.

There actually wasn't much in the way of organized activity, but Brother Curtis was good for an adventure, whether it was dragging the boys along on church business, or just dropping them off to play bumper pool at the Boys' Club a short way away. A few times, he left them in a park or dropped them off at the movies while he disappeared on an errand, eventually returning to bring the boys home. Bobby didn't like to admit it, but he often grew scared waiting for Brother Curtis to come back for them because he didn't really know where they were or how to get home.

Brother Curtis navigated the bus routes of southeast Portland as if he'd designed them personally. He'd flash his monthly pass and hand out twenty cents to each of the boys from a small coin purse he carried. The boys would put their change in the fare box and get a paper transfer from the bus driver so that they could ride for the rest of the day without having to pay again, and climb the stairs onto the bus. Bobby and Billy liked to sit on a seat by themselves, while Brother Curtis usually sat on one of the bench seats near the door. He was well dressed when he went out, despite his secondhand clothing, but lagged a few decades in style. For one thing, he was the only one on the bus wearing a fedora. Bobby once asked him about the hat, and Brother Curtis explained that everyone in Chicago, where he was from, wore hats when they went out. The answer seemed to imply a certain disapproval of the lack of sophistication among the citizens of Portland. He wore a trench coat as well, and used to sweep it to one side like he was opening a curtain when he reached for the coin purse in his pocket.

Brother Curtis also brought with him a small, wheeled cart on which he carried groceries or other things they'd accumulate during errands, which he'd drag along, bump-bump-bump up and down the stairs of the bus. There was always a plan for the day, even if mundane.

They would go to the Pop Shoppe to return empty bottles, and then to the roller rink at nearby Mt. Scott Park, where Brother Curtis would sit on the bleachers and watch the boys skate. Sometimes they tagged along while Brother Curtis stopped by the church thrift store or visited another member of the ward.

They'd eat at cheap restaurants or fast-food joints. Bobby particularly liked hamburgers at Herfy's, a chain that featured a statue of a Hereford cow in front. Other times, the boys would hang around the apartment, watching *The Six Million Dollar Man* or *The Rockford Files* on Brother Curtis's old television, or playing Monopoly. Occasionally, Brother Curtis produced larger events that included watching the Portland Winterhawks, a minor-league hockey team, play at the Lloyd Center downtown. He took Bobby, Billy, and, early on, Manny and some of their siblings to the Bagdad Theater, a Hollywood relic that seemed out of place in Portland. This landmark theater was built by Universal Studios in 1927 with, for unknown reasons, Middle Eastern architecture and decor. In earlier decades, usherettes wore Arabian costumes and the theater offered vaudeville-style shows. In 1975, the Baghdad hosted the premiere of the Hollywood blockbuster *One Flew Over the Cuckoo's Nest*, which boosted its standing. Bobby thought the place was cool. The Paramount, which had been built about the same time in an Italian rococo style, was equally interesting to Brother Curtis. He was always drawn to things that had even a tenuous historical, sophisticated flavor to them.

On the eve of his tenth birthday, Bobby stood in the doorway of his house wearing, for the first time in his young life, dress slacks, a white shirt, and a clip-on tie. Behind him, the usual chaos reigned throughout the house. Jimmy had taken to singing Rod Stewart's hit "Da Ya Think I'm Sexy?" and Robert Palmer's "Bad Case of Loving You (Doctor, Doctor)" at the top of his lungs. At the same time, their younger sister was watching some loud cartoon on television.

Brother Curtis had planned a special outing to celebrate Bobby's birthday. It started like every other adventure, when Brother Curtis came to the house and talked Bobby's mother into letting him take Bobby out to dinner. This seemed excessive, but obviously the old man had taken a liking to Bobby, and, in truth, this was more of a birthday celebration than he was likely to get any other way. So Bobby's mother relented with little fight. Things became a bit more awkward after Brother Curtis arrived with clothes—nice dress-up clothes—for the boy to wear. Bobby's family could not repay Brother Curtis for this. Like the rest of the kids, Bobby wore the kind of used clothing that announced that the family lived in a category commonly known as "ghetto poor." This man from the church was increasingly providing more, both monetarily and emotionally, to Bobby than was his family, which left them with an underlying unease. At the same time, how could they stand in the way? Bobby wasn't doing well in school; he could barely even read. The only other option would soon be the drugs and crime that were practically an adolescent rite of passage in Felony Flats. And so the large and small gentlemen, dressed in their best clothes, rode the bus downtown and had dinner at the nicest restaurant that Bobby had ever entered—not a difficult distinction to achieve, of course—a decent red-leather-booth steakhouse. But in Bobby's eyes, they might as well have been dining at the Ritz.

3

Manny did his very best to avoid Brother Curtis at all times, particularly when his mother was at school or at work. He was convinced that he was under constant surveillance by the old man. There were knowing looks, Manny thought, that seemed to say "No one believes you." For much of the time, Manny secluded himself in a shed in the backyard, where he and his brother kept a growing collection of bicycle parts, some of them stolen. Other times he'd ride the bus without any particular destination, or walk aimlessly around the mall.

Manny grew distant from his old friends Bobby and Billy, whom he figured were involved in whatever nasty things Brother Curtis was up to. Manny was not able to grasp the fact that Bobby, who was younger, lacked the family structure that Manny had enjoyed at least earlier in his life, nor did he understand the emotional manipulation at play. Instead, he saw the new clothes his friends had gotten, the skateboards, the trips to skating rinks and movies. He figured they were willing participants, that they were all in the game together. And he sensed that they didn't like him anymore, were mad at him, and looked at him differently. Manny began an exile from the church and the neighborhood.

There were times, however, when Brother Curtis couldn't be avoided, like when Manny was in the car and his mother had to pick her husband up from work. Frank Curtis was more than an active member of the LDS church. He was also an employee. He worked part-time at the church's charitable arm, Deseret Industries, a few blocks from the veterinary clinic where he'd first lived and a short bus ride from the Duke Street neighborhood. Most people knew Deseret by its sizable thrift store, sandwiched between fast-food joints and big-box stores on a main route through southeast Portland. The thrift store housed donated clothing crammed onto round racks and shoes assigned to tall metal shelves, all of which contributed to a faint lingering, musty smell. There was discarded furniture, kitchen appliances, and some popular paperbacks mixed in with Mormon books. The church is a prolific publisher, and the thrift store benefited from its position at the end of that pipeline in an array of books devoted to raising children and Mormon history. Of course, there were also numerous copies of the Bible and the Book of Mormon, the church's main religious text. Brother Curtis was sometimes assigned to bring in newly arrived discards from the loading dock behind the building. The job allowed him to scavenge incoming treasures before they made it to the shelves, and he was able to grab a lot of useful furnishings and kitchenware. He brought home games, basketballs, skateboards, and the like to give out to kids he knew. At other times, Brother Curtis worked in the building behind the thrift store, called the Bishop's Storehouse, where needy church members picked up boxes of groceries to get by when money was short. The storehouse is part of the church's welfare system to help families, through the massive Mormon tithing income.

When he lumbered over to the Pontiac after a shift, still in his uniform—a red knit vest over a white shirt—Brother Curtis often would be carrying a box of groceries from the storehouse. The kitchen in Felony Flats was stocked with jars and boxes bearing the familiar Deseret logo, featuring a bumblebee and hive from the Mormon philosophy of "industry, harmony, order, and frugality."

By the time Manny was twelve, he and his brother were coming and going from home without explanation, let alone permission, traipsing in occasionally for food and a change of clothes. Manny became insolent and often ditched school. He figured everyone in the world knew what had happened with Brother Curtis. They would see him differently now, as damaged. Having lost authority, Raquel acquiesced in her husband's ideas for handling the boys. It was arranged that she would bring Manny and Jeff over to the apartment Brother Curtis kept at the salvage yard and he would straighten them out.

The salvage yard sat in the middle of a run-down residential street, but it was no small place. Dead cars filled the property, their entrails strewn between a tall wooden fence that hid the yard from the street and a chain-link version that marked the end of the property in back. The entire perimeter was topped with a loose coil of razor wire. One front corner of the yard was occupied by a large old wooden garage, the kind with ground-to-roof double doors that opened out on either side. Some part of this structure had been made into shotgun-style living quarters that ran front to back along the side of the garage, beginning at a nondescript door on the side of the building, behind yet another chain-link fence. No one knew why Brother Curtis was there, but he had been since he moved out of the veterinary clinic, even as he supposedly joined households with his new wife and her children.

Manny and Jeff went inside. Their mother spoke briefly with Brother Curtis and then drove away. Brother Curtis came in and was followed shortly by a neighbor whom Manny vaguely recognized from church, and the man's son. Manny guessed the son to be in his late teens, maybe pushing twenty. He stood larger than both his father and Brother Curtis, which made him a giant to Manny. The men were angry, their lectures peppered with phrases like "straighten you out" and "get what's coming to you." Manny was scared witless, convinced that something awful was about to take place. A belt buckle was undone.

And then, unexpectedly, Raquel came back. Manny had left the bag of clothes he'd been made to pack in the backseat of her car, and at some point his mother had noticed it and returned. The second she opened the door, Manny bolted. Everyone followed, and the whole chaotic scene moved onto the street in front of the garage. Manny cried and hollered incoherently about Brother Curtis and the neighbor. And then Brother Curtis grabbed Manny by the collar and landed one of his giant hands hard against Manny's face. Manny momentarily imagined seeing stars like in the cartoons. Raquel seemed shocked and, at the same time, perplexed. But Brother Curtis's slap brought only a brief interlude to the unfolding drama. Manny grabbed the bag of clothing and swung it, knocking the old man to the ground. Manny had always been oddly particular about his appearance, regardless of how cheap his clothes were, and had packed an iron in the bag because he'd figured they were going to go to church. Now, with Brother Curtis on the ground, Manny took off running down the street.

Brother Curtis was seen to and appeared to be recovering, albeit slowly. Raquel drove off down the street after Manny. For a block or two, mother and son argued through the car window as Manny continued determinedly down the sidewalk and Raquel cruised slowly next to him. Finally, Manny relented and climbed into the backseat.

The event marked both his most defiant move against parental authority and his first act of physical violence. Within days, it was decided that Manny would move to Las Vegas and live with his father.

Most of the boys from Felony Flats practiced petty criminal activity to acquire money or goods they weren't likely to receive any other way. Bobby Goodall was no exception. He participated in the break-in of a nearby apartment with one of the boys Brother Curtis had brought to church. They were after a stereo and some eight-track tapes.

Somehow Brother Curtis found out and scolded Bobby about breaking the law. After that, Bobby kept his crimes from Brother Curtis to avoid repercussion. Meanwhile, Bobby and Billy cut school and regularly shoplifted from the Plaid Pantry convenience store up on Duke and 82nd, near where they caught the bus. Bobby was skilled at sticking bottles of MD 20/20, a popular variety of "bum wine" better known as Mad Dog, down the waistband of his pants without being detected.

Brother Curtis allowed the boys, who were by now between ten and twelve years old, to smoke cigarettes as long as they kept it outside. At the salvage yard apartment, the boys had created a smoking lounge on the roof, accessed by the fire escape. They'd even brought folding lawn chairs up there. From the roof, they could see the entire yard and down the street, past the weather-beaten houses to the VFW at the end of the block, where oldsters gathered to play bingo and swap stories.

Brother Curtis bought cans of beer and let the boys drink until they passed out in his apartment. Bobby, in particular, tended to black out when he drank excessively, a condition that would plague him for life. Particularly when he was looking for booze and cigarettes, Jimmy came along when Bobby went over to Brother Curtis's place.

One evening while Bobby was on the roof there, he heard Jimmy yelling inside the apartment. Bobby shimmied down the stairs in time to see Jimmy with a baseball bat in his hands threatening Brother Curtis. Bobby froze and watched the scene unfold. Jimmy was a big kid, and he was loud. He also had an explosive temper, which everyone knew, so pretty much anything could happen here. But mostly Bobby was focused on what Jimmy was hollering about. He called Brother Curtis a pervert, in between issuing threats to kill him, and something about his pants. The words slowly came together for Bobby like a puzzle as his brother continued to rant. Apparently, Jimmy had been asleep or passed out on the sofa. When he woke up, Jimmy figured that Brother Curtis had taken off his clothes. Now Jimmy was threatening to kill the man.

". . . you ever fucking touch me again, you fucking pervert."

Bobby was unclear about exactly what had happened. At the same time, a paralyzing mixture of panic and shame moved through his chest toward his stomach. He wanted to run away, hide, become invisible, find a place where no one knew him. There was a connection, he saw, between whatever happened to Jimmy, what had made Jimmy so upset, and the private things that Brother Curtis did with him.

After Manny had moved to his father's place in Las Vegas, Raquel walked into Frank Curtis's apartment in the salvage yard and found her husband in the bathtub with a young boy. It was a moment of clarity. She left both Brother Curtis and the church, and wrote a letter to their Mormon bishop telling him what she'd learned. In time, Raquel and the rest of her younger children ended up in Las Vegas, where she and Manny's father reunited. Then the family later moved back to Portland. Frank Curtis disappeared.

And then he came back.

When Bobby was about to turn thirteen, Brother Curtis started coming by his house again with renewed offers to take him out and about. Bobby hadn't understood why the man had left him in the first place and continued to be dumbfounded at his ability to find Bobby, although his family hadn't moved very far in the years since they were all close. Brother Curtis was by now living in an apartment complex on Killingsworth Street near the Portland airport, which was a way from the old Felony Flats neighborhood. By coincidence, Billy was for some reason staying with his aunt, who lived in a trailer park nearby. His mother had moved the family from their house in Felony Flats sometime earlier. Brother Curtis's intervention allowed the boys to hang out again. And Bobby had missed Billy, who was about his only real friend.

Brother Curtis's apartment was on the ground floor of the big complex, directly in front of the pool, which made it smell faintly of chlorine and dampness. The boys liked to swim when they came over in the summer. And, as before, Brother Curtis always fed them. Occasionally, Bobby or Billy went to a Mormon ward with the old man, but not often and not to the same place they'd gone before. There were other, younger, boys around now, and Brother Curtis seemed to be more focused on them. He didn't seem keen on having the groups mix.

One day during the summer, Bobby paddled alone around the pool at Brother Curtis's apartment. Billy was gone, his muddled family situation having prompted relocation again. Brother Curtis had brought Bobby along when he stopped to pick up a younger kid he knew from the church. From the pool, Bobby could see Brother Curtis talking to the boy inside his apartment. Bobby was relieved to finally be the older one in the group and enjoyed this newfound status. And at the same time, he was filled with anger and resentment. He didn't even know this kid, but he knew Brother Curtis would take him places and give him things. This new kid was more important now, Bobby deduced. The attention and the affection that had come with Brother Curtis would soon be gone.

SEATTLE, WASHINGTON

—

1997

4

In nearly two decades of practicing criminal law, Timothy David Kosnoff had come across all manner of characters. It was fair to say he was well versed in the undesirable traits of the human species. Nonetheless, Kosnoff remained a believer that most people possessed some measure of decency and was still surprised when occasionally confronted with evil deeds that exceeded the spectrum of bad decision making.

Some years back Kosnoff had moved to Seattle from the urban grit of Chicago. He'd begun his legal career the traditional way: working in the public defender's office, representing indigent people who'd been accused of crimes. Much of the time, that included drug-addled citizens who'd turned violent or stolen to support their habits. Kosnoff used to describe other of his clients as African-American men who'd been arrested in a park for the crime of being there. The justice system in Chicago was broken into numerous small, specialized courts—drug court, gambling court, traffic court, and the like. Kosnoff had found himself spending more time on the road than in the courtroom. He'd long had the wanderlust to head west, lured by the promise of something new. California was too complicated. He'd been to Washington and liked it. He liked to hike and fish. Shortly after getting married, he'd talked his way into the only job he could find, as a prosecutor in the town of Friday Harbor, in the San Juan Islands of northeast Washington, accessible only by boat or plane. Mostly, the job consisted of prosecuting drunken citizens for disorderly conduct, but Kosnoff did it zealously. In time, however, he missed a more active law career. Eventually, Kosnoff landed in Seattle and hung out his own shingle, which brought with it the freedom to decide which cases he'd take and how he'd run them, but also plenty of financial headaches and long hours. Certainly, Kosnoff now represented people with money, many of whom were engaged in various aspects of the illegal drug business. But he returned to the pool of lawyers assigned by the court system to defend the indigent, for which he was paid by the state. He'd always seen himself as a kind of equalizer. Working on behalf of thieves, killers, and the like made the system fair; he balanced the scales of justice, in theory, anyway, by representing the accused. This fervent belief had fueled him through the tough cases. And in the spring of 1997, he needed to find it, to tap into it, once again.

A light rain fell as Kosnoff stared at the paperwork piled on his wooden desk, though the weather was not responsible for his dismal spirits. He was defending a man named Shawn Swenson, who, at twenty-five, was facing life in prison for murdering the owner of a small recording studio in north Seattle. Swenson and another man had posed as would-be recording artists in order to get into the studio to steal digital recording equipment. But things had gone horribly wrong. The recording studio owner, who was gagged with duct tape, died of suffocation. Kosnoff presented the argument that Swenson had been interested only in making off with the recording equipment and had been in the car during the owner's murder. In the criminal justice system, defendants were better off as dim-witted than cold-blooded killers. Given the circumstances, it was also the only available option.

The case was, in all aspects, awful. Every court appearance had been colored by a crowd of heartrending survivors mourning the loss of a father, son, husband, or friend and yearning for justice. They were unlikely to ever make sense of what happened, but their attendance served as an outlet for their rage and pain. Tim Kosnoff was their enemy. He'd taken to referring to his entrances into court as "walking the grief gauntlet." And though he remained a dedicated advocate for his client, in private moments, he had to admit that the job was wearing.

The criminal defense business in general was getting to be a lot less rewarding than it used to be. Back in 1993, Washington had led the nation in passing the first three-strikes law, an initiative financed heavily by the National Rifle Association. The law prescribed mandatory sentences for most crimes and stripped much of the creative strategy out of defense work. And even without the constraints of mandatory sentencing, Kosnoff was slowly losing his zeal for defending criminals. It takes a certain unwavering enthusiasm for and earnest belief in humanity to stay in the defense game, particularly with clients who are rarely innocent and occasionally evil, but almost always the victim of their own idiotic decisions. Everyone comes in the door stewing in despair, with his future, maybe even his life, resting on a lawyer's ability to fight as if his own life depended on it. Not surprisingly, the profession is beset by burnout.

Distraction was, therefore, a welcome visitor. It arrived on this particular morning when the secretary whom Kosnoff shared with his office mate put through a call from a young man in need of a lawyer. Even during busy times, Kosnoff took calls. His clients included the transient, incarcerated, or otherwise hard to reach; he'd learned to seize the moment when people phoned him. Kosnoff shuffled papers and doodled notes while the kid on the phone laid out his situation in formal, awkward speech. He'd apparently been impressed by a small, square advertisement Kosnoff had placed in the phone book so long ago he'd forgotten about it. The kid introduced himself as Jeremiah Scott.

He also revealed that he'd contacted a few other lawyers, all of whom had, it seemed, declined the job. This didn't bode well, but Kosnoff was willing to play along awhile longer. It was clear that Jeremiah possessed little knowledge of the legal system beyond what he'd likely gleaned from watching television, but he seemed determined.

Jeremiah indicated that he'd recently celebrated his eighteenth birthday by deciding that he wanted to sue the Church of Jesus Christ of Latter-day Saints, in which he had been raised. This was a problem for Kosnoff, of course; he made his living representing people accused of committing crimes, not victims. What Jeremiah was proposing sounded like a civil—not a criminal—lawsuit, in which one person makes a complaint against another, usually for money, through the court system. Kosnoff had never represented anyone in a civil suit.

And yet he kept on with the conversation. Jeremiah Scott, whoever he was, had an interesting story. He said that back in 1991, about the time he turned twelve years old, he'd been molested by a Sunday school teacher, but not at church. Kosnoff wasn't immediately clear on how this all came about, but he saw that the church was somehow involved. Jeremiah also mentioned that he'd accumulated a criminal record as a minor. Kosnoff, all of whose clients had criminal records, was unfazed by this bit of information. But he figured it was a likely reason the kid hadn't gotten very far with other lawyers he'd contacted.

There was something earnest about this Jeremiah. So for no good reason, Kosnoff invited Jeremiah and his mother, who seemed also to be involved in this legal pursuit, to come to his office and discuss the matter more seriously. He issued his usual instructions: Jeremiah was to write down whatever details he and his parents could recall about what had happened, and make a list of people who could vouch for his story. At the least, Kosnoff thought, he'd find the kid a lawyer. What the heck? Kosnoff knew plenty of people who might take the case. In fact, he shared an office with a solo-practice attorney who handled civil litigation.

Their office in Bellevue, Washington, was really on the east side of Seattle, separated from downtown by Lake Washington. A bedroom community at the time, the location offered cheaper office space than Seattle proper. Plus it was an easy commute from home, ten or so miles east on yet another lake, in another Seattle suburb.

Over the years, Kosnoff had gotten into the habit of working from home a fair amount of the time, coming into the office mainly to meet with clients and other attorneys. He lived with his wife, Mary Ann, and their ten-year-old son, Nathan, to whom he was devoted. Everything about Mary Ann was far from the world of Kosnoff's criminal law career. She was a concert pianist and could rightfully be described as both perky and elegant, which she pulled off effortlessly. She regularly practiced yoga and believed that thinking about horrible things polluted the mind. It went without saying that the details of most of Kosnoff's cases didn't make their dinner conversation.

Like many solo players in the law, Kosnoff shared office space—meaning lobby, receptionist, and conference room—with another attorney. Joel Salmi, Kosnoff's office mate, practiced civil law, mostly defending people and corporations from lawsuits filed against them by other people and corporations. It was a lucrative business for a one-man operation. Kosnoff thought Jeremiah Scott's claim might be a case for Salmi.

In the days that followed, the lawyers began to kick around another idea: Maybe they could work on the case together. Salmi was busy with his own caseload and would appreciate the help. But there was something more. Kosnoff was intrigued by the idea of representing a victim. This was not an entirely impulsive or fanciful idea. Another criminal lawyer in town, a man he respected, had started handling cases on the civil side of the law. The move had made Kosnoff ponder such a change during what was becoming a regular review of potential career options. If anything came of this case, and he wasn't at all sure anything would, it might be a way for him to try out civil law. Kosnoff and Salmi had engaged in hypothetical musings about working on a case together for some time. They shared a casual style with a deep reserve of professional seriousness that could be tapped whenever the occasion called for it. Ties and hard-soled shoes were rarely seen in either office, unless one of them had to appear in court. Still, both were unquestionably in the legal game to win.

Salmi had no taste for defending criminals, which he'd considered too much of a commitment for too little compensation. He'd always liked Kosnoff, though, and really liked his spirit. The man got hold of a case and gave it his all; he possessed unbelievable energy and enthusiasm for a midcareer lawyer. So Salmi easily agreed to sit in on the meeting and offer an opinion at least.

The week of Jeremiah's appointment brought near-constant rain, not unusual in Seattle, a city washed by a slow, steady drizzle at least half the year. But spring had offered no relief to a particularly cold, wet winter, and even veterans of the gray were losing patience with the sun's late appearance, the kind of weather that makes the Pacific Northwest famous for suicides and depression.

Jeremiah arrived at the law office late in the day, to accommodate his schedule at Bellevue Community College. Sandy Scott, his mother, came along with him. She was attractive without being remarkable, a pleasant-looking woman with dark hair. She also looked on the young side to have an eighteen-year-old son.

Kosnoff was running late when he appeared in the small waiting room. At forty-three, he had already acquired a noticeable amount of gray hair that was invading inward from his temples, creating a striking contrast to his often tanned face. Kosnoff was an avid tennis player and sometimes rode mountain bikes with his son. He ushered the Scotts into a conference room and introduced Salmi, saying that he had experience handling cases like this one. The lawyers—neither particularly large but both exuberant—shook hands with overly friendly greetings, shared appropriate disdain for the weather, and praised Jeremiah and his mother for successfully navigating their way to the office, as if they could have missed a large building next to the largest mall in the middle of the not-very-large city in which they lived.

Everyone took a seat at the rectangular wooden table facing a wall lined with legal books. After a few more minutes of small talk, Jeremiah began methodically describing the series of events that had led him to want to file a lawsuit, this time in more detail. He read from a typed white sheet of paper he had prepared, as instructed, for the occasion. Kosnoff and Salmi took notes.

When he was about twelve, Jeremiah said, he'd been repeatedly sexually abused by a member of his church, a man who had taught Sunday school and been active in Jeremiah's Boy Scout troop. The man was elderly and without relatives, and he had come to live with Jeremiah's family. He'd required the boy to accompany him on doctor visits and other errands around town. And then he'd molested him in his bed at night. Kosnoff wrote the words "Frank Curtis" and "Sunday school" on his yellow pad.

Kosnoff and Salmi both noticed that Jeremiah was oddly emotionless when he described the events that had led him into this legal pursuit. He spoke matter-of-factly, offering nothing more than what was asked. He seemed almost dead inside.

Jeremiah's mother was none of those things, however. Sandy Scott was visibly nervous throughout the meeting. She fidgeted and spoke in overly controlled statements, as if the wrong phrase might set off an explosion inside her. She was obviously uncomfortable while Jeremiah recounted what had happened to him. Every so often, Sandy interrupted her son's narrative to add details or clarification.

Jeremiah continued, telling the lawyers that he had first revealed that he'd been molested about two years after the incidents occurred. The information had come out when Jeremiah himself was investigated by the police for molesting a boy whom his mother babysat. Kosnoff knew the scenario well from the criminal courts. Nearly all molesters had themselves been victims. Sandy added that her church leader had apologized after she'd told him that Jeremiah had been molested. She said that he'd told her that he'd known the man had abused a boy in the past, but the man had promised not to do it again.

After Jeremiah finished his story, Sandy asked what would be involved in filing a lawsuit—how it would work, what would happen, how long it would take, and so forth. She wanted to know what would be required of Jeremiah. Salmi sketched out an outline of how a lawsuit might proceed and offered a quick education on the workings of the legal system. And then everyone arranged to meet again.

It was dark outside by the time Jeremiah and his mother left the lawyers' office. Kosnoff and Salmi rehashed the meeting only briefly before going home. Salmi was much more interested in the case now that he'd heard the Scotts' story. He'd once defended a handful of Protestant churches that had been sued for the bad deeds of employees. But Salmi had never been involved in a case in which a church had known that someone was an abuser before an incident had occurred, as Sandy Scott had described. In the legal world, that fact was huge. It meant that the church might have liability for what happened to Jeremiah.

Kosnoff and Salmi agreed to keep working on the case together and, in the days that followed, began tossing about ideas. Eventually, they worked out a plan—Salmi would handle most of the legal arguments and Kosnoff would take care of developing the facts of the case. Kosnoff would be doing much of what's considered the grunt work, but it was a way to see if civil law suited him. Salmi was more familiar with the legal arguments, having used them in defending previous cases. The two lawyers would split any award. Since Jeremiah had no money to pay up front, they'd have to accept the case on a contingency basis, meaning that they would fund the work from their own pockets and then take a percentage of any money awarded at the end. But given the nature of the case—it was a liability claim with only one victim—they reasoned they could easily handle it.

Salmi was not a risk taker, which had paid dividends in keeping his stress level low. He was a gentleman lawyer who represented insurance companies and other corporations. He knew that complicated contingency cases could take over a lawyer's life and send a small firm careening into bankruptcy if they dragged on and got expensive.

A very small percentage of lawsuits in the United States actually go to trial, and that's the way it's supposed to be. Trials are expensive for everyone involved, including the government. The legal system is designed to encourage opposing parties to work out their differences and settle claims among themselves before entering a courtroom. It's a long process, one in which there are many opportunities for argument and resolution.

Based on his past cases, many of which involved liability matters, Salmi thought Jeremiah's claim seemed pretty straightforward. He told Kosnoff that if even half of what Jeremiah said was true, the lawsuit was probably worth a couple hundred thousand dollars and would take about a year. They'd each get paid a decent amount for the work done and Kosnoff would get a chance to try out a bit of civil law. The men left the office thinking the project could be, professionally speaking, fun.

5

Tim Kosnoff embraced his new pursuit enthusiastically. He spent much of the time that he wasn't working on Shawn Swenson's defense researching information for his new civil lawsuit. He and Salmi met a few more times with the Scotts and then put the preliminary parts of Jeremiah's case in motion. The first order of business was to find out more about the man named Frank Curtis who had molested Jeremiah. Because Sandy Scott had recalled that her Mormon bishop told her that the man had promised not to molest again, it was a good bet that he'd abused someone else before he moved into the Scotts' house. So the lawyers hired a private investigator in Oregon named Bill Anton, whom Salmi had worked with before, to look into Frank Curtis's background.

Meanwhile, Kosnoff did some of his own digging. By the time he met with Sandy and Jeremiah Scott a couple of weeks later, he was able to confirm a fact that everyone involved had suspected but no one really knew: Frank Curtis was dead. On May 15, 1995, about two years earlier, at age ninety-two, he'd succumbed to heart disease, officially categorized as "natural causes." He'd been interred at the Portland Memorial Funeral Home and Mausoleum, three miles from the house where he'd lived with Jeremiah and his family.

Kosnoff presented this information as a huge relief for everyone. The police had investigated the crimes involving Jeremiah, and Frank Curtis had eventually pleaded guilty to molesting the boy. But because of his age, he was never incarcerated. The death was great information for the lawyers. In some ways, it was better to present the record of the confession than it was to have the man himself. Jeremiah wouldn't have to face Frank Curtis, and a jury would not see an "elderly gentleman" who might seem sympathetic. Still, Jeremiah seemed surprised to learn that his abuser was dead, even given the man's advanced age. In private, Sandy told Kosnoff that Jeremiah went through periods where he seemed withdrawn. At other times, he was, by all outward signs, utterly unaffected by revisiting what had happened to him. Sandy worried constantly about her son.

Salmi, meanwhile, had drawn up a legal complaint outlining all the ways the Scotts had been harmed, part of the paperwork that would be filed in court if the case continued. It is standard procedure in a civil lawsuit to send a copy of a complaint to the intended defendants in hopes that a settlement might be worked out that will save everyone the time and money of a protracted courtroom battle. After several edits, Salmi and Kosnoff sent their best draft to the headquarters of the Church of Jesus Christ of Latter-day Saints in Salt Lake City. The complaint named the church, along with Gregory Foster, the Scotts' former bishop in Portland, as defendants. Based on what he knew from working on other liability cases, Salmi figured the church's lawyers might be eager to get the matter resolved since it seemed likely, based on Sandy Scott's conversation with the bishop, that church officials may have known, and not disclosed, that Frank Curtis had molested someone else before he'd moved in with the Scott family. Kosnoff too thought things looked good for this new case. When he and Salmi talked in the office later, they began to entertain the possibility of a settlement before the end of the year.

Tim Kosnoff did not possess much of a background in organized religion. He'd grown up in Goshen, Indiana, a small town where his was one of only a few Jewish families in a predominantly Catholic neighborhood. And his family was not particularly observant. The Kosnoffs' Judaism was more cultural history than spiritual connection. It had not made him a part of something so much as it had made him different. In elementary school, he'd raised his hand with the other kids in class whenever the teacher asked who had gone to church on Sunday so as not to stand out. He'd had a bar mitzvah presided over by a cantor from a neighboring town. But that's not to say that he didn't understand the concept of religious connection. He'd had several Catholic and Protestant friends whose lives were intertwined with their churches, and his wife had been raised Catholic. All of them had given him a healthy respect for the general good deeds and moral compass that he thought went along with most church-affiliated groups. But Kosnoff's devotion was to social justice and the law.

After graduating from college with no particular plan for the future, he'd gone to work with farm labor activists in Ohio. Mostly, he swept floors, answered phones, and performed other odd jobs. But the job also offered a young Tim Kosnoff his first real look inside the courtroom. The group's ragtag lawyer was continually pitted against attorneys in expensive suits who represented the big canning companies. Kosnoff went along with the labor group to the majestic federal courthouse where these dramas unfolded. He was astonished that the powerful corporations could be confronted and defeated through the strength of a legal argument. At the same time, his older sister was heading off to law school. The converging events influenced Kosnoff to apply to law school immediately. He'd managed to take a late LSAT and was accepted into the Illinois Institute of Technology's Kent College of Law in Chicago.

Now he and Salmi were trying to flush out the details of Jeremiah's story and, at the same time, grasp the practice of Mormonism. Both were proving to be complicated tasks. Neither lawyer was familiar with Mormon religion or culture. Sometime ago, a Mormon family had lived down the block from Kosnoff, and they'd seemed like nice people. Salmi had been involved in a lawsuit once in which it was alleged that the Mormon supervisor of a government agency was favoring his brethren over non-Mormons. These random snippets represented the sum of their collective knowledge about the Church of Jesus Christ of Latter-day Saints and its members.

And, in truth, religion didn't make much difference to either of the lawyers. As far as they were concerned, this was a matter of law. The church was a corporate entity that had played a significant role in a scenario resulting in the sexual molestation of young Jeremiah Scott. It was about negligence and liability. Actions resulted in harm. Straightforward tort law. Of course, Kosnoff and Salmi knew that they'd likely have to show just how such a horror could have been perpetrated. They also began to realize, the more they worked on readying the case, that they'd have to explain the relationship between the Mormon church and its members, something the lawyers didn't really understand.

After their first meeting, Kosnoff directed Sandy and Jeremiah to make a written accounting of all the ways their lives had overlapped with Frank Curtis. The idea was that this would help the Scotts tell their story more succinctly, a task they would have to do several times later, as the case progressed. Mother and son dutifully complied, spending hours compiling facts and filling in details that stretched back eight years. During later meetings in the book-lined conference room, Kosnoff was impressed by how well both Scotts had done their homework.

Sandy Scott had always been active in her church, which is a hallmark of Mormonism. Mormon women gather in something called the

Relief Society, a group in each ward that meets to discuss family and women's issues, brings meals to sick members and new parents, and otherwise helps the needy. In time, she was "called" to teach a Sunday school class at the Brentwood Ward, the congregation to which they belonged. This was an honor. Mormon members are called to service when their church leaders are "impressed" through an inspiration from God that a member should take on a particular role. The underlying idea is that these people would not be called unless there was a message from God, and they are therefore worthy of holding the position.

Sandy described to Kosnoff and Salmi how, by the late 1980s, she was teaching a class of girls in her ward. Part of the Sunday school routine included gathering all the children into a big recreation room to sing Bible songs. That's where Sandy first met Frank Curtis, an older fellow who led a Sunday school class of elementary school boys. Brother Curtis, as he was known in the church, seemed to be a happy, grandfatherly sort of character, eager to chat up someone, anyone really, who had time to listen. He took to calling Sandy the "Lady in Red," because she often wore her favorite red dress. Her husband had given her the dress, despite their perpetually tight budget, for her birthday. Sandy had thought Brother Curtis was a nice old guy. It was no secret that he was also a lonely character. No one had known much about whether he had a family or where they might be, only the vague information that he lived in some kind of lower-income retirement home.

Despite his advanced age, Brother Curtis was a hulking presence, largely because he was overweight. He carried more than two hundred pounds unsteadily on his five-foot-eight-inch frame. He'd gotten into the habit of cornering Sandy and her two children at the end of the hallway after church, where he'd inevitably ask about the family's plans for lunch and the rest of the day. (Sandy's husband often had to work on Sundays, so she took her kids to church without him, an arrangement that pleased no one.)

Brother Curtis was far from subtle about wanting company, and he'd tell Sandy how nice he thought it must be to have a family around. He was a good cook, he said, and he'd sure love to come over and make them a meal. They'd really enjoy it, he promised. Sandy finally relented and Brother Curtis became a fixture at the Sunday table. Before long, he was also calling during the week in search of a dinner invitation. At least twice each week, Sandy made the fifteen-minute trip to Brother Curtis's studio apartment in a run-down complex that was part of the county's welfare network for seniors to pick him up for lunch or dinner. He would visit with the kids, and he struck Sandy as being a nice guy stuck in a sad situation.

By this time, Brother Curtis was approaching his eighty-fifth birthday. He confided to Sandy that one of his greatest disappointments in life was having ended up alone. What he wanted most, he told her, was to live out his final days in the company of a family. Sandy came to see Brother Curtis as a test of faith. She believed that the right thing to do was to bring him to live with her family in their home. Everything she'd learned from the church had seemed to support this idea, and beyond that, she believed it was what God would want her to do, that if they sacrificed, as the Gospel taught, there would be blessings in heaven. She viewed the whole situation as an opportunity to help a good man.

Sandy's then husband, Kent, had been a harder sell. He'd worried about the extra cost to their already strained household. There would be doctor visits and other errands, and the Scotts had only one car. And what, he'd worried, would happen if Brother Curtis needed more care?

As she'd done with other major decisions, Sandy Scott had turned to their bishop, Greg Foster, for guidance. Mormons are taught to seek counsel from their bishops in all things, from spiritual questions to financial problems and parenting concerns. At the same time, no one in the LDS church is ordained. The church operates through a lay ministry. Its leaders do not come to the job from any formal education or training like, say, that of a seminary education in the Catholic church. Instead, they hold a day job while serving as volunteer group leader. So it's not unusual for a person's spiritual leader also to be his doctor, plumber, or accountant. Greg Foster, the Scotts' bishop during this time, was a lab manager at Citizens Photo, a retail camera and film processing business in Portland.

At their initial meeting, Sandy had told the lawyers that she'd met with Bishop Foster for nearly an hour in his office in the nondescript ward building and laid out a plan for making Brother Curtis a permanent fixture in her home. Sandy's parents lived near Seattle and her children didn't see them all that often. It would be a good thing for the kids, she'd told Foster, to have this grandfatherly figure around who really seemed interested in them. Bishop Foster had been less than enthusiastic about the idea, which came as a surprise to Sandy, given what she'd perceived as the spiritual merits of her plan. The bishop told Sandy a story about having had his own mother-in-law move in, and how it had been time-consuming and quite draining on the family and their budget. He'd advised her to reconsider. Older people needed a lot of time and energy, he said. Perhaps this was more than she could handle.

Sandy heard only a call to sacrifice. And the more she'd thought about it, the more she'd decided helping Brother Curtis was a call that her family should heed. Faced with the spiritual argument, Kent relented. They'd been taught that this sort of action would bring them all blessings in the next life, which was promised to be a time of great happiness and reward. The religion puts a lot of emphasis on people carrying their own weight and saving for the next life, where the real reward is received.

So despite Bishop Foster's reservations, Frank Curtis moved into the Scotts' home on an autumn weekend in 1989. The move hadn't been much of an ordeal, given how little the man possessed. He had a bed and a small dresser, but that was about it in the way of furniture. He had some clothing and a box or two of personal things. Jeremiah and

Sandy recalled that Brother Curtis had an old photo album that held a lot of pictures of other families and children he'd known over the years, a big, fake-leather book full of sticky pages with plastic covers. The book obviously had been carried around for a while. Brother Curtis liked to look through the pages, the Scotts said, and tell little stories about the people in the pictures—where they lived, how old they were, and, occasionally, some activity they'd done together.

Taking in Brother Curtis required some reconfiguring inside the Scott household. The children's bedrooms were on the top floor of the house, along with a bathroom. Kent and Sandy's bedroom was on the main floor with the kitchen and living room. Downstairs was a semifinished basement, where the kids played and where, during the day, Sandy homeschooled her children. She'd been unconvinced that her children would receive the attention and education she wanted them to have in the local public school.

Sometime before Brother Curtis's arrival, Kent and Sandy decided to move into the basement and give their bedroom to the octogenarian, since he had difficulty getting up and down stairs and frequently needed to visit the bathroom during the night. So the basement, which was significantly colder than the rest of the house, was made into a master bedroom and Brother Curtis was moved into the bedroom on the first floor. Homeschool moved to the kitchen table.

With lingering exasperation, Sandy told Kosnoff and Salmi about the constant battles that had erupted around food. Brother Curtis liked to cook and seemed to know a fair amount about gourmet food. He'd clearly learned how to prepare meals while working in restaurants, judging by the excessive amounts of food he made and the huge messes he created in the kitchen. And his culinary expertise seemed to be connected to a dark, pre-Mormon past. The old man had entertained the Scotts with exciting tales of how he'd worked in the kitchens of restaurants in Chicago and Detroit, where he claimed to have cooked for Al

Capone and equally shady, though less famous, gangsters. Jeremiah was fascinated by his yarns, Sandy said. This glorifying of crime troubled her, but she'd mostly thought it harmless.

The more pressing practical concern was the grocery bill that grew out of Brother Curtis's elaborate menus. Sandy had never spent so much money on food in her life. The family was going broke fast. She'd begged Frank to scale back, told him they couldn't afford this kind of thing. Oh sure, he'd said, of course. And then, soon enough, there he'd be with another tab for payment. The cycle had become a well-worn routine. Sandy would scold Brother Curtis for the grocery bill. He'd retreat from the kitchen, help out here and there, and then want to make his special this or that dish because, after all, they'd done so much for him.

Sandy said she'd felt bad because Brother Curtis hadn't had much else to share and he'd seemed so happy and proud to cook for them. And, she said, the food was good. But Kent and Sandy had quarreled over money and Brother Curtis. And then Sandy scolded Brother Curtis for spending too much on food. Adding to the stress, Brother Curtis's cooking projects had become distracting during the children's academic lessons, now that the kitchen was also the schoolroom.

The Scotts were also contending with Brother Curtis's transportation needs. Years earlier, he'd had a pacemaker installed. That, along with myriad other ailments, meant that the man seemed to have an appointment with one doctor or another, or a prescription that needed filling, or a test, or something else as often as three times a week. This meant that Brother Curtis had to take the bus, but he wasn't steady enough on his feet to climb up and down stairs on his own. So Jeremiah had accompanied Brother Curtis on the bus to the doctor and wherever else he'd needed to go.

During their trips, Brother Curtis had entertained Jeremiah with more tales of his early gangster years. He'd committed a lot of bad deeds, he said. Brother Curtis told Jeremiah that he'd killed a man, been involved in the occasional shoot-out, and stolen lots of things. The fact that three of Brother Curtis's fingers were severed only accentuated these tales. Brother Curtis had seen and done far more interesting things than any other adult Jeremiah had known.

Brother Curtis also showed great interest in whatever Jeremiah was involved in. He helped with Jeremiah's Boy Scout troop at church. At other times, the Scotts recalled, Brother Curtis kept to himself and stayed in his room without explanation. He often made little dogs out of yarn. Not anything that was particularly interesting or creative, but just small, crude-looking yarn animals with glued-on wiggly eyes that he'd give to kids at church or try to sell at senior citizen gatherings.

Kosnoff and Salmi continued to make notes during the meetings in which Sandy unfolded parts of her family's history. They were sizing up how she and Jeremiah might look to a jury. They also pondered how Sandy Scott might hold up under the harsh cross-examination of an opposing attorney, which would most certainly happen if, by some unexpected circumstance, the case went to trial. Kosnoff thought she'd likely fare okay in the end, but it might take some practice.

In any event, she and Jeremiah both continued to enlighten their lawyers on the Scott family history. Things had remained tense inside the Scott house, she said. Sandy and Brother Curtis squabbled more over the grocery bill and increasing interruptions of the children's schooling. Kent and Sandy argued about money and Brother Curtis. And then, without explanation, Brother Curtis left one day while the family was out celebrating Jeremiah's eleventh birthday. No note. No good-bye. No nothing. Just gone. Kent and Sandy had called around to other church members with no luck, and then called the hospitals and, finally, reported Brother Curtis missing to the police.

A few months later, he resurfaced.

Toward the end of that year, Brother Curtis wrote a letter to the Scotts apologizing for taking off without saying good-bye. He said that he was in Michigan, visiting his daughter, a person no one had ever heard him mention. And he wanted to come back. He hadn't wanted to leave on bad terms and he missed the Scotts. His letter was followed by a phone call in December. Brother Curtis wanted to come for the holidays. It wouldn't be a long visit, he assured them, but he'd like to see them and the children and his other friends in the ward.

When Brother Curtis arrived before Christmas, it was immediately evident that the man had more than a short visit in mind. He arrived with boxes of his belongings. But the Scotts stood firm. In the interim, the family had shifted their house back to its original state, and Sandy and Kent had reclaimed their bedroom. Brother Curtis couldn't very well sleep on the sofa, given his age and girth, so it was decided that he would stay in Jeremiah's room upstairs. The boy had recently received a big water bed from his grandparents. And, while Brother Curtis had difficulty getting himself in and out of bed, Jeremiah's room had seemed the best place to accommodate him.

As weeks turned to months, Brother Curtis remained in the Scotts' home, and things became stressful. Sandy noticed that Jeremiah seemed particularly tired. He was getting up frequently during the night, in order to help Brother Curtis down the stairs to the bathroom. Sandy had thought it was sweet that her son was helping the old man, but she was worried about him. At the same time, Brother Curtis lavished attention on Jeremiah, staging adventures outside or playing video games. Every now and then, he surprised Jeremiah with little gifts.

Jeremiah and his sister, who was seven, slept in bedrooms next to each other on the top floor of the blue house. Despite being three years apart, the kids spent a fair amount of time together because they were homeschooled and because the Scotts were trying to follow the Mormon prescription for family bonding. As much as they could with Kent's work schedule, the Scotts had tried to have a weekly Family Night, which included the four of them talking together about Scripture and other lessons. They also went to church together whenever possible, though they attended different Sunday school classes. Jeremiah and his sister shared the regular petty arguments of siblings, but they'd also learned to entertain each other with made-up games and jokes. Sometimes they passed clandestine notes.

Such a correspondence marathon had been going on one afternoon while Jeremiah was playing video games in his room. His sister saw the folded piece of paper slipped underneath her door—it was Jeremiah's turn—and opened it: "Frank is raping me." She didn't understand what the note meant. So she threw it away and went outside to play.

As the months wore on, Sandy and Kent argued more, debating the situation with Brother Curtis, including the religious blessing connected to housing him, and then deciding that he'd have to leave. The grocery bill issue returned, though Brother Curtis had scaled his kitchen productions back a bit after Sandy strengthened her resistance.

In the meantime, homeschool ended. The Scott children were going to public school and Sandy had started a small day care in their home to bring in extra money. Jeremiah had developed a habit of oversleeping, or at least not getting up first thing in the morning like he used to, and he was often late to school. Sandy had been convinced that her son was tired from getting up to help Brother Curtis in the middle of the night. Nonetheless, it was irritating to have to hound Jeremiah repeatedly to get going in the morning. The last straw had come one morning in the spring of 1992, Sandy said. She recalled how she'd walked upstairs and opened Jeremiah's bedroom door. She was hit immediately by the putrid smell of urine, and then saw the quart jar full on the floor. This was not the first time Brother Curtis had peed in containers, and Sandy had admonished him about it, telling him to get help to the bathroom if he needed it. Sandy had had enough and told Kent that Frank Curtis had to go. Kent hadn't been particularly inclined to argue on the man's behalf. Blessing or not, Brother Curtis created hardship and chaos in the house. He'd have to find another advocate.

Frantic calls were made. Brother Curtis was sent back to the senior housing center. Kent helped the old man get his things boxed and then carried the boxes down the stairs. There were some brief, strained good-byes, and then Brother Curtis left the Scotts' house for good. Jeremiah remained silent about the awful things Brother Curtis had done to him at night in his bed.

6

A week or two after Salmi and Kosnoff sent their complaint to the Church of Jesus Christ of Latter-day Saints in Salt Lake City, they headed to a Seattle high-rise to the law offices of Stafford Frey Cooper, a white-shoe firm that defended Fortune 500 clients from civil lawsuits throughout the Pacific Northwest. Lawyers at the LDS church headquarters had contracted Stafford Frey to handle the Scott matter locally. Specifically, the job went to a partnership of legal experience and religion, pairing an up-and-coming Mormon lawyer named Marcus Nash with Thomas Frey, a senior partner in the firm. After some preliminary phone calls, it had been arranged that the lawyers would all meet at the Stafford Frey Cooper offices to discuss the pending lawsuit of Jeremiah Scott.

Kosnoff wasn't entirely sure what to expect, but he was ready to present what he thought were the merits of his case—chiefly, the fact that Sandy Scott's bishop had told her in 1993 that he'd known something about Frank Curtis having molested children but hadn't mentioned it earlier. The church's lawyers would no doubt see that their client had a problem there, he thought. Kosnoff and Salmi had sued for $1 million, which they figured would be countered and negotiated until it ended up in a settlement that was somewhere around $75,000 to $100,000. Maybe $150,000 if things went well.

Things did not go well at all.

Jeremiah's lawyers were ushered into the firm's glass-walled conference room overlooking Seattle and offered water and soda in crystal glasses. Frey and Nash came in and everyone shook hands. Frey was a balding man with a round face and years of civil defense experience under his belt. He oozed self-assurance. As the conversation unfolded, Kosnoff found Frey both arrogant and patronizing. Nash had come to the firm directly from law school at the LDS Brigham Young University a decade earlier. He was polite and seemingly less contemptuous than Frey, but he deferred to his senior partner.

Frey was unwilling to acknowledge or discuss any of the issues in the Scott complaint. Instead, as Kosnoff would recall later, he presented a lecture on what a general nuisance these sorts of cases were, not to mention the harm they caused to the good works of religious institutions. Frey also railed about how frequently sexual abuse cases were being filed in recent years in a way that Kosnoff found stunningly insensitive to the victims. Frey continued his lecture until Kosnoff decided that his opponent had slipped into intimidation and bullying. Kosnoff also pondered whether Frey was baiting him by belittling his client's complaints, so he was determined not to lose his cool. He'd defended a lot of criminals against career-climbing prosecutors and was a scrappy fighter, but he didn't take professional sparring personally. Right out of law school he'd worked briefly for a Chicago firm where he learned the rules of engagement in high-stakes defense work. One of the firm's senior partners defended midlevel mobsters. Kosnoff had always marveled at how, despite their relentless arguments and drama in the courtroom and in the press, the lawyers had managed to maintain an amicable relationship with federal prosecutors. Still, as Frey grew increasingly acerbic, Kosnoff's blood began to boil. He wanted nothing more than to get out of the man's office.

"If you want to understand my theory of the case," Kosnoff finally said, "I would be glad to discuss that with you. But all I'm getting is disrespect."

Frey and Nash offered nothing. Salmi thought they might follow up with an offer by phone later, but that didn't happen either. Kosnoff's desire to go to court was growing. He wanted to get his opponents onto more familiar turf, where he felt more equipped for a contest. With no promise of resolution, or even movement, from the church, Salmi and Kosnoff, and their client, faced a challenge. In order to continue, they would have to declare a legal war against an enormous and well-funded corporation, and open up Jeremiah's life to public review. The church's lawyers had, in effect, thrown down the gauntlet.

Joel Salmi was in downtown Portland working on another case one afternoon late in the summer when he ran into an attorney he knew at Starbucks. Gary Rhoades and Salmi had once worked in the same office building, before Rhoades joined Dunn, Carney, Allen, Higgins & Tongue. The firm had been around for decades and handled mostly business law—employment and tax cases and commercial litigation—but also represented some individuals in civil matters. Dunn, Carney was the sort of big legal corporation where lawyers specialized in practice areas, under which various departments of civil law are organized, all with the support of paralegals and secretaries and big budgets. Salmi had always thought of Rhoades as both a good lawyer and a good guy in general. As they sipped coffee and caught up on each other's lives, Salmi got an idea.

Kosnoff and Salmi had concluded earlier that the Scott case would best be filed in Oregon. Jeremiah lived in Washington, but Gregory Foster, the Scotts' former bishop, would be named as a defendant, and he lived in Oregon. This meant that they could file the case in either state. There was another reason to file in Oregon, one that every civil lawyer in the Pacific Northwest understood. Typically, juries can award punitive damages above and beyond what is considered actual compensation for some harm, in order to punish the defendant for wrongdoing. This sort of big money tends to be awarded in cases that involve egregious behavior on the part of a corporation that a jury decides to punish. For reasons rooted in the earliest days of its statehood, Washington law prohibits the award of punitive damages to plaintiffs in civil lawsuits. But the award was available in Oregon.

The lawyers at least wanted to hold on to the option of seeking punitive damages, primarily from the church, for its role in creating a situation in which Frank Curtis was allowed to prey on Jeremiah. Even if they filed the case in federal court, which was another possibility, the court would follow the law of the state in which it was located. So it was pretty clear that whatever else happened, the case was going to take place in Oregon. Yet neither Salmi nor Kosnoff was licensed to practice law there; they were licensed in the state of Washington. They'd need to partner with an Oregon lawyer such as Gary Rhoades. Another advantage of teaming with Rhoades, of course, was that Dunn, Carney had resources. The deal would likely be that Rhoades's firm would work on the case—mostly representing the Scotts in the courtroom—either for a set fee or for a percentage of the reward. Salmi outlined the basic facts of the case for Rhoades at the café, and then they talked more on the phone in the days that followed. Rhoades was interested enough that he agreed to bring the case to the partners at Dunn, Carney.

Kosnoff, meanwhile, was consumed with the murder trial of another client. The case of the beloved recording studio owner's killer was going downhill. Shawn Swenson's accomplice had accepted a deal from the prosecutor, in which he pleaded guilty and then testified against Shawn. The jury responded with a first-degree-murder conviction that was likely to earn Shawn decades in prison at his sentencing the next month, and there wasn't much Kosnoff could do about it. But he was still trying to find a way to lessen the sentence.

Kosnoff also was cramming like he hadn't done since law school. The rules governing civil lawsuits are different from those of the criminal court where he'd spent his career. So Kosnoff had been hitting the books. Large texts on civil practice, statutes, and rules in Washington and Oregon had become a regular part of the interior decoration at his office and home.

On a Friday afternoon the following October, Kosnoff and Salmi huddled around the speakerphone in Salmi's office for a phone conference with Bill Anton, the private investigator the lawyers had hired to look into Frank Curtis's past. The Alexander Christian Ltd. investigations firm had been directed specifically to find out what was known about Frank Curtis in the Mormon wards where he had belonged before he met the Scotts in 1989. Mostly, the lawyers wanted to find the family of the boy they thought Frank may have victimized before he'd come to the Scotts.

Kosnoff was a firm believer in the importance of learning early in the game as much as possible about the players, including potential witnesses, and what they might say. He didn't like surprises. He'd seen things go sideways when people turned out not to be what they'd seemed.

Bill Anton reported that Frank Curtis had divorced a woman named Raquel Saban in 1979. They'd been married for less than a year. The investigators had briefly spoken to the woman at her daughter's house a few miles outside of Portland. But Salmi had told Anton they wanted to focus on the church wards for now. As it would later turn out, Frank Curtis had been a member of three different wards in Portland from the late 1970s to the early 1990s, mostly owing to changes in ward boundaries and population. All of them were located in the same general low-income, working-class neighborhood.

Sandy Scott had told Kosnoff some months earlier about a bit of investigative work she'd done shortly after learning that Frank Curtis had molested Jeremiah. She'd remembered Frank having talked about other boys while he lived with the Scott family and had mentioned one in particular, a boy named David Johnson. She'd given his name to the police. Still stinging from the revelation of Frank's atrocious behavior, Sandy had been determined to find Frank and have him put away. To that end, she'd called every Johnson listed in the Portland phone book and the Mormon directories she had until, finally, through one family member to another, she found someone in David Johnson's family. Eventually, Sandy had talked directly to David.

"I introduced myself, and said, 'I have a son that was molested by Frank and I was wondering if anything of this nature had happened to you,' and he admitted it happened," Sandy said later. At the time, the Johnsons hadn't heard from or about Frank in years and were no help finding him. The Portland police also had interviewed the Johnsons. But the lawyers needed more details than had interested the police. Now, on the phone, Bill Anton reported that the investigators had found and interviewed David Johnson's father, Phillip. The elder Johnson was a devout Mormon and a member of the same Portland ward where Frank Curtis had belonged in the early 1980s, years before he'd met the Scotts in another ward. Johnson seemed cooperative and, through a long conversation at his home in Portland, had relayed the following story:

Frank Curtis had moved into their ward in about 1982. A couple of months later, he'd been called by their bishop, a man named Gordon Checketts, to be a scout leader and Sunday school teacher. Frank had taught a group of children that included David Johnson, who was about eleven years old at the time. Shortly afterward, Frank had called the Johnsons and suggested that David come to his apartment to study the Mormon teachings with a couple of other boys from the church. His best friend, a boy named Steven Penrose, also was in the ward and was being taught by Frank Curtis. The boys went to Frank's home together. Johnson said they were both abused.

Kosnoff made notes as the investigator relayed highlights from the interviews. Both lawyers were thinking versions of the same thing: There's no way they'd let their son go to some old man's apartment, church or no church.

Anton continued, saying that David's father had revealed that his son had sometimes been reluctant to go to Frank's place, but that he'd chalked it up to David not wanting to study. As far as the Johnsons had been concerned, Brother Curtis was an upstanding elder in the church who'd been called by the bishop to teach Sunday school. Johnson's wife, who had been at home briefly during the interview, added that her son had spent some Friday and Saturday nights at Brother Curtis's place, and that he had once bought David a bike.

The truth about the abuse had apparently unraveled after Steven Penrose's brother got wind of what was going on and told their mother. She then got the truth out of Steven and told the bishop that Brother Curtis had been molesting boys. During their interview, Johnson told the investigator that he had never spoken directly to his son about the incident but thought that his wife had. David was a shy, trusting kid, who didn't talk about things much, Johnson said. But he ultimately provided a phone number for his son. There was something else, Anton told the lawyers. Johnson said he'd learned, after the incident with David Johnson had come to light, that Brother Curtis had molested children in another ward. Phillip Johnson had gone looking for Brother Curtis, he told the investigator, but Brother Curtis had disappeared.

This was getting complicated. The information from the investigator, combined with what the lawyers had learned from the Scott family, began a list of potential victims of Frank Curtis.

FRANK CURTIS TIME LINE OF VICTIMS

Before 1982	Unknown children learned about by Phillip Johnson	Portland?
1982–83	David Johnson and Steven Penrose	Portland
1991	Jeremiah Scott	Portland

Anton continued his phone report for quite a while, with Kosnoff and Salmi alternately interrupting him to clarify details. If Frank Curtis had molested other victims in 1983 involved with the Mormon church before he met Jeremiah in 1989, as it now seemed, they wanted to know everything about it. Particularly, since it appeared from Anton's investigation that multiple people connected to the church might have known about Frank Curtis's proclivity for sex with children.

Having completed the highlights of his investigation, Anton concluded the call. Salmi told Kosnoff that they should begin to focus more on the church leaders, trying to determine how much the bishops and higher-ups knew about Frank Curtis's abuse and when they knew it. In particular, they needed to find out whether Greg Foster, the Scotts' bishop, knew about the Johnson and Penrose boys. This would be key to determining the extent to which the church itself had been responsible for placing victims, specifically their client, in harm's way. It was becoming increasingly obvious that they needed to know more still about Frank Curtis's earlier life. Even in the short time that they'd been working on the case, the man had become legendary for the stories he told about his past and for his unexplained disappearing acts. The bulk of this investigative work would fall primarily to Kosnoff, the lawyer most familiar with criminals.

Nearly all government business in Portland takes place in buildings that look down upon two adjoining grass plazas covered by a canopy of leafy trees. Originally, one of the squares was designated for women and children, and features all female gingko trees. The other was intended for men, no doubt a place designed to discuss important business of the day. Both are filled with numerous statues depicting pioneers making their way west, with children and Bibles in hand. The plazas are divided by Main Street, in the center of which is a very large bronze elk standing grandly atop an octagonal granite fountain.

Justice of all levels is administered in the surrounding buildings, which could not look more like government structures, except for one: the Mark O. Hatfield United States Courthouse, home to the United States District Court for the District of Oregon, sometimes jokingly known as "the Schick Razor building" for its uncanny, though presumably unintended, resemblance to the popular man's shaver. About a year after the building opened, the Honorable Ann Aiken was named to preside in one of its courtrooms. A former state appellate court judge, Aiken was a longtime member of Oregon political circles and was married to the former head of the state Democratic Party.

Lawsuits get to federal court in one of two ways. Either the case involves an issue of federal law, or none of the plaintiffs lives in the same state as any of the defendants—a situation known as a "diversity jurisdiction." Since none of the defendants resided in Washington, where Jeremiah Scott lived, Kosnoff and Salmi decided to file their case in federal court in Oregon. Judge Aiken also sat on the bench in Eugene, within the same federal district. She heard more cases there, including this one. The lawyers would log a fair amount of windshield time traveling back and forth to Eugene.

Within months, the lawyers' filing decision met with a fateful technicality. Along with Gregory Foster, who had been the Scotts' bishop when Frank Curtis moved into their house, and who, they alleged, had known that Frank had molested children earlier, the Scott lawyers had named the Corporation of the Presiding Bishop of the Church of Jesus Christ of Latter-day Saints, the Corporation of the President of the Church of Jesus Christ of Latter-day Saints, and the Church of Jesus Christ of Latter-day Saints as defendants. On first glance, the lengthy list of Mormon entities might appear to be overkill from aggressive lawyers. In fact, it was an attempt at capturing as many tentacles of the octopus that forms the Mormon church's business empire as possible.

Put simply, to file a lawsuit against an entity is to identify the potential source of a jury award or settlement. But in the case of the Mormon church, the whole is the sum of many legal parts, some of them overlapping, some controlled by others—ranging from complex corporate business entities to spiritual organizations—and, in all, not a construction that the church wishes to reveal.

The Mormon church is a private entity, and its wealth is a well-guarded secret. The most comprehensive estimate places its total assets at between $25 billion and $30 billion.

At about the time Kosnoff filed his complaint, journalists Richard and Joan Ostling, in their book *Mormon America: The Power and the Promise*, estimated the church's revenues, without adding in the earnings of church-controlled business entities, at between those of Union Carbide and Paine Webber. The church took in an estimated $4.9 billion in U.S. income in 1995, according to the Ostlings' estimate. Were it not a religious, and therefore nonprofit, entity, the Mormon church would rank among the top third of Fortune 500 companies by revenue. The church functions very much like a diverse, multinational corporation. The Mormon umbrella covers agricultural, manufacturing, sales, and development arms, as well as a massive investment portfolio that includes utility, financial, and media companies. The Ostlings, using an earlier *Time* magazine report, estimated the church's vast assets, including real estate, stocks and bonds, church-controlled businesses, and other investments, to be nearly $30 billion.

There are some inherent benefits in church-owned businesses that have kept the Mormons awash in cash. Members are encouraged to do business with Mormon-owned businesses, which increases the financial base from which the LDS church receives its 10 percent. Given its ten million members, the Mormon empire has a guaranteed market for its products. Also, the workforce of the Mormon corporation is largely made up of volunteers, significantly lowering its overhead.

The Mormon corporate structure would lead to the Scott legal team's undoing in federal court. LDS lawyers filed legal briefs in which they argued that, while the other Mormon entities named as defendants in the lawsuit were corporations of the state of Utah, the Church of Jesus Christ of Latter-day Saints is actually an *unincorporated* entity. It has members in every state, including Washington, where Jeremiah Scott, the plaintiff, also lived. That meant the case did not qualify as a diversity jurisdiction and therefore had no reason for being in federal court.

Judge Aiken agreed. On November 30, 1998, eight months after the Scott case was filed in her court, she signed an order dismissing the lawsuit. In retrospect, neither Salmi nor Kosnoff could come up with a particularly good reason for having filed the case in federal court. It might have been a particularly bad idea, in fact, had Aiken let the case proceed. Federal court judges can be impatient about civil tort matters plugging up their dockets. The general feeling is that these are cases best handled by state superior courts, leaving federal judges free to handle matters of federal law. The result, often, is that even complicated civil matters are hustled through the court process with less time for research and investigation than would be afforded in a state court.

Ten days after the Scott case was dismissed in federal court, Kosnoff and his team moved across the plaza to the Multnomah County Courthouse for the State of Oregon and filed a new lawsuit against Gregory Foster, the Church of Jesus Christ of Latter-day Saints, and four different corporate entities of the church. The lawyers wanted to make sure they had all of the financial entities of the church in their sights.

In the new complaint, Jeremiah's lawyers accused Greg Foster of having known about Frank Curtis's proclivity toward molesting children when Sandy Scott came to discuss letting Curtis move into her home in 1989. As long as they were starting over again in a new court, the lawyers decided to throw in everything they thought might be relevant. The new lawsuit included accusations that the church had displayed a pattern of behavior that placed children in harm's way, and a claim for intentional infliction of emotional distress.

But there remained a minor hitch in moving forward. Kosnoff and Salmi had to obtain permission from the Oregon courts to appear on behalf of Jeremiah Scott because they were licensed to practice only in Washington. In the interim, Gary Rhoades would act as Jeremiah's primary attorney in any court proceedings. He and a young associate named Jim Hillas had taken on the case at Dunn, Carney. Kosnoff and Salmi continued to work in Seattle and waited to hear from the court. The case, it seemed, was getting ever more complex, and the prospects of compensation for Jeremiah were no closer in sight. But what the lawyers did not yet know was that things would grow more complicated, and darker, than they ever imagined.

7

Despite his best efforts, Tim Kosnoff wasn't very good at ignoring things that bothered him. And Jeremiah Scott had said something that continued to nag his lawyer. He'd told Kosnoff and Salmi that his father, from whom Sandy was divorced, was against his suing the church. Jeremiah's father was still active in the Mormon church. He'd remarried and started a second family with his new wife. He wouldn't want to cooperate, Sandy had said. Kosnoff was intimately familiar with the popular hatred of lawyers, and lawsuits generally were lumped into that same negative view. Still, it seemed like there must be more to this. Jeremiah was the man's son, after all. Kosnoff had some experience with parents whose children had been victims of criminals, many of whom he'd defended, and they were usually fervent in their pursuit of retribution, even where it was clearly not due. The more he learned about the situation, the more Kosnoff started to realize that the church exerted much more influence than he'd understood.

Sandy Scott's parents were raised Mormon and in turn baptized Sandy and at least one of her three siblings. The family stopped going to church, but Sandy continued to participate in church activities with friends. When Sandy's family moved from their home in New Jersey to Bellevue, Washington, she connected to a Mormon ward there, where she met Revis Kent Scott, a furniture salesman who led a youth group at her ward. He'd grown up outside of Salt Lake City, where people called him Kent or Kenny. The name stuck when he moved west to attend college in Washington. Kent's people were Mormon dating back before his grandparents. He'd been raised in the church and, as prescribed by the religion, dutifully spent a couple of years on a mission. The church encourages young men between the ages of about nineteen and twenty-five to commit to a two-year mission at a location of the church's choosing before they start their careers. (Mormons now send young women around the world as well, but it's not considered mandatory.) At any given time, there are more than fifty thousand Mormon missionaries out proselytizing. Many, if not most, of the eager and earnest are sent abroad. As a result, Mormon membership is growing more from outside the United States than inside it.

Mission work is considered a rite of passage and an honor. Kent returned home ready to move on to the next milestone for a Mormon man: marriage and family. He and Sandy were married in the Mormon Temple in Bellevue. Temples are more sacred places of worship than the average meetinghouse where Sunday services are held. Marriage in a temple is thought to be eternal, in that husband and wife are "sealed" to each other for this and all other lives. Thus, the ceremony is reserved for only the spiritually and morally qualified. A temple marriage requires complete adherence to church doctrine.

Varying degrees of this personal testing continue throughout the lives of even long-practicing Mormons. The religion dictates that members of the flock prove their worthiness before being permitted entrance into a temple for any reason, even to witness the marriages of their own children. Worthiness is determined in an interview with a church authority, during which every aspect of the prospective temple-goer's faith, from tithing to engaging in spiritual activities, is evaluated.

(This inquiry includes sexual behavior as well. In 1982, for instance, church authorities determined that oral sex constituted "an unnatural, impure or unholy practice." Consequently, engaging in such behavior, even with a spouse, could leave members outside the temple door.) In the end, applicants hope to be issued a Temple Recommend, which is essentially a pass to get in.

The details of what takes place during a temple ceremony are known only to the initiated. The Mormon marriage ceremony features a kind of dramatic play symbolizing how Mormons believe the afterlife works: God ushers men into heaven, and men, in turn, usher in their wives, which is a key reason for marriage, particularly for Mormon women. Brides promise to obey husbands, so long as they obey God, and both pledge to sacrifice all in defense of the church.

Sandy and Kent Scott were committed to keeping faithful. Within a few months of marriage, Sandy was pregnant, an event that was, predictably, met with celebration. Adherents to doctrine believe that parents are called upon by God to provide bodies for "spirit children" waiting in heaven to come to earth. And the more the better.

Jeremiah was born in April 1979. Three years later, the family expanded and he gained a sister. Children born to parents who've been sealed in a temple marriage are automatically sealed to their parents for all eternity and possess the full complement of Mormon blessings and privileges so long as they remain faithful. Basically, everyone starts with a clean slate and it's up to the individual to keep it that way.

With her marriage established and two babies born, Sandy settled into a role that's often derisively referred to by church critics as a "Molly Mormon." Traditionally, Mormon women defer absolutely to their husbands and church authorities in all things, devote their lives entirely to caring for their husbands and children, adhere strictly to church doctrine, dress in a pleasing yet chaste manner, and are consumed with church activities.

Money was always tight in the Scott household, a situation aggravated by their religious practice. Mormon church members are required to give 10 percent of their income to the church in tithing. The family moved around Washington and Utah before finally settling into a small house in southeast Portland. The Scotts' new home was an average three-bedroom affair, with a fireplace and a basement. It was located near an elementary school in a lower-middle-class neighborhood, a few blocks from a main street defined by a string of used-car lots, a Fred Meyer department store, IHop, the Super King Buffet, and a cluster of commercial buildings that looked to have been built in the 1960s. The neighborhood bordered a lower-income area that was gentrifying with each new homeowner and a little help from city officials, but would forever be known as Felony Flats.

Jeremiah Scott's lawsuit progressed very little for months after it was filed. The case suffered long periods of inaction, partly because of the slow grind of the civil court system, and partly because the church's lawyers were doing everything they could to stall. Time can be a weapon in civil justice. The state of Oregon had no court rules that required a speedy trial in a lawsuit such as the Scotts'. It's generally up to the plaintiff's side to keep things moving along, and usually in the best interests of the defendant to slow them down. A lot can happen while the clock runs: Witnesses move or die, memories fade, lawyers get busy with other cases, plaintiffs lose interest in fighting, and court cases get more expensive.

Any hope the Scott team had for a quick settlement had faded by early 1999. The LDS church had made clear its intent to fight every step of the process. Salmi and the lawyers at Dunn, Carney had done substantial defense work for insurance companies, so they were certainly familiar with the standard strategies involved in defending a lawsuit. It's also common to try to get a lawsuit dismissed on procedural or technical grounds before the case unfolds in court. The church had filed all the standard defense motions and more. Kosnoff and his team were deluged with paperwork. Every legal brief filed by the church had to be researched and answered, and each resulting hearing required the lawyers to prepare and argue in court. Routine procedural matters became protracted arguments. The church also continued to argue that certain corporate, asset-holding entities of the church could not be sued because they were separate from the greater church to which Jeremiah Scott had belonged.

While the process of motions and answers crawled along, Kosnoff resumed his research in earnest. The church's lawyers had successfully petitioned the court for an extension of time to file paperwork, a slow-down that allowed Kosnoff to work on the handful of defense cases that were keeping him financially afloat. He was negotiating a deal for two minor thieves and defending another who, against any inherent impulse of self-protection, chose to rob drug dealers and was now in jail—a dangerous combination. Adding to that, one of Kosnoff's long-time clients was facing domestic violence charges. This wasn't a new occurrence. The client habitually shared bed and board with exotic dancers. The relationships inevitably went south, usually dramatically, and ended in an arrest and a call to his lawyer.

And yet, despite the demands of other cases, Kosnoff was con-sumed with learning more about his new opponent. He possessed an insatiable intellectual curiosity that had sometimes cost him when time was money. Now, faced with a religion and history he didn't know much about, he couldn't resist a little obsession. On one Monday morning, Kosnoff sat at his desk at home and picked up a piece of paper on which he'd scribbled the phone number of a woman in San Francisco named Linda Walker. He dialed but didn't reach her and left a message.

Kosnoff had gotten her number from a woman named Sandra Tan-ner, who ran a ministry for ex-Mormons in Salt Lake City. The Inter-net is home to numerous forums that link former Mormons possessed of varying levels of anger about their experience, most of which Kos-noff tended to ignore. But he'd found another population of pseudo, quasi, and genuine academics who studied the religion and culture of Mormonism. Sandra Tanner and her husband were part of a network of writers devoted to debunking myths in Mormon literature. In a conversation earlier, she'd mentioned to Kosnoff that there were some big lawsuits against the church in Texas. She'd also left Kosnoff with the distinct impression that there were more sexual abuse cases in Mormon communities than he'd assumed and urged him to contact Linda Walker, who, she said, had worked with lawyers on the Texas cases.

Kosnoff had already learned some of the church's ugly history on his own, and not just because he enjoyed mucking around in the details, though that was certainly true. There was a more pragmatic reason. With the exception of Bill Anton, whose bills were already driving up the cost of this case, there was little money for investigators or any other employees.

For weeks Kosnoff had been glued to his computer screen, having benefited from a fortuitous advance of capitalism in the legal industry. It so happened that a company called LexisNexis, owner of the world's largest database of public records and periodical archives, had recently solicited Tim Kosnoff's business. Such a courting of lawyers typically includes a trial period in which the would-be subscriber is allowed to access the company's databases for free before committing to the regular, hefty fee. Big law firms regularly spent as much as $30,000 a month for such a service. Kosnoff, in need of information as cheaply as possible, had signed up for a trial membership and was taking full advantage of this temporary unfettered access to magazine and newspaper articles and legal opinions.

There was a lot to absorb, some of which bordered on the outrageous. Among other things, Kosnoff was interested in a lengthy 1994 article from a weekly publication in Phoenix called *New Times*. The story reported child sexual abuse claims among Mormons in Arizona and surrounding states. Of particular interest to Kosnoff, though, was that the article reported numerous civil lawsuits against the church for having played a role in some truly horrific crimes.

In some of the cases, church leaders had advised wives and children to be more understanding and help their abuser to heal. In other instances, they'd counseled pedophiles and, upon gaining a promise to change behavior, had placed the abusers back into positions in which they had easy access to children—scout leader, Sunday school teacher, Little League coach, even spiritual leader. In nearly every case in which a Mormon molester had made it into the court system, church leaders and, at their direction, members mounted a campaign of support, extolling the offender's character and urging his release.

The story noted one particularly astonishing case, that of Richard Kenneth Ray, who ultimately confessed to having sexually abused more than thirty children and a few animals. Ray was finally convicted after molesting a non-Mormon toddler in the care of his wife. The child's parents became suspicious when their toddler started acting out inappropriate sexual behavior, and they called the police. At least three church officials had known of Ray's propensity to abuse over the years. Before he was sentenced to fifty-eight years in prison by an Arizona judge, the court received a barrage of letters from church members on Ray's behalf, including one from a Mormon official who noted that Ray had been "a great influence for good" in the lives of hundreds of young people: "In view of the good things he has done throughout his life, I believe firmly that the sooner he is let back into society, the better for all it will be."

In another case, a Mormon bishop had directed the wife of a molester who had sexually abused their young children to continue living together as a family, even as child welfare workers took steps to remove the children. The mother also heeded the bishop's direction that she not allow her children to testify against their perpetrator father, effectively preventing him from being prosecuted.

Tale after tale brought more appalling details, until Kosnoff was nearing saturation. Despite years of working in the dregs of human degradation, those stories were discomforting. It was, after all, about kids. And Kosnoff was the father of a young boy.

Kosnoff also read with some surprise that the Church of Jesus Christ of Latter-day Saints all but controlled the Boy Scouts of America. According to the story, membership was practically mandatory for young Mormon boys, and troops were frequently led by men who doubled as leaders in the church. What followed, of course, was case after case of pedophiles like Frank Curtis having been installed as scout leaders. Kosnoff noted a book called *The Miracle of Forgiveness* by a Mormon leader named Spencer W. Kimball, which had been quoted in a discussion of the religious rationale for what seemed like an epic lapse in judgment, but more important, strikingly similar to the story of his client.

This reminded Kosnoff of something that he'd learned somewhere along the way, perhaps from Sandy Scott, that excommunicated Mormons may rejoin the church after a year or so of repentance. Frank Curtis could easily have fit in with the Mormon sexual perpetrators portrayed in the story. Kosnoff was more convinced than ever that the church, having previously been hit with what had to be major financial claims involving these cases, would settle with Jeremiah Scott, just as Joel Salmi had predicted.

Linda Walker was likely out having an early lunch when Tim Kosnoff first called her. She had reached middle age some years earlier and decided that the freedom to come and go as she pleased was her reward for decades spent at the mercy of bosses and children. Such a luxury would prove hard to sustain in the long run, but it was enjoyable while it lasted.

Linda often said that she didn't like to pay rent, which was why she'd adopted a side career as an apartment manager. Her present job was located in a charming upscale neighborhood high above San Francisco's infamous Haight Street. From her home, Linda also ran something called Child Protection Project, a nonprofit clearinghouse organization and website through which she had helped out on sexual abuse cases against the Mormon church. When she heard Kosnoff's message, Linda was immediately skeptical, but also curious, so she called him back.

Within about five minutes she began peppering Kosnoff with questions about his background and the case and had no compunction about lecturing him on how to run his lawsuit. The woman was nothing if not brazen and warned Kosnoff that he'd better join with a big law firm soon or he'd wind up bankrupt, sleeping in the street.

"You can't do this alone," Linda told Kosnoff. "You'd better go find a big law firm with a lot of money. You don't know what you're getting into." She added, "You need to learn a lot more about Mormons."

Linda's knowledge had come firsthand, having been born into a long line of Mormon followers. Her parents had divorced, an event that brought with it a move from Utah to Southern California with her mother, whose religious practices had lapsed. But Linda had continued to spend summers with the Mormon side of the family in Utah, and later briefly attended Brigham Young University in Provo. She lasted a year before returning to California, where she married a law student. Two children and a divorce later, Linda worked with local civil rights organizations and raised her kids in Los Angeles, where she became something of a low-level political consultant, and eventually ran the campaigns of several local judges.

Having come along fairly early, Linda's children were grown and gone by the time she hit her midforties, a circumstance that left her in need of something meaningful to do. She returned to Utah to pursue a personal project that was supposed to last about sixty days but went on for several years. Prompted by the death of a close family member, Linda began researching rare genetic diseases that are concentrated in families that practiced polygamy. Given that the LDS church didn't ban the practice until the late 1800s, many Mormon families, including Linda's, have roots in polygamy. She ended up working for researchers at the University of Utah, interviewing people for genetics studies focused on women in plural marriages. In this role, Linda had also learned about abuse of all kinds in those communities.

Linda explained to Kosnoff that she'd started Child Protection Project to help girls trapped in abusive polygamy, but over the years that mission had grown to include mainstream Mormon sex abuse victims. Lots of people called her, she said. Linda Walker possessed a unique combination of skills that made her valuable in investigating these kinds of claims: She understood the nuances of both Mormon culture and the legal system.

She warmed up to Kosnoff a bit after about half an hour on the phone, or at least was persuaded that he was somewhat legitimate. She could be mistrustful about things, but not entirely without reason. A few months earlier, a Mormon legal team had successfully had her removed from work on a case in Texas, after alleging that she was soliciting clients, which is prohibited. Linda was working for two lawyers there, interviewing people about a case against the LDS church involving a Mormon man named Ralph Neeley who'd repeatedly molested an eight-year-old girl in the ward building in Jefferson County, Texas. Neeley was convicted for the crime. Long before, victims argued, Neeley had told his local bishop what was going on, and church officials did nothing to stop it.

Linda presented this story as a sort of cautionary tale. Shortly into the job, she'd discovered that the people she was interviewing about Neeley frequently confused his bad acts with those of his friend and Mormon brother, a man named Charles Blome. One thing led to the next until, in the end, the Texas lawyers Linda worked for filed a second lawsuit against the Mormon church, this one for negligence involving Blome. The man was a youth leader who'd molested several of the young boys in his charge, for which he was serving time in prison. Mormon officials had early on alerted Blome to a sheriff's investigation and he'd burned evidence—the prosecutors alleged this included nude photographs of victims—before investigators could get hold of it. Linda had found a key witness, which helped to push an outraged Texas jury into awarding a $4 million judgment against the church, about a million more than what the plaintiffs had asked. Before the case went to trial, however, she was booted off the case at the request of the church's lawyers, who were holding up the lawsuit with misconduct complaints about her and the lawyers who'd contracted her.

There was no doubt of Linda's passion. It made her both a dogged team member and challenging when it came to strict adherence to the rules and procedures of the law. She had a voracious need to right perceived wrongs, to empower the Davids against the Goliaths. At the slightest provocation, Linda would wind up into an animated force of righteous indignation that was hard to temper.

Over the phone, Linda's enthusiasm came barreling at Kosnoff in a let's-go-get-'em kind of way, which could be too much in the staid world of the law. But he seemed to take it well. They were becoming kindred spirits in this new project, and Linda was beginning to let go with more information. Indeed, it was hard for her to hold back with an eager audience on the other end of the line. Linda told Kosnoff that the Mormon church had conducted its own investigation into allegations of sexual abuse a few years back, for which, Linda said, she'd been interviewed. The man overseeing the investigation was a church accountant, she said, who had been deposed by the lawyers who had sued the church in Texas. The report was likely a survey of the church's potential liability, something that would be important to Kosnoff's case. While it wouldn't shed any new light on what happened between the Scott family and Frank Curtis, and their spiritual leaders, the report would be germane to what is known, in legal terms, as "pattern and practice." To a jury, demonstration of pattern and practice would show that

Jeremiah's abuse was not a fluke or an accident, but rather part of regular behavior for which the church should be punished. It could make Kosnoff's case exponentially bigger.

By the time they hung up, Linda had assigned Kosnoff a list of books to read and rattled off numerous civil lawsuits in other states. She'd also told him that he would need to hire her, which, he believed, wasn't likely to happen anytime soon. He had no idea how important Linda would become in his quest to discover the legacy of Frank Curtis.

8

On a Monday morning in April 1999, Tim Kosnoff left his house
at dawn and drove south through the misty gray. He sipped coffee, but he was already plenty alert. The drive from Seattle to Portland
takes about three hours, depending on the traffic, a long, uncharacteristically scenic stretch of Interstate 5, the megahighway running from
Canada to Mexico that is notorious for its stupefying dullness.

Kosnoff used the time to contemplate the six depositions involving members of the Johnson and Penrose families that he was about to
orchestrate. He had never before conducted a deposition. With rare
exception, depositions—essentially interviews given under oath before
a civil lawsuit reaches the courtroom—didn't exist in Washington's
criminal law system. Typically, in criminal cases, witnesses make their
statements to the police, and those statements become part of the court
record. Kosnoff had questioned the hell out of cops and witnesses on
the stand, mostly to raise doubt about a client's guilt with a jury. But
today he'd have to get six strangers to reveal the details of Frank Curtis's abusive behavior in a Portland ward of the LDS church some seventeen years earlier. More important to the case, Kosnoff needed to

show that the church knew that Frank Curtis was a molester before he met Jeremiah Scott at Sunday school.

Despite his lack of experience in this particular legal exercise, it made sense for Kosnoff to depose the Johnson and Penrose families. Criminal practice tends to make lawyers more cagey and agile. All the people who would be questioned during the next two days were coming in because they had been ordered by a judge to do so; it was doubtful they were interested in helping Jeremiah Scott. And what little the lawyers had gleaned about Mormon culture told them that these folks were unlikely to cooperate in any effort to punish their church.

Kosnoff navigated his 1988 Peugeot across the Interstate Bridge that connects Oregon and Washington over the Columbia River, forming a dramatic entrance into Portland. By now, the sun had burned off some of the mist and was trying to break through the clouds. The morning traffic was heavy.

The law offices of Dunn, Carney, Allen, Higgins & Tongue are located in the upper floors of a high-rise downtown office building. The firm was walking distance from the courthouse and had become the central meeting point for nearly everything that happened on the Scott case. Kosnoff briefly spoke with Gary Rhoades, who would be present for much of the questioning, along with Lisa Thomas, their paralegal. Jim Hillas, the other Dunn, Carney lawyer, was occupied with other matters. It had taken weeks of negotiation and scheduling to make these depositions happen. In the end, the lawyers decided it best to have the Johnson family members come in one by one on the first day and the Penroses the next.

By this time, the church had hired a respected Portland lawyer by the name of Stephen English, who was head of the litigation department at the venerable law firm of Bullivant, Houser, Bailey and the former chairman of the litigation section of the Oregon State Bar Association. English mainly represented international corporations in a variety of ways, including eviscerating tort claims filed against them.

He was tall and lean and stood with exceptional posture, which created the effect of his looking down on people. Accentuating that, he tended to peer over the top of his round, rimless glasses. He arrived with another lawyer from the firm and they were ushered into the conference room. Another lawyer named Janet Knauss was there representing the Scotts' former bishop, Greg Foster. She was significantly younger and less experienced than English.

While a court reporter finished setting up her equipment, the lawyers engaged in preliminary rule making. Phillip Johnson and his wife, Catherine, arrived on time and were ushered to seats in the lobby outside the conference room. Kosnoff explained that Phillip would be questioned first and that his wife would have to wait in the lobby. Phillip and the lawyers took seats at the table, and Kosnoff began the proceedings by reintroducing everyone so that each person's presence could be memorialized by the court reporter. He gave Phillip a standard speech about how things would proceed: His answers would be used in court; he should ask if he didn't understand something; he had to wait until questions were completed before answering; he had to give verbal answers rather than a head shake so that the court reporter could record his response; and so forth.

While Kosnoff knew these people through the investigator's report, this was the first time he was face-to-face with them. He started with some preliminary questions to get his first subject talking and to create an outline of the Johnsons' life. Phillip (who went by "Phil") told the room that he'd grown up in Portland, where he met Catherine, whom most everyone called "Cathy." Both had been members of the Mormon church for their entire adult lives. Excepting a brief stint in Southern California shortly after they were married thirty-four years earlier, they'd lived in and raised their seven children in Oregon.

Phil was cresting fifty-five, and had, for the past eighteen years, worked for the church in a low-level capacity. Church work was certainly more stable than his previous jobs—in earlier years he had worked as a forklift operator—but hard times were a constant in the Johnson household.

It was clear from Phil's answers that the Johnsons had done their best to steep their children in the religion and culture of Mormonism. They observed weekly Family Nights, regularly attended religious services and Sunday school, and enrolled their children in the church's scouting programs. Both Cathy and Phil had been called over the years to serve as youth teachers in the ward where they lived. Throughout their lives, save for once, the Johnsons had possessed Temple Recommends to attend services in a Mormon temple. Devout as they might have been, Phil admitted that he and Cathy had also been denied entrance for not having kept up their mandatory 10 percent tithe to the church.

Kosnoff periodically glanced over the eight pages of notes he'd made to prepare for this deposition, based on conversations with the investigator and the other lawyers on the Scott team, and his own research. As much as anything else, this was a chance to get a better grasp of the workings of the church and to establish that its members were true believers who trusted completely, perhaps blindly, in their religious leaders. To that end, he asked Phil to explain the various steps that young men moved through as they progressed in their religious training.

Starting at about age twelve, a worthy Mormon male may receive confirmation into something called the Aaronic priesthood, so long as he adheres to certain moral standards and attends church. At about fourteen, he may be considered a teacher, again dependent on maintaining certain requirements of religious worthiness. If all goes as planned, that same lad will, at the age of eighteen or nineteen, become a member of the Melchizedek priesthood and thus be considered "a priesthood holder." A man of this standing enjoys the full rights of the church, may be called to hold a leadership position, and may baptize others. LDS church members believe that a brotherhood among priesthood holders—as well as a corresponding sisterhood among women in the church's Relief Society—obligates them in service to one another. They are expected to be actively concerned for the welfare of other members and families. The church ward itself is considered a family, with the bishop (leader of the ward) acting as father. Women cannot hold the priesthood, which is why they must be "sealed" to a husband or father in order to gain entrance into their afterlife—the Celestial Kingdom.

Each ward, or congregation, is led by a bishop and one or two assistants, called counselors. Wards are organized into stakes, headed by a stake president, who functions much like a district manager. The bishop is assisted by two counselors, and the three together are known as a "bishopric" that governs the ward. Phil Johnson had been a first counselor to the bishop in a ward in California many years ago. As luck would have it for Kosnoff, Phil had also served as clerk of the ward in Portland, which meant that he had handled membership records. Evidence of the existence of some permanent record kept on individuals by the church opened the door for the Scott team to request Frank Curtis's membership records. Those records, Kosnoff hoped, would show how Frank had moved around from ward to ward, and that church officials knew about his tendency to molest boys.

This theory was confirmed as Phil answered question after question about membership records. When members leave a ward for whatever reason, Phil said, their records are forwarded to Mormon headquarters in Salt Lake City. Phil also said that he'd known bishops to make a notation or "red flag" on a record if there was a problem with that member.

The Johnsons had first met Brother Curtis shortly after he moved into the Portland ward, to which they belonged, in the early 1980s. Brother Curtis was nearly eighty years old at the time. He attended weekly LDS services, called "Sacrament Meetings," and was an elder, meaning he was a priesthood holder who'd attained a certain status within the church.

Brother Curtis was called to lead boys who were ten to twelve, David Johnson's age, in Sunday school and Blazers—young Boy Scouts. It was not uncommon for Brother Curtis to visit at the Johnson home, sometimes for dinner or Sunday lunch. There are few single adults within the Mormon membership and they are typically "fellowshipped," or invited into the homes of Mormon families. At some point, Brother Curtis had suggested to Phil that his son David should come to his home to study Articles of Faith. The Articles, believed to have been written by the prophet Joseph Smith in 1842 and adopted by the church as a standard work in 1880, lists the thirteen basic points of the Latter-day Saints' faith. Young men progressing along the path into the priesthood, as David was, are expected to learn, sometimes even memorize, such works.

Brother Curtis had told Phil there would be other boys with David, including Steven Penrose, David's best friend in the church. Phil and Cathy Johnson had thought it was great the way this elder in their ward had taken an interest in David, a quiet, somewhat shy middle child. On at least one occasion, Phil recounted, David had been reluctant to go to Frank's house, but his parents had sent him along, anyway. Kosnoff knew this from the investigator's report that he and Salmi had gotten last year. Phil had thought David didn't want to go because he just didn't want to study. At Kosnoff's request, Phil attempted to place this event in time, finally settling on 1983, which was later determined to be off by at least a year. Given the boys' ages and other events, it was more likely 1982.

As the deposition progressed, and they fell into a rhythm, Kosnoff sensed Johnson was opening up, and he tried to keep the momentum going.

"What did he say that, looking back on it, should have aroused your suspicion or concern?" Kosnoff asked.

"I asked him why he didn't want to go over to this person's house, and he mumbled something about 'he makes me sit on his lap,'" Phil said.

"Did he say anything else besides Curtis making him sit on his lap?"

"No."

"What was your reaction when you heard this?"

"Totally naïve," Phil said. "I couldn't see what he was objecting to."

Kosnoff hadn't known what to expect from this question-and-answer drill, and was surprised at how forthcoming Johnson was, as if he genuinely wanted to talk about what had happened. Kosnoff was choreographing much of the unfolding narrative from information contained in reports they'd gotten from the investigations firm. As a defense lawyer, Kosnoff had often gotten only one shot at a witness—at trial. He was accustomed to making a careful study of the details in people's backgrounds in order to anticipate what someone might say. In general, criminal lawyers tend to view litigation much more like a street fight than like the more genteel chess game of civil lawyers, and Kosnoff was no exception.

Phillip Johnson, though, was not resisting Kosnoff's inquiries. He was a large man without being obese, and Kosnoff thought he seemed tired. He sat sort of slumped in his chair at the table looking worn out. Of course, by this time, they'd all been in the conference room for more than two hours. Kosnoff began asking Phil about when he found out that his son had been molested by Frank Curtis, and was taken aback by his oddly specific answer:

"On the fourteenth of August, nineteen eighty-three," Phil said.

"You remember the specific day?" Kosnoff asked.

"It was a Sunday."

"How is it that all this time you can remember that it was—the specific date?"

"I wrote it down."

Mormons, particularly the heads of Mormon families, are encouraged to keep journals in order to record family histories, as well as for spiritual reasons. Journaling, they believe, helps them focus on the blessings they've received and deal with anger and frustration. Kosnoff definitely wanted to know more about the existence of a journal, which might contain events recorded more accurately than they were remembered. He also made a mental note of the possibility that other people, including Brother Curtis, possessed personal journals. Phil said he was not particularly faithful to his journal, but he did tend to record major occurrences. He'd dug up old entries after he received a subpoena for the deposition.

Phil continued, saying that he had learned about David's abuse from their bishop at the time, Gordon Checketts.

At this point, Steve English interrupted Kosnoff with a blanket objection to anything the Johnsons and Bishop Checketts had discussed. Unlike at trial, objections made during depositions are simply noted and ruled on later, and the questioning continues. The conversation between the Johnsons and Bishop Checketts was already a major issue in the case, because the church believed it to be a confidential conversation between a church member and his religious leader. As such, the church's lawyers maintained, the information was considered privileged and could not be used in court.

Despite the interruption, Kosnoff continued to ask questions and Phil continued to answer them. Phil said he remembered Bishop Checketts calling the Johnsons into his office in the ward building on a Sunday. David was already there when they arrived, but they hadn't known why.

Bishop Checketts, Phil said, had broken the news that Frank had been molesting David. Phil said that he'd learned the abuse had been going on for more than a year. And then he said something even more important to the lawyers in the room: Bishop Checketts had mentioned that he'd learned from the bishop of another ward, where Frank had previously been an active member—Phil seemed to think this was in Chicago but was uncertain—that Frank had molested children there as well.

English tossed off a handful of objections during Johnson's story. Lawyers do this for a couple of reasons: There is always a chance that a judge will keep the testimony out of court for the reason stated in the objection, and because it breaks the flow, or momentum, of the opposing counsel. Occasionally, this sort of gamesmanship takes the form of a lawyer asking the court reporter to read back previous answers because they weren't heard, or requesting a break, or just objecting. Technically, there are only a handful of reasons for a lawyer to object in a civil deposition. But that doesn't mean he might not try out a few others. English frequently objected to something on the basis that it "mischaracterizes previous testimony," which meant nothing in the long run but did break the flow of conversation between Kosnoff and his witness and so was somewhat effective. Kosnoff assigned more sinister motives to the church's lawyers, having decided that they were trying to send a message to Johnson that the church might be harmed by his answers.

Conspiracy theories aside, what Phil was saying, if correct, was potentially damaging to the LDS church, as it meant there was one more leader, in addition to the bishops Greg Foster and Gordon Checketts, who may have known that Frank Curtis had molested children long before he wound up in the home of Jeremiah Scott.

Johnson also said that neither he nor his wife reported Frank to the police.

"Why not?" Kosnoff asked.

"I've tried to think of that, why I didn't do it. I guess—I don't know what I thought," Phil said. "I guess among the things that I did think about was that the church was doing what it could. I have no idea what Bishop Checketts did after he revealed this to us, but I guess I felt that it was in somebody else's hands, that we would just move on with our life."

However odd or naïve this might have sounded, Kosnoff didn't pay it much mind. He was preoccupied with matters of strategy. The private investigator's report had noted that David Johnson, along with his younger brother and some other boys, had been sexually abused by another perpetrator—a barber whose shop was across from their school—at about the same time they were preyed upon by Frank. Further digging had revealed that the barber had been arrested for the crime. Collectively, the events were a shocking coincidence of unfathomable pain. At the same time, the entire situation was a big help to the Scott team: Faced with similar incidents of sexual abuse involving the same child, the same people had reported only the non-Mormon abuser to the police.

Morning had long since moved into afternoon, and everyone in the room was eager for a change of scene. Rhoades had come and gone a few times already. Phil was clearly fatigued, but Kosnoff was determined to squeeze out every detail that might help his case. And they were deep into the sort of emotional story that might outrage a jury, for good reason.

As long as he was probing what Bishop Checketts said and did with the Johnson family, Kosnoff made a point of having Phil also discuss how the matter of Brother Curtis's abuse was handled with David. Phil had told the Scott team's private investigators that he hadn't known the details of what happened to his son in Brother Curtis's apartment because they'd never talked about it. Now he confirmed that David had not received any sort of psychological counseling from the church or anywhere else. But he had been disciplined:

"At the time that we met with Bishop Checketts, he let us know that he had been—that Frank had been molesting David. And also a result of that meeting was that Bishop Checketts suggested that David be put on probation because he had chosen to continue to return to this situation," Johnson said.

"With Curtis?" Kosnoff asked.

"With Curtis."

Phil went on to explain how the event played out in the church. David was eleven years old at the time and working toward receiving the right of full priesthood at the end of his teenage years. (In fact, Frank Curtis had used this same religious training to "groom" David and Steven Penrose, when he projected himself into a mentoring role to the boys in the church.) One of the main duties of Mormon boys of David's age is to act as a deacon and pass the Sacrament—bread and water—to other members during church services. When Checketts placed David and Steven on probation, it meant that they would not be allowed to perform that, or any other, duty in the church for an unspecified period of time—until the bishop was impressed that David was ready to resume his role in the church.

"Checketts was blaming David in part for his molestation by Curtis, is that what you're saying?" Kosnoff asked, his outrage starting to show. English immediately objected. Meanwhile, Phil tried to hedge about the bishop's decision, even though it was clear at this point that he hadn't been happy about it.

"I knew we were going to get into this, and I . . . looking at this incident sixteen years later, what was said and what was decided appear to be totally out of line," Phil said. "Knowing what we know today about the dynamics of child abuse, they may have been totally wrong, looking from our perspective today."

Kosnoff wasn't about to let up on Phil until he had this whole incident preserved for a jury.

"Was David placed on probation?"

"Yes."

"Probation is a form of discipline?"

"Yes."

"David was disciplined by Bishop Checketts because he had gone back and endured abuse by Frank Curtis?"

"Yes."

English jumped in again, this time objecting that Kosnoff's question called for Phil to speculate. "It also gets into the interpretation by Bishop Checketts of church doctrines and the appropriate response thereto," English said. "I think it's protected by the First Amendment issue."

Kosnoff ignored English and remained focused on Johnson.

"Well, did you agree with Bishop Checketts at that time that David was blameworthy for what had happened to him by Curtis?"

"I'm afraid so," Johnson said.

"Did your wife?"

"I'll say that we just simply concurred with what he suggested doing."

"In reference to Bishop Checketts telling your son that he was to blame for the molestation," Kosnoff asked, "did that also occur with respect to the barber or are we talking just about the Curtis incident?"

"Just the Curtis incident."

Phil Johnson finally left the conference room some four hours after he'd walked in. Kosnoff and Rhoades huddled briefly in Rhoades's office down the hall to review what they'd just learned. The information about Bishop Checketts having disciplined the kids was outrageous, as far as Kosnoff was concerned. Years later, he could still get riled up about it.

"That wasn't just Checketts, it was Checketts's belief system," he later reflected. "What is wrong with you that you would have such a twisted, pathetic, outrageous understanding of the situation?"

At the time, the attorneys were, in general, pleased with Johnson's forthrightness, and particularly his testimony about membership records and Checketts's response. It was now crucial that they get hold of Frank Curtis's membership records, which had been among their requests to the church earlier. It now seemed quite possible that either Checketts or someone else in the church might have placed a "red flag" or made some other note in the record about Frank having been accused of molesting children.

Less than an hour later, Cathy Johnson was sitting in the conference room answering many of the same questions Kosnoff had asked her husband. Like her husband, she was courteous and cooperative, though it was clear that the subject of abuse was extremely troubling to her. She sniffled and wept softly through much of the deposition. When Kosnoff asked questions about Frank Curtis having molested David, Cathy lost her composure and began to sob. The lawyers took a short break while she pulled herself together, then they moved on.

Cathy said that she had gone along with Checketts's decision to punish her son for his role in the abuse, though she hadn't agreed with it.

"What did you say to David about the fact that he was being punished for what Frank Curtis had done to him?" Kosnoff asked.

"Well, the only thing we could say was that this is what the bishop's responsibilities were toward children that have been . . . that probably have been molested, you know," Cathy said. "For anything that a child does, you know, if they're not worthy to hold a position for a little while, then, you know, certain responsibilities are taken from them for a little bit. And this wasn't going to last for very long, I'm sure, but it was just something that the bishop just felt like, you know, David just wasn't ready to continue passing the Sacrament at that particular time."

Cathy also told the lawyers that her son had left the church because he felt uncomfortable and ostracized at Boy Scout meetings, as if everyone knew he had done these awful things, regardless of whether that was real or imagined. David, she said, later began using drugs and was somewhat disruptive in school, which she attributed to the sexual abuse. But the family hadn't sought counseling because David had been so unwilling to talk about what happened. Kosnoff finished questioning Cathy Johnson within an hour. From a legal standpoint, there wasn't much more to gain from her. Besides, David had arrived and was waiting outside with his father.

David was then twenty-eight, married, and raising three young children. Their youngest child, David Jr., was eight months old. Kosnoff thought David looked skinny and, frankly, unhealthy. He seemed shy and distressed, though it was unclear how much of that might be owing to the pending deposition.

It was already four o'clock in the afternoon. David worked in construction and couldn't easily get off work. His was a pretty good job, particularly considering that, before the mill, David had done roofing and painting, both of which left him at the mercy of the weather and the business acumen of other contractors. David had dropped out of school in the ninth grade.

Without much warm-up, Kosnoff got right into asking David about Frank Curtis.

It was evident quickly that David was going to have a hard time remembering—and reliving—the details. He said that Brother Curtis had seemed, at first, a pretty nice guy. He'd prepared some minor lessons in religion for David and Steven Penrose, and then they just sort of hung around until it was time to go home. This went on periodically for about two months, and eventually the boys started having sleepovers at Brother Curtis's house. By this time, the old man had moved from his apartment into a trailer park.

Brother Curtis had allowed the boys to watch television and, one evening, showed them a pornographic videotape featuring a man and woman having sex. Neither David nor Steven had ever seen such a thing. The porn became a routine at Frank's, a forbidden and exciting secret they shared.

"As we were watching the pornographic movies, he'd want us to come sit on his lap, and slowly grabbed our hands, asked us . . . wanted us to touch him," David told the lawyers. "I didn't really want to go there too much, but eventually I got into messing with him."

At Kosnoff's prompting, David methodically went through the litany of horrors that had occurred in Frank's trailer during the next year or so. Brother Curtis had engaged the boys in mutual masturbation, oral and anal sex, and all manner of other violations. And because his trailer was small, whatever was happening with one of the boys was happening in front of the other. One of them would end up sleeping in Brother Curtis's bed, an arrangement made all the more unpleasant by the fact that he was often lax in his personal hygiene. He was a big, stinky man. He could also be scary.

"The tone of his voice was kind of threatening, at times, I can remember," David said.

"Can you tell me a little bit more about that? How would he use his voice in a threatening tone or manner?" Kosnoff asked.

"When he wanted us to do something, he'd tell us in a lower, deeper, stricter voice, 'Could you do this for me?'"

It was clear to everyone in the room how painful this was for him to relive, but they were all still engaged in legal combat, and Kosnoff needed to mine everything he could while he had the chance. He kept at it.

"Looking back on it now as an adult, do you have any idea why you did it even though you didn't want to?"

"I guess in a way I was doing it because my friend was doing it. I can't recall if my friend started doing this before I did."

"Did you look up to Steven?"

"Yeah. He was about the only friend I had."

David insisted that he couldn't remember much of what Brother Curtis had said to him and Steven while he was with them, and after a few more tries, Kosnoff came to believe that David was telling the truth. He tended to glance down and avoid looking anyone in the eye while answering, but Kosnoff didn't think he was dodging. Mostly, Kosnoff was pleased that David was still talking at all.

Why, Kosnoff asked, had David never told anyone what was happening with Brother Curtis?

"I guess I thought I could get in trouble . . . that I could be the one liable for what was happening. For some reason, that's the way I felt."

David went on to confirm something his father had said earlier in the day, that Brother Curtis had given David a bicycle. The Johnsons had been impressed, if a little confused, by this act of generosity from a man who seemed to need help paying his utility bills. David had wrecked the bike soon after he received it.

"I hated him," David explained. "I didn't care for him at all . . . and I felt used, real used. And I mean, I thought because he was in the church he was supposed to be a good person, teach me the right ways, but [that] didn't happen."

Toward the end of their time with Brother Curtis, David said, Steven had dragged along his younger brothers, one of whom eventually told his mother that bad things happened there. The Penroses went to Bishop Checketts, who then met with the Johnsons. Somewhere along the way, Frank Curtis had left town.

Oddly, David said that he couldn't remember having been placed on probation by Bishop Checketts, though he did remember the meeting in the bishop's office: "I know he asked me questions of what happened, but I was young, I was embarrassed, I didn't want to say nothing, so I didn't say nothing really that I can remember."

English, who hadn't said a word since David sat down, objected after Kosnoff made reference to the Johnsons having said that Checketts put David on probation. But, for whatever reason, he didn't object when Kosnoff asked David about his conversation in the bishop's office, which might have been a clergy-penitent privilege issue.

Kosnoff moved on to the incident with the barber. David, his brother Kevin (who was a couple of years younger), and Steven Penrose had all been abused by the barber at about the same time as the incidents with Frank Curtis. The barber lived across the street from their school, and David said he'd initially gone there for a job sweeping up the shop. Instead, he wound up being paid by the barber for sexual favors. This went on for a couple of weeks until the barber was caught, though David couldn't remember how that had happened.

The following year, when he would have been entering the sixth grade, David said, he was held back in school and placed in special-education classes, having been diagnosed as "emotionally disturbed." The special-ed track continued until, in the ninth grade, he resumed mainstream classes with his peers. Shortly afterward, David dropped out of school.

None of the other lawyers asked questions once Kosnoff was finished. It was after five o'clock and everyone seemed eager to end the long day. Tomorrow, they knew, would be just as taxing.

Kosnoff made his way to the Days Inn, a nondescript motel in downtown Portland, where he was becoming a regular. There was no room service, gym, or business center here—just a clean room with a television and a bathroom. Mostly, it was cheap at $39.99, which had become increasingly important with each passing month. At some point, Kosnoff developed a habit of keeping a pillow and bedding from home in the back of his car because they helped him sleep better.

At the motel, he opened a beer and called Mary Ann. It was good to talk about more pleasant things, like his son and school. Kosnoff was exhausted and exhilarated at the same time. There was something else too. Whatever understanding he'd previously possessed of faith and religion was fading. It was too difficult to reconcile what had happened during the boyhoods of these young men with any sort of spiritual organization. These were fairly unsophisticated people, sure, but the naïveté that had come with their faith was puzzling. And how could a religious leader not want this molester arrested? "They forced these people to be religious zealots who will place their need to belong to this religious organization over the safety of their children," he reflected years later. "It was evil."

Tuesday started much more quickly than Monday, since most of the technical staging and rule making remained in place from the Johnsons' depositions. Don, Joanne, and Steven Penrose arrived at the Dunn, Carney office together. It was immediately evident that they would not be as polite and cooperative as the Johnsons had been. Collectively, they seemed edgy and unhappy from the moment they walked in the office.

Kosnoff had an idea why. Don had made clear that he thought he'd been duped by the investigators because they hadn't told him that there would be a lawsuit filed against the church when they had questioned him the previous October. He'd also said that he did not believe the church was responsible for what happened to his son. Frank Curtis had done these horrible deeds. (The Johnsons had not been in favor of a lawsuit against the church either.) Kosnoff had gotten the you're-a-greedy-lawyer message loud and clear from the Penrose family.

Tuesday's agenda was much like that of the previous day. Don Penrose would take the first turn in the conference room, followed by his wife, and then Steven. Janet Knauss, the lawyer representing Greg Foster, announced that she would be concurring with all of Stephen English's objections, according to an agreement the two of them had made after depositions ended the day before. Jim Hillas, the Dunn Carney associate working on the case, joined the group in the conference room, but Kosnoff was still doing the questioning.

Don answered preliminary questions matter-of-factly and provided a fairly complete oral history of the family. By coincidence, Don, like Phil Johnson, was employed by the church and had been for many years. He'd also been called to various leadership positions over the years. The Penroses had ten children, ranging in age from one to thirty-four, half of whom still lived at home. At one point later in the deposition, Don remembered that he'd forgotten one of his children when he was listing them earlier and corrected himself.

Like the Johnsons, the Penroses lived in a low-income suburb of Portland. Bill Anton, the investigator, had been contracted to serve the family with notice to appear at the deposition and had commented that the Penrose home looked a bit like that of the Old Woman Who Lived in a Shoe, owing to a frenzy of children young and old coming and going from the house. In fact, when Anton had gone there to serve the subpoenas, Don had chased after him, Anton told Kosnoff, yelling about Steven: "You'll never get him!" Neither Kosnoff nor Anton could figure out why.

Kosnoff and Salmi had read in the investigation report about an awkward, if not surreal, event that happened the first time the investigator went to the Penrose house to interview the family, back in 1997. Don Penrose had been getting ready to take his son to a Boy Scout meeting. They stood on the driveway, as daylight slowly began to fade, in front of a house badly in need of maintenance. Don Penrose had talked to the investigator about Steven, his older boy, and confirmed that he'd been molested by Frank Curtis while he was supposed to be studying for his religious training. And then Penrose's younger son, who was standing next to his father, looking up at the adults and listening to their conversation, suddenly blurted out that Frank Curtis had molested him too. Don Penrose turned and corrected his son. No, no, they were talking about something that happened to Steven a long time ago. But the boy was insistent. Soon it became clear that he was telling his father, evidently for the first time, that he too had been a victim of Frank Curtis. Not only had this man learned that yet another son had been molested by this church brother he'd trusted, but he'd experienced this tragedy in front of a stranger, out on the driveway, completely exposed.

In his deposition, Don provided much the same information as Phil had regarding matters of the church and Frank Curtis. He had been aware that Steven was going to Brother Curtis's house for work in Blazers and religious study. Don recalled that Steven was coming home with scouting-related knives and various other items that Brother Curtis had given him, which the Penroses were somewhat curious about, but not enough to make inquiries.

The mood remained tense in the conference room, and Don could barely keep his hostility in check during much of the questioning. He answered question after question by saying that he could not recall important things—including when he had found out that Brother Curtis was molesting his son. He did not remember meeting with Bishop Checketts about the molestation. Kosnoff was losing patience with what he perceived was Don's refusal to give him any information.

"Did you subsequently learn that your son had been repeatedly sexually abused and sodomized by Frank Curtis?" Kosnoff asked, finally.

"Yes," Don answered.

"Was that something that happened every day of your life?"

"No."

English immediately objected and went on to accuse Kosnoff of being argumentative and of harassing Don.

Later, Joanne Penrose sat down in the conference room without any hint of friendliness. It was clear that, like her husband, she wanted no part of this proceeding. Joanne mentioned that, while raising ten children, she'd worked as a manager at a restaurant for several years until she decided that her kids needed their mother at home more. Despite her hostility toward the process, Joanne was able to fill in many of the blanks that her husband had left. As time wore on, Kosnoff sensed her resistance starting to soften.

Joanne was the one who had first heard what was going on from one of her younger sons. He'd been approached by Brother Curtis while he was with Steven. From there, she said, the news just sort of snowballed from one child to the next, until the story came out. Joanne went into great detail about how she'd called a meeting with Bishop Checketts and told him what had happened. She had been under the impression that Bishop Checketts had notified the police, but couldn't be sure if he'd told her that or if she'd just assumed it. She and Don had not been able to afford therapy for their sons at the time, and Steven had pretty much refused to talk to the bishop or anyone else about what had happened, anyway.

Later, Joanne said, Steven had felt that people treated him differently at church, and he stopped going, just as David Johnson had. She thought her son felt guilty, embarrassed, and uncomfortable. He'd gone on to have more serious behavioral problems, started drinking and using drugs as a teenager, and had a minor brush with the law. Ultimately, like David Johnson, Steven had dropped out of school.

As a young girl, Joanne said, she had been molested by two relatives, a trauma that had led her to see a therapist much later in life, to help her sort things out. She realized that her son must have felt some of the same issues. She'd tried then to get him into therapy, she said, but didn't think he'd ever participated.

It was after two thirty in the afternoon by the time Joanne left the conference room. Kosnoff was keeping a close eye on the clock because he wanted to make sure he left enough time for Steven Penrose. The Scott team didn't know what to expect from Steven, who had already announced his intention to be as difficult as possible.

Bill Anton had found it difficult to locate Steven to serve him a subpoena to appear for questioning. It was clear that the man didn't want to be found, nor did his parents seem to want him found. Eventually, Anton had served Steven at his job at a local store. Shortly afterward, Steven had called Dunn, Carney and said to one of the lawyers, "There's no way I'm going to testify."

When Kosnoff called Steven to follow up, Steven had said only that he wasn't interested in talking about things that had happened fifteen years ago and didn't matter anymore. Ultimately, Steven had no choice in the matter. He'd been ordered by a judge to show up. Steven had told Kosnoff on the phone that if he came he wouldn't remember anything, indicating that he wasn't planning to answer any questions. His impending deposition had been the subject of numerous phone calls and emails among Kosnoff, Salmi, Rhoades, and Hillas during the days leading up to the deposition, as they ruminated on what was motivating Steven's obstinacy and how best to handle it. While the Penroses had remained active in the church, it didn't appear that Steven was particularly devout. The obvious question on everyone's mind was whether Steven felt that he had to protect the church or his parents, or if he was simply not inclined to cooperate and didn't want to talk about Frank Curtis.

Kosnoff had reviewed strategies with Jim Hillas before the depositions. Most of the time, lawyers handle a hostile witness by asking leading questions that include facts the lawyers want the witness to agree with on the record. It's a bit like the classic joke: "And after you stopped beating your wife with the candlestick, what happened?" But there are other things that lawyers can do to move along a reluctant witness. Hillas had suggested, for example, that Kosnoff review what Bill Anton had been told by the rest of the Penrose family the year before, to remind Steven that they had already heard much of his story. After that, Kosnoff was just going to have to wing it.

In contrast to David Johnson, Steven Penrose was well built and good-looking. Even though he showed up for the deposition, he arrived cloaked in attitude.

Following some preliminary questions that were largely inconsequential—Kosnoff's attempt to create a rhythm—Steven made good on his promise not to answer. He dodged one thing after another, telling the lawyers that he couldn't remember most of the things that others had testified about, although he remembered that Frank had parts of three fingers missing from one of his hands. Finally, Kosnoff decided that he wasn't going to get much out of Steven and started a verbal sparring match that lasted several minutes.

"Did Frank Curtis do sexually inappropriate things with you when you went to his apartment?" Kosnoff asked.

"I don't feel comfortable in answering that question."

"Nevertheless, you must."

Knauss didn't let this opening pass without making objections regarding Steven's emotional pain. So far, much of what had been said by witnesses was not particularly good for the church's position. But a judge might later excise whole parts of the testimony, making them unusable in court. Steven held his ground, and Kosnoff launched into an interrogation about who might have influenced Steven's testimony, though it was likely that Steven was acting on his own.

"I never said I was abused, I said I didn't want to talk about that," Steven said.

"Well, you have been sworn. You've been served with a subpoena to testify here today. What right or authority are you asserting in support of your position that you don't have to answer my question?"

This prompted a whirl of objections from the other lawyers, who wanted to carve out whatever use they could make of the controversy. Kosnoff agreed to a ten-minute cooling-off period and then resumed his questioning.

"I said I don't think I really need a legal thing. I said I don't want to talk about the abuse and I'm not going to talk about it," Steven said.

"Okay. You understand that the subpoena to testify here today that you received is an order?" Kosnoff asked.

"So?"

"Are you saying that you are not willing to obey that order?"

"I'm here."

"But you're not answering my questions."

"I'll answer any questions that you ask except for about the abuse."

"Did Frank Curtis abuse you?"

"I don't feel comfortable in answering that question."

"Do you understand that there are legal consequences for refusing to answer a question put to you as a person who has been legally served with a subpoena to testify in deposition?"

In the end, Kosnoff halted the deposition, refusing to continue until there was some resolution to the standoff with Steven. The truth was that Steven's version of events with Frank Curtis was of negligible importance to the case of Jeremiah Scott, but Kosnoff was incensed. He was ready to try to have Steven held in contempt of court, which was unlikely to happen for all sorts of reasons. In the meantime, Steven left the law office with his parents.

Kosnoff sensed a hint of smugness in English as they shook hands on the way out. He spoke briefly with Rhoades and Hillas, and then loaded his notes into the car for the drive back to Seattle.

The Scott team's list of Frank Curtis's victims was turning into something more complex, with events charted on a changing time line to keep track of the growing number of players. Revised, it now looked like this:

FRANK CURTIS TIME LINE OF VICTIMS

Before 1982	Unknown children	possibly Chicago
1982–1983	David Johnson, Steven Penrose	Portland
1991	Jeremiah Scott	Portland

9

As Tim Kosnoff reviewed the depositions of David Johnson, his family, Steven Penrose, and his family, as well as the reports gathered by his investigator, he became more convinced that a larger pattern of abuse existed. Frank Curtis had molested Jeremiah Scott in 1991. He had abused David Johnson and Steven Penrose in 1983. There was a suggestion of an earlier abuse case, perhaps in Chicago. The more Kosnoff learned, the more he realized how much he didn't know. What had Frank Curtis been doing between 1983, when he left town after molesting David Johnson and Steven Penrose, and 1991, when he started to abuse Jeremiah Scott?

It was clear from what the victims said that Curtis had an established methodology for ingratiating himself with families of young boys, creating trust, and then seizing opportunity when it presented itself. What if Curtis had gone from one opportunity to another, year after year, perhaps even decade after decade? There could be a long sequence of abuse incidents, laddering through the years, many if not most involving the Mormon church.

His mission now, Kosnoff realized, was to find these other cases, if they existed, and use them to build an impregnable legal argument against the church. And although the challenge was daunting, Kosnoff also found it somehow irresistible.

Kosnoff had expected the LDS church's lawyers to wage a significant battle over records and had told Salmi and the rest of the team as much. Some amount of squabbling over what specific information has to be produced is standard procedure, and such matters often wind up in front of a judge to sort out. The object of the game is to get hold of as much as possible while limiting what the other side is allowed to learn.

Kosnoff had thrown tremendous effort into researching other LDS cases, particularly a recent lawsuit in West Virginia in which a mother alleged that the church had known for years that her husband was abusing their children and did nothing to stop it. The woman's husband ultimately pleaded guilty to thirty-seven counts of child abuse and was sentenced to up to 185 years in prison. In the civil lawsuit that followed, the Mormon church argued that church officials had learned about the abuse in their role as clergy, and so anything to do with those conversations was off-limits to examination. Linda Walker had pointed Kosnoff to other LDS cases in which the same argument was used, along with the church's position that releasing nearly any kind of records would violate First Amendment protections of the free exercise of religion.

In short, the Free Exercise Clause of the First Amendment to the U.S. Constitution prevents the government from discriminating against people because of their religious views. The idea that people are free to follow whatever religious beliefs they choose is ingrained in American history. Interpreting that concept has kept judges busy for centuries, however, because religion usually involves some practice. Courts have had to differentiate between what is considered "belief" and what is "conduct." In general, conduct is not protected—for example, people aren't allowed to sacrifice human life in the name of religion—but the line between legally protected belief and illegal conduct is subject to the interpretation of a judge or jury.

The church argued that its discipline records were part of the Mormon belief in the process of repentance. For the court to require the church to produce its records, the LDS lawyers argued, would be to unconstitutionally bring questions of faith into the courtroom. Further, they maintained, such an examination intruded into the private relationship between a man and his spiritual leader.

Kosnoff and the other lawyers on the Scott team had anticipated that the church would raise the same issues in the Scott case. They just hadn't expected it to happen immediately. Nor had anyone expected the volume of motions the church's lawyers were filing with the court on the issue.

Even getting a document as simple as a membership directory was subject to months-long dispute. The request for directories had started with another tip from Linda, who'd told Kosnoff early into the case that every Mormon ward had a membership directory that was regularly updated. The directories were an essential part of LDS life because there were so many gatherings and volunteer jobs that needed to be coordinated. Linda had used both ward and stake directories in other cases, and pointed out that they would be particularly valuable for finding people who might have interacted with Frank Curtis or any of his victims in what Kosnoff now knew to be at least three different wards where the man had been a Sunday school teacher or Boy Scout leader. The Scott lawyers had figured it was routine to include the Portland area ward directories in a request for production to their opponents and really hadn't given it much more thought. Except that nothing was routine in this case. At first, the church had agreed to, but did not, produce any directories. Then English and his crew said that the directories were not available from the church headquarters, and that they hadn't figured out how or where to get them. Finally, the church agreed to provide any ward directories that it could find but wanted the court to issue a protective order on the information. Such a move would mean that the directories would first be produced exclusively to the judge, who would have to read through the information and determine what was confidential beyond what the attorneys needed to work their case. The LDS lawyers used the same pattern of action on other record requests, including the Scotts' own church membership records. All of this maneuvering had the direct effect of delaying and preventing the Scott team from gaining evidence. Kosnoff was getting frustrated by the church's lawyers and their drawn-out process. Criminal court cases move much faster than does the civil side of the justice system. Civil cases are more often won and lost in the paperwork and the run-up to court than they are in the courtroom. Jim Hillas once joked that criminal cases could be over in three months, but if you gave a civil lawyer three months, he'd panic.

The church's lawyers were issuing their own demands for everything they could think of that might help their defense. Kosnoff had been laid up early in 1999 recovering from hip surgery, the result of a fall off a ladder at home. Now he was catching up and had taken on the role of responding to the church's requests. To that end, he had Jeremiah and Sandy Scott chasing down Jeremiah's employment records at the camera shop where he worked, and diaries, drawings, even schoolwork that Jeremiah had completed during the periods of time while Frank Curtis lived with the Scott family. Some of the requests, Kosnoff thought, were plain ridiculous. He was losing patience with the church's demands, and with his colleagues, who he felt were giving their opponents too much leeway on requests for Jeremiah's medical and counseling records and other records the church was demanding the Scotts to produce. At one point, Kosnoff blew up in an email after Lisa, the paralegal at Dunn, Carney, sent a list of questions about some of the responses that were still outstanding.

Look, guys, I don't understand your email at all. I sent you most of these materials more than a month ago. . . . Everyone seemed to acknowledge (and ORCP [Oregon Rules of Civil Procedure] *rules make clear) that if it is not in Jeremiah's possession, he does not have to go out and hunt it down. Now I am being asked at the eleventh hour to chase down docs which may be in the possession of third parties and that I better do it ASAP or the depositions won't go forward. I am NOT going to chase down any docs which may exist at any doctor's office, employer, juvenile hall or other third party at this point. That is their job which I am not willing nor required to do for them. I am NOT happy about this.*

Tim

There was more stress on the Scott team than the tortuous legal nitpicking of their opponents. Kosnoff and Salmi had taken out a credit line at the bank to fund the costs during the last year and a half or so, and Dunn, Carney was sinking more and more time into the case with no payment on the horizon. Earlier, the arrangement among the lawyers had turned into one of ownership, in that Kosnoff and Salmi could hardly pay for Dunn, Carney's services on contract. So the firm now owned a significant stake in the outcome of the case. Collectively the lawyers for Jeremiah Scott had already spent about $30,000 on everything from court reporters to postage, and that didn't include anyone's legal time. Kosnoff was devoting more hours to this case and was less able to work on other cases that would generate income.

After months of crawling through the preliminary arenas of the court system, *Jeremiah Scott v. Gregory Lee Foster, The Church of Jesus Christ of Latter-day Saints, et al.* was finally assigned a judge under whom the case would proceed. But at the last minute the church's lawyers made a request to remove the judge and have the case reassigned. Each side of a civil case has an opportunity to request a new judge after one is selected and before court hearings really get going, in the interest of fairness and eliminating any perceived conflict. But it's a move that's used sparingly. Even in major cities, legal circles tend to be tight-knit, and the chances are high of having to face a certain judge again. It doesn't make sense to unnecessarily risk making enemies on the bench. But word moved through Dunn, Carney that the judge had ruled against another church on various issues in the past, and the Bullivant, Houser, Bailey lawyers weren't taking any chances. The case would go back into the pool for assignment to another judge.

Kosnoff spent this downtime lining up more people who might be able to support his case. He'd found two professors at Arizona State University who'd published a study of Mormon women survivors of child sexual abuse in 1996. Their results would be good for the case if the lawyers could get them admitted into court. In more than half of the cases reviewed, victims reported that they'd gone to their bishops for help and were either not listened to or not believed. The victims in the study were told by their church leaders that they should "forgive and forget" the abuse, that it was their fault, or that they should stop thinking about what happened and instead read the Bible and pray.

The study's authors, both women, were former active Mormons, one of whom had been on the faculty at Brigham Young University. The professor, Martha Beck, was the daughter of a well-known Mormon scholar. After lengthy phone conversations, Kosnoff had persuaded her and her colleague to review the circumstances in Jeremiah Scott's case, thinking that they might be able to testify as experts in court.

He also tracked down a woman named Colleen, whose son had been molested in the 1980s by his Mormon Boy Scout leader in Portland. Colleen's son had committed suicide after settling a lawsuit against the church. Kosnoff listened to her story over the phone. The family had once attended the same ward as had Frank Curtis but not likely at the same time since they didn't remember him. Greg Foster had been among the family's home teachers when Colleen's son was molested.

Kosnoff came to realize that there were eerie similarities in the ways that the scout leader, a man named Timur Dykes, and Frank Curtis had groomed young boys. Both men had worked their way into positions of trust through the church; they'd sought and been given leadership roles with boys, and they were able to gain the parents' trust and permission to take their victims on outings and otherwise spend time with them.

Colleen said that her son eventually had told her that Timur Dykes was abusing him and she'd turned to both her bishop and a non-Mormon child abuse hotline. The bishop had wanted to handle things inside the church, Colleen told Kosnoff, but Portland police became involved because the hotline employees were obligated to report what they'd learned. Timur Dykes was convicted of a lesser offense and sentenced to probation and sex offender treatment, mostly because no other boys corroborated the allegations. The bishop had interviewed the boys and reported to the police that there were no other victims. Colleen was upset that Dykes was never excommunicated from the church, though he'd received some lesser discipline. Kosnoff was amazed to hear that the man was allowed to continue working with young people and later convicted after molesting seventeen more boys. Colleen's son had joined a lawsuit that the other boys brought against the church. They settled for a relatively small amount of money, she said, a few thousand dollars. (A later lawsuit by victims of Timur Dykes ended in an $18.5 million verdict against the Boy Scouts of America.) Ultimately, Colleen told Kosnoff, her son had lost himself in drugs and other crimes and had attempted suicide numerous times before he finally succeeded in 1994.

Kosnoff didn't know what to say. Colleen's story was obviously deeply painful, beyond what he'd even imagined. And at the same time, it was good for his case. His research was indeed showing a pattern and practice of the LDS church ignoring child sexual abuse. Colleen agreed to testify in the Scott case. These assorted finds kept Kosnoff going. Each phone call he made led to three more. He talked to anyone who might have something to add, however tangential, to his growing knowledge of sexual misconduct within Mormon culture. Tim Kosnoff had always been driven by his emotions. Now he was possessed by a passion that had drained out of his criminal defense career, or perhaps had gotten buried in the legal minutiae around making deals for the lives of broken people that had become his career, and unwavering in his pursuit of retribution.

"The church was the dark side," Kosnoff would say years later, reflecting on the case. "They were feeding my need to be a white knight."

Throughout the battles over church records, Kosnoff and Salmi became increasingly distracted by another, weirder, problem. As it turned out, when Joel Salmi had called Bill Anton, to look into Frank Curtis's background before he and Kosnoff filed the lawsuit, Anton had assigned much of the legwork to one of his associates, a woman named Ginger Goforth.

Ginger typically did not interact with clients. That was Bill's job. It was his agency. He'd talk to his clients, who were mainly attorneys, to find out what sort of information they needed, and then assign the job to someone on his staff who would perform the legwork in the field. Neither Joel Salmi nor Tim Kosnoff had even known Ginger Goforth existed. That is, not before she became the subject of a legal attack directed at eliminating the information Ginger had gathered in interviews with former bishops Greg Foster and Gordon Checketts.

Ginger had been the one who tracked down Frank Curtis's ex-wife, Raquel Saban, and interviewed her on the driveway of her daughter's house in Gladstone, a suburb of Portland. Ginger also had interviewed Joanne and Don Penrose, the Johnsons, and a couple of other families with whom Frank had been friendly. Now that Greg Foster was named as a defendant in the case, his attorney wanted to keep anything he'd said to Ginger far out of the courtroom. Ginger had reported that

Gordon Checketts had confirmed, during her conversation with him, that he'd known that Frank Curtis molested children and, despite what Joanne Penrose may have thought, had not reported it to the police. Ginger's legwork in the early days had helped to shape the Scott legal team's requests for information and records. Now they faced the possibility that a judge might forbid them from using anything gleaned in those interviews because of the manner in which it was obtained.

Greg Foster was represented in the case by Janet Knauss and her boss, an attorney named Jeff Kilmer. He and Steve English alleged that the former bishops, as well as some of the Johnson and Penrose family members, had been duped by the investigator because she had not told them that she was working for lawyers who were planning to file a lawsuit against the LDS church. The fact of the matter was that there was no legal obligation for her to reveal that information. Instead, the scenario fell into a murky area of the law about a controversial practice called "pretexting," used by investigators to gain information. Essentially, an investigator uses a "pretext," such as conducting research of one kind or another, to ask questions. People are more likely to cooperate without knowledge of a lawsuit on the horizon.

Oregon did not require private investigators to be licensed, nor did it regulate them until 1998, after the Scott case was already in court. So while there was no violation by the investigators—they were not seeking personal identification information like Social Security numbers that would be used illegally—the LDS church argued that the Scott lawyers having gained and used the information was unethical under the guidelines that govern officers of the court. Ginger and Bill, they posited, were acting as agents of the lawyers. The church also took issue with the fact that Ginger had recorded her phone conversation with Greg Foster. In fact, Oregon was one of several states that required only one party's consent to record a phone conversation. There was something else, however. The church contended that Checketts and Foster could be considered a part of its organization, and Foster was named as a defendant. The argument followed that interviewing the former bishops without notifying their lawyers was a violation of court rules. But complicating this assertion was the fact that the interviews took place before the lawsuit was filed. While they did not believe that Ginger and Bill did anything wrong, the Scott lawyers worried that the judge might accept the church's position.

The controversy came as a surprise to the Scott team. Initially, the argument had seemed preposterous, a wild departure from the issues and yet another roadblock to receiving information from the church. But the more the debate continued, the more everyone on the Scott side realized that this seemingly innocuous technicality could end up seriously hurting their case. In a hearing on various motions, the church asked the court to make Kosnoff and Salmi hand over all of Ginger's notes and reports. They were incensed. They had enough problems fighting the church on issues they'd expected without being blindsided by something they hadn't known had happened on their own side of the lawsuit. At the hearing, Salmi argued that the church was trying to gain access to information and materials ordinarily considered to be "work product" that were otherwise off-limits under the law.

The judge required the Scott team to produce the investigator's reports and notes that were free of any "thoughts or impressions," which are considered strategy, and therefore confidential. Salmi filed a sworn affidavit saying that he had had no knowledge of the investigator's practices, and knew only the results they'd received in reports. Dissatisfied, English and Kilmer pushed on. Ginger, who no longer worked for Bill Anton's Alexander Christian Agency, where she'd been employed during the investigation, was made to file a sworn affidavit as well. In it, she stated that she had told everyone the same story: She was doing research for Joel Salmi and Tim Kosnoff in Washington State, and that the results might be published. She had not, she stated, posed as a college student, or an author, or said that she worked for the church, all of which had been alleged in court by one or the other of Checketts,

Foster, or the Penroses. It was an unusual move, but it seemed to quiet the church's growing fervor around Ginger, if only temporarily.

In any event, the Scott team was focused on something much more important at the time. Through a combination of information sources, it appeared that Frank Curtis had, as the Scott team had grown to suspect, been excommunicated from the Church of Jesus Christ of Latter-day Saints. Linda Walker had looked at a few of Frank Curtis's membership records the church had been made to produce in response to early discovery requests, along with other information from the Scotts, the private investigators, and her own research, and figured out that Frank Curtis had been baptized more than once. The only logical explanation for this was that he'd been excommunicated at some point and then rebaptized back into the church. The Mormon excommunication is not a permanent banishment. After some period of repentance and counseling, an excommunicated member may be rebaptized into the church at the discretion of church leaders. The church later acknowledged in court that Frank Curtis had been excommunicated.

This single fact was huge to the case. The Scott team had become convinced that the Mormon church had disciplined Frank Curtis for molesting children, and that records existed that would prove that church officials knew this man was a molester before he ever met the Scott family, let alone moved into their home. This conviction, and the unrelenting church defense, would turn the legal argument over church membership and discipline records into an epic battle that grew bigger and continued longer than anyone anticipated.

IO

The Multnomah County Courthouse is about a century old and has, over the years, become an odd mix of architectural restoration and practical renovation. There is no adequate place for metal detectors, for instance, so the security scanning of visitors occurs near the front door, forcing entrants to snake through a small anteroom and, during peak hours, out onto the sidewalk, as if waiting to get into a popular nightclub. Inside, the building's dramatic marble staircase and accompanying heavy wooden banister are obscured by the chaos at the front door, where the metal detector shares a hallway with a snack bar and, farther down, an ATM.

One morning in early December 1999, Tim Kosnoff, Joel Salmi, Gary Rhoades, and Jim Hillas made their way through the human traffic and upstairs to the courtroom of Judge Joseph Ceniceros, to whom their case had finally been assigned. In the hallway outside, people milled around on the white tile floor, some huddled together to discuss legal maneuvers in hushed tones. This was the third or so major hearing over issues relating to discovery evidence in the Scott case. The

Scott lawyers were hoping Ceniceros would sort out the issues, so they could move on.

Stephen English was not at the hearing, which likely meant he was in trial elsewhere; the church was represented by another lawyer from Bullivant, Houser, Bailey by the name of David Ernst, who was known for defending food makers from claims that stemmed from outbreaks of illness. Greg Foster, the Scotts' former bishop, was represented by Jeffrey Kilmer that day. By this time, Salmi's and Kosnoff's applications for admission to the Oregon Bar for this case had been approved, so at least they could appear along with the Dunn, Carney lawyers for their own client. Each group of lawyers arranged themselves around and behind the wooden tables on either side of the courtroom. There were microphones on the tables, but the courtroom was empty except for the lawyers involved in the case and the judge's clerk, who was busy with paperwork at a desk in front of the bench.

The Honorable Joseph F. Ceniceros had been a judge for more than twenty years, having served in the smaller district court before presiding in county circuit court. He was generally liked by most of the Portland legal community. Cenisceros was known to be infinitely approachable, not big on formality, and possessed little patience for attorneys who wandered off the issue at hand in an attempt to impress His Honor with their vast knowledge of the law.

Judge Ceniceros was simultaneously involved in a capital murder trial, which limited his ability to thoroughly digest the voluminous briefings filed by the attorneys in the Jeremiah Scott case. Though a crime had occurred in this case too, neither a victim nor a suspect was in the courtroom. Instead, the legal rules surrounding religion were on trial here. Much of the information that the Scott team had been denied by the church and Greg Foster hinged on a couple of issues that Ceniceros was going to have to rule on soon, for they were holding up the case.

The arguments went to the heart of the legal separation between church and state. As they all knew by now, the LDS church's position was that the First Amendment prevented the court from intruding into the practice of Mormonism, which included examining any church records, reports, conversations, and other actions that might show that church officials knew that Frank Curtis had a propensity to molest children before he moved in with the Scott family. The issue of access to records was inevitably a part of every hearing, but today there was something else that needed sorting out, concerning Greg Foster. The Scott team alleged that Foster had a legal duty to warn the Scotts that Frank Curtis had molested children before. They had to establish that Greg Foster had what in legal terms was called a "special relationship" to Jeremiah Scott, or they risked losing their claim against him. And again, they were hit with the First Amendment. Kilmer, Foster's lawyer, argued that, in order to establish such a relationship, the court would have to examine the doctrine and practice of Mormonism, which was off-limits because such an examination violated the Free Exercise Clause of the First Amendment.

"What they are alleging is that Bishop Foster, because of his relationship as a bishop with the plaintiffs, had a special relationship there that required him to act in a particular way under the law that wouldn't have been required had he been the next-door neighbor," Kilmer told the court. He went on to point out how this would require an unconstitutional probing into Mormon doctrine.

"[Bishop Foster] is accused of having information—all of which is disputed I want to say, but that is not relevant either—that he did not communicate and that he had an obligation to communicate. In order to get into that, you have to get into these issues of the practices of the church and the relationship of the parishioner to that practice."

The Scott legal team had decided earlier that Jim Hillas, the junior member, would make the arguments in this hearing. He'd invested hours in the earlier work on briefs and knew the arguments backward and forward. Hillas wondered how far Kilmer was going to go with this argument, since he didn't seem to be slowing down. Jeffrey Kilmer was a senior partner in the Portland law firm of Kilmer, Voorhees & Laurick, which represented banks, insurance companies, and construction firms. He was nearing sixty years old but remained energetic. He seemed completely at home in his surroundings at all times. Kilmer had spent most of his career, including an earlier stint as chief deputy district attorney, inside this same courthouse, which made him more of a peer of the judge. He'd even served as a temporary judge, "judge pro tem" in legal terms. An old-school lawyer, Kilmer liked to ratchet up the drama from time to time.

"It's entirely possible that if you belonged to the Church of the Holy Palm Tree that the minister in that church did not have the kind of relationship with his parishioners that would create a special relationship," Kilmer said.

Kosnoff was growing impatient waiting for Kilmer's diatribe to end. He was convinced that Kilmer had nothing and that he'd opted for style over substance. As far as Kosnoff was concerned, this whole issue was simple: Foster knew that children were at risk of being harmed by a pedophile and he didn't warn Sandy Scott when she'd asked him about Frank Curtis moving into her house. But the argument was not that simple where religion crossed civil law. Kilmer was working on getting this whole question of what Foster knew or didn't know into the protected territory of the relationship between a bishop and his ward members.

"The Church of the Holy Palm Tree may say, 'Look, we're nothing but a sham and a fraud. We hold ourselves out to be religious only to get a deduction for our members so they can contribute money to us and we all take a trip to Hawaii and worship the holy palm,' and in that case the jury could say that there is no special relationship there. But in order to say that, there would have to be some factual inquiry into the relationship."

Ceniceros motioned to Hillas that it was his turn to present an argument. Hillas, fair skinned with strawberry hair and freckles, looked younger than his thirty-three years and was only a few years out of law school. In the days leading up to the hearing, Hillas had read and reread all the research he'd done earlier to find cases that supported the motions that the Scott team was filing. Despite an annoying cold, which tampered with his professional court voice, Hillas was ready. He began by pointing to a recent case in Washington involving very similar facts in which the Washington Supreme Court allowed the case to go forward, finding that there was no First Amendment conflict. The relationship, Hillas said, was not based on the pastor's religious ties, but on the fact that he was the victim's counselor and that they had a special relationship of trust and confidence.

"We're not asking this court to consider Mormon doctrine, to decide whether it is a duty," Hillas told Judge Ceniceros. "We're simply alleging as a fact that plaintiff had a special relationship with the church because he was a member, and that he had a relationship of trust and dependence."

Earlier, Ceniceros had wondered aloud whether the fact that they were involved in a religion made this any different than if Jeremiah and Bishop Foster had been in the Boy Scouts or any other organization. And he seemed to be responding to Hillas's similar, straightforward arguments now. Ceniceros also had made comments throughout this and the earlier hearings that let everyone know he was troubled by the involvement of religion and needed to see a clear line between a relationship based on religious dogma and a relationship based on trust, irrespective of the teachings of any church. Hillas was on a roll now, bringing up cases from the Washington Supreme Court and, for backup, a federal court ruling from the Fifth Circuit Court of Appeals.

"The Washington Supreme Court . . . they just come right out and say as other cases have said, the First Amendment does not provide churches with absolute immunity to engage in tortuous conduct,"

Hillas said. "We are simply trying to hold Bishop Foster to the standard of care of a reasonable person in his position. We don't care that he is a member of a church; we are not trying to say that he was motivated by church doctrine. We're simply saying he had a duty to plaintiff based on his relationship and that's where we go. The fact that he was a member doesn't preclude us from bringing that claim."

Ceniceros signaled that he was looking to move things along. In the end, he accomplished that by approving and denying many of the motions from both sides without actually ruling on the question of whether or not there might be an intrusion into religious practices. Foster could be deposed within certain parameters. Ceniceros was seeking practical solutions wherever possible, even if it came down to semantics. The Scott lawyers agreed to reword some of their allegations to sidestep direct religious conflicts and drop others, like accusing Bishop Foster of failing to discipline Frank Curtis. While they were still not through all of the arguments over discovery materials, Kosnoff was happy to have broken the stalemate on at least something that would free them to get more of the information they needed to make their case. It had been four hours and they were all due back in court the next day to argue yet more points of contention in what was still the first phase of the lawsuit, so everyone was eager to bring an end to the hearing. The bigger questions around religion would remain unresolved.

Tim Kosnoff continued to work on a few defense cases as discovery continued in the Jeremiah Scott lawsuit. In one instance, he'd been asked to represent a man who was in federal prison in California, and traveled there for a couple of days to visit with him. The man had come to the United States from an African country as a child but had never become a citizen. He'd landed in prison for some crime and had gotten into a fight with a guard. The man had beaten the guard severely in the incident. As crimes go, beating a prison guard is nearly nonnegotiable, and the penalties are harsh. The man had ended up with a twenty-five-year sentence. He hadn't connected well with his previous lawyers, and the federal court public defender's office asked Kosnoff if he'd step in and handle the appeal. It was a temporary distraction from the Scott case that had the added benefit of bringing in money. Kosnoff reviewed the man's case and found a few areas where the prosecutors had over-reached. In the end, he managed to win a reduced sentence, but the man still faced deportation to a now-unfamiliar country where he knew no one. The whole situation was sad. He looked forward to refocusing on the Scott case, where the facts were on his side. In his most cynical moment, Tim Kosnoff continued to believe that if you had good facts, you should win in court.

Following this short respite, he returned to the agonizingly tedious conflict over church records. One of the first things Kosnoff and Salmi had done was to request Frank Curtis's church membership records, including records of any disciplinary action that church officials had taken against him. After that, the lawyers requested all records of church discipline for child sex abuse, because they planned to show that the church had a pattern of not protecting children from known sex offenders in a request for punitive damages later in the case. Oregon law didn't allow plaintiffs to ask for punitive damages up front. Instead, after certain benchmarks were met during a case, the plaintiff's side was allowed to amend a complaint to include punitive damages. That point was still a long way off in Jeremiah Scott's case.

The church lawyers had filed motions to exclude nearly every-thing, even Frank Curtis's discipline records, claiming that they were protected by clergy-penitent privilege. This was no surprise. In gen-eral, nearly every state law contains some provision that allows for religious confession: the cleansing of souls by religious exercise. The idea is that citizens should be allowed to unburden themselves of sin and seek forgiveness, usually involving a priest in the Catholic confes-sional. Police and prosecutors usually cannot force clergy members to reveal the details of what they learn in confession. Defense lawyers use the clergy-penitent argument often. The Mormon church's lawyers, in particular, used the argument nearly every time the church was involved in a lawsuit. The practice of Mormonism added a certain unique twist on the usual arguments around shielding information, however, because it operates with a revolving lay clergy. In educating himself on the religion, Kosnoff read about cases where courts in other states had wrestled with the question of who should be afforded such a shield against examination within the Mormon church. Mormons believe that every male in good standing over a certain age holds the priesthood of God, able to baptize and minister to their Mormon brothers. The Scott team had purposely referred to Frank Curtis in court filings as "a high priest," a term that the church's lawyers called irrelevant because it applied to so many people, to point out that he had been considered worthy and respected within his Mormon ward.

Complicating the religious hierarchy issue, the church's volunteer ministers, such as a bishop or stake president, are appointed without a set schedule and serve for no set period of time. When Mormon elders believe that someone is "called" by God to a position, he serves until he can no longer continue for some reason or until someone else is "called." So it was much more complicated to establish who, among Mormons, should be legally afforded the privilege of not having to reveal information similar to, say, an ordained priest of the Catholic church. Judges who'd ruled in the cases Kosnoff read first had to analyze these relationships to find out who was acting as clergy and penitent. And that got problematic in court. The church's lawyers argued that the examination intruded into its practice of religion, just as they had with the question of Greg Foster's relationship to Jeremiah Scott and Frank Curtis. Stephen English and his team held firm to the argument that most of the records the Scott legal team wanted were shielded by clergy-penitent privilege. They extended their theory to cover church officials whom the Scott team wanted to depose—specifically Gordon Checketts, the former bishop who had learned from Joanne Penrose that Frank Curtis had molested her son and David Johnson. The conversations were ecclesiastic, the LDS church's lawyers contended, and could not be disclosed.

Joel Salmi had told Kosnoff that he was concerned about this issue. He knew from having defended claims against churches and similar organizations that, in order to win a significant award, they needed to clearly establish that the LDS church had prior knowledge that Frank Curtis had been molesting children before he became a Sunday school teacher in the Scotts' ward. Bishop Checketts was the best and most clear example they had of the church having known. Of course, records, if they ever got them, would solidify that argument. Frank Curtis had been rebaptized because he was a member in good standing by the time he met Sandy Scott a decade later, while he was teaching Sunday school in a different ward. The ward boundaries around Portland had shifted over the years and some had been combined or sprouted anew based on population changes. If Checketts had followed the procedure that Phillip Johnson described, there would have been a "red flag" of some kind placed in Frank Curtis's membership file indicating that there was a problem. The Scott lawyers needed those files.

Each camp filed volumes of legal briefs on the clergy-penitent issue, in which they cited cases in other states that bolstered their argument, and then enumerated those points further in multiple hearings. And then the Scott team received an unexpected assist. While Judge Ceniceros had ruled earlier that the church had to turn over Frank Curtis's general membership record, which showed the dates he belonged to various wards in different locations, the judge had held off on deciding the fate of the disciplinary records. Church lawyers warned that such a thing would bring the court into protected religious territory. Instead, Ceniceros directed the lawyers to make a closer examination of the church disciplinary process. This had seemed like yet another expensive and unnecessary delay to the Scott team, but they had no choice. For its part, the church was required to designate someone who could answer questions on the procedure. They offered up a man named Dr. Lloyd Hale, a plastic surgeon who was a stake president over eight wards in suburbs of Portland and had been involved in more than seventy-five church disciplinary hearings in one or another capacity he'd served in the church.

On a Thursday morning in late 1999, Joel Salmi began to question Dr. Hale in the Dunn, Carney conference room about disciplinary procedures inside the Mormon church. It seemed appropriate for Salmi to lead this deposition since he was most familiar with liability issues and, besides, Kosnoff had handled most of the others. Kosnoff and Gary Rhoades were seated at the table, along with Dave Ernst and Jeff Kilmer, who was there mainly to observe and to protect Greg Foster's interests. Ernst was representing Dr. Hale on behalf of the church, although the doctor had also met with one of the church's lawyers from Salt Lake City in the days leading up to his deposition. Dr. Hale was forthright and interesting, however, and provided a better look at the inner workings of Mormon discipline than Kosnoff or any of the other lawyers had seen before.

At Salmi's prompting, Dr. Hale explained that there is no official religious exercise of receiving confession in the Mormon church, as exists in Catholicism. Mormons counsel with their bishop or stake president about any matters over which they are troubled, including moral transgressions. Salmi was working to show that the interactions that the church claimed were protected under the clergy-penitent privilege were, in fact, not confidential. He pressed Hale on the nature of conversations involving church officials.

"If it's not the bishop and the stake president and there's another third person around, that would not be considered a confession, would it?" Salmi asked.

"In my mind, it would not," Dr. Hale said.

"And likewise, if a statement is made in a public meeting and the bishop is present, that would not be considered a confession, would it?"

"No."

"Isn't the . . ." Salmi stopped in midsentence. David Ernst had leaned over and started whispering to Hale while he was answering.

"Did you want to take a break?" Salmi said to Ernst. "I'd just like the record to reflect that counsel is consulting with the witness. And if you want to take a break, that's perfectly fine."

Ernst snapped back at him from across the table and the two lawyers began to argue while Dr. Hale, Kosnoff, and Kilmer watched.

"If that was important for you to say that on the record, that's fine," Ernst said. "I've never heard you do that before and you've done that many times with your witnesses, but if it meant something to you to be able to put that on the record, that's fine."

"No," Salmi said. "I'm just asking you, did you want to take a break to consult with your client."

"If I needed to take a break, I probably would have told you that," Ernst said.

"Okay."

"But if it was important for you from a professionalism standpoint to put on the record that I was talking with him, as you've done hundreds of times in depositions and we've never said anything to you, that's fine."

The lawyers agreed to take a break. A few minutes later, everyone was back in place around the table, but as soon as Salmi resumed questioning Dr. Hale, Ernst started objecting again. This time Kilmer joined in as well. Salmi persevered, ignoring both of them. He looked straight at Dr. Hale.

"Let me give you an example," Salmi told the doctor. "If a member reports to the bishop of a church that their child has been molested by another member of the church, do you consider that a confession?"

"No, because I consider that the member is reporting an incident," Dr. Hale said.

Kosnoff could barely contain his excitement. Salmi's performance was magnificent. Hale was surprisingly straightforward, Kosnoff thought. And his testimony was huge. It would, Kosnoff hoped, finally allow them to prove that at least one, if not two former bishops had learned that Frank Curtis was molesting children.

Dr. Hale's deposition lasted all day. Between breaks and the myriad objections of Kilmer and Ernst, Salmi managed to glean more important points. For instance, the doctor described disciplinary proceedings as being more administrative than ecclesiastical in nature. Essentially, a Mormon bishop or stake president convenes a hearing—sort of like church court—when he learns of some major transgression. The matter is reviewed by a designated group of twelve other men known as a "high council." The transgressor may or may not be present and other people may be called as witnesses. Usually, if the perpetrator of the sin attends the disciplinary hearing, he's already owned up to his bad acts and is working toward forgiveness. Discipline is considered the first step toward repentance in the Mormon faith. In any event, the accused is questioned by his bishop or stake president, and if it's established that some major moral sin was committed, there are consequences. A sinner may be punished by restricting his privileges within the church, or he may be excommunicated. Acts including murder, child molestation, and apostasy against the church are considered cause for excommunication.

Dr. Hale said that a report of the disciplinary procedure is sent to the Office of the First Presidency, which is to say, Mormon headquarters in Salt Lake City. Kosnoff continued to believe the church must have records of having excommunicated Frank Curtis for child sexual abuse, and that's why the LDS lawyers were putting up such a vigorous fight.

Dr. Hale also confirmed that only a bishop, stake president, or mission president is authorized to hear confessions from members. So anyone else in the chain of information was, arguably, not legally protected, because he wouldn't have been participating in a confession. In what was perhaps eagerness to show that the Church of Jesus Christ of Latter-day Saints was concerned with protecting children, Dr. Hale said that the church had a policy of encouraging known sex offenders to turn themselves in to authorities. A warning is placed in the membership file of a Mormon who is excommunicated by the church for child molestation, he said. This was yet another confirmation of the "red flag" that should have existed in Frank Curtis's membership files.

Salmi, Kosnoff, and the Dunn, Carney lawyers spent the next few weeks passing documents back and forth by email, crafting a twenty-six-page, skillfully written brief using excerpts from Dr. Hale's deposition. The church held to its position. Three months later, Judge Ceniceros issued a letter ruling that statements made by Frank Curtis to a bishop or stake president and during a church disciplinary hearing were protected from disclosure under the clergy-penitent privilege. At the same time, he ruled that statements made by anyone else about Frank Curtis's behavior, outside of a disciplinary hearing, were fair game. While whatever went on during the disciplinary hearing itself was protected by the clergy-penitent privilege, Judge Ceniceros decided the report of results of the hearing, which, according to Dr. Hale, was forwarded to the church headquarters, was discoverable. The church had to produce any sort of "red flag" attached to the records of Frank Curtis. And the bishops would be deposed about what had been reported to them by the parents of children who had been molested. Finally, Kosnoff told Salmi, things were turning around. This, they figured, would be the beginning of their march toward victory.

11

Even as Kosnoff was encouraged by the judge's ruling, he needed to concentrate on what was happening with Jeremiah Scott. Earlier that year, Jeremiah sat in a conference room high above the streets of downtown Portland, with a video camera pointed at him and a stenographer recording every word he said. For two days, the tale of a young boy's life, his achievements and missteps, and the intimate, painful details of the events that had brought together the roomful of lawyers surrounding him, unfolded one question and answer at a time.

Jeremiah and his mother were deposed by the lawyers for the church during the same couple of days. Jeremiah went first in the conference room at Dunn, Carney. The entire Scott team of lawyers, Kosnoff, Salmi, Rhoades, and Hillas, was there, along with Jeffrey Kilmer and an associate named Pamela Stendahl. But this was Stephen English's show. He would be asking the questions.

By this time, Jeremiah already had answered pages of inquiries submitted by the church's lawyers. He'd been evaluated by a psychiatrist chosen by the church's lawyers, and another selected by his own lawyers. Still, Jeremiah remained unfailingly polite. Perhaps too much so:

His stoic demeanor often masked how much he'd been harmed. It had taken Kosnoff reading through police reports, in fact, to really understand what an emotional catastrophe lay in his client's background and how far back the story stretched.

In the weeks leading up to this deposition, Kosnoff and Salmi had prepared Jeremiah for the fact that every last detail of his life, and in particular events he most wanted to forget, would be painstakingly picked apart by the church's lawyers. This was simply how the game of law worked, the price of filing a lawsuit. In order to defend their clients, English and, later, Kilmer would look for cracks in Jeremiah's claims. That Frank Curtis had molested Jeremiah Scott was really not an issue here today. The lawyers would be looking for ways to reduce their clients' role in the whole situation and minimize the harm Jeremiah had suffered because of it, to reduce the compensation their client might have to pay. Harm, in a legal claim, is measured in money.

All the emphasis on family in the Mormon religion had not saved Jeremiah's parents' marriage. They divorced in 1993, an event that required Jeremiah and his sister to move with their mother to her parents' house in Washington, where the suburbs of Kirkland and Redmond intersect, about fifteen miles west of Seattle. The area was a boomtown, home to the prosperous Microsoft and Nintendo corporations, and in every way it epitomized the American dream. Tall pine trees line the streets, barely obscuring the view of snow on distant mountain peaks. Blocks of homes situated on large plots of green grass surround churches, grocery megastores, and the family-friendly fast-food joints where Little Leaguers collect after games.

Jeremiah's grandparents' house was good sized but nothing extraordinary. It stood behind a lawn that sloped down to the street, and had rectangular basement windows that faced the front not far off the grass. In their new life, Jeremiah and his sister attended public school and their mother ran a small day care in the basement. Everyone appeared to be settling in to life in Washington.

All of that ended one afternoon in the fall of 1993, when Redmond Police Detective Rick Springs came to the door with two social workers. Detective Springs told Jeremiah's mother, Sandy, that the parents of one of her day-care charges, a precocious four-year-old boy, had told his parents something that seemed unthinkable: Fourteen-year-old Jeremiah had molested the boy while he was in Sandy's care. The detective directed Sandy to wait outside while he and Jeremiah talked in his room. Jeremiah told Springs that on a particularly hot day back in August, Sandy had asked him to help her with the children. The kids had been outside playing and were a sweaty mess. Jeremiah's mother had asked him to take this little boy into the bathroom and help him get cleaned up.

After a lengthy interview, Jeremiah told Detective Springs that he'd gotten in the shower in order to wash the little boy, and that he'd had an erection thinking about some girls in school. Jeremiah's penis, he said, had brushed against the boy's bottom. And then he'd rubbed the boy a bit.

Eventually, the detective asked Jeremiah if anyone had ever inappropriately touched him. Jeremiah was, after all, only fourteen at the time, which made it more than likely that he was repeating behavior he'd learned from someone else. Jeremiah revealed things he'd never told even his parents—things that had happened in the blue house in Portland. Jeremiah told Detective Springs the same things that he was now telling a roomful of lawyers and the video camera: that Frank Curtis had regularly sodomized the then ten-year-old during the time they'd shared a bedroom. At first it was every night, Jeremiah said, and then sometimes less often, like three or four times a week, followed by a reprieve of a week or so. And then the cycle would begin again.

In the conference room, English asked Jeremiah to explain Frank Curtis's abuse. The Scott lawyers knew this story. Salmi was handling objections and would interject periodically when he thought English was belaboring some point, or asking Jeremiah to speculate on what his parents thought, hoping that a judge might toss something out later. But there were no big fights today. The lawyers seemed to be on their best behavior. Kosnoff was watching Jeremiah to see how he was holding up through this, which was really a preview of how he might come across to a jury. Jeremiah continued his narrative of the dreadful time with Brother Curtis.

"One of the things that really brings it back is . . . he had . . . he had really raspy, heavy breathing, and he would . . . when he did this, he . . . almost always, he breathed really hard. He was really old and I would get this feeling of old breathing in my ear and it just—that's one thing that I remember very clearly about it. And he . . . the Mormons wear garments and he was—"

Jeff Kilmer was momentarily perplexed at the mention of garments, and he interrupted Jeremiah for clarification. Like most Mormon adults, Frank Curtis wore religious garments underneath his clothing and to bed. Mormonism prescribes that those who have been baptized, approved for admission into the temple, and thus follow the teachings of the church wear sacred garments next to their skin as a reminder of the covenants they've made with God. Both men and women wear white (to symbolize purity) long-underwear-like suits decorated with symbols of obedience, truth, life, and discipleship in Christ.

"The Mormons wear garments," Jeremiah continued, ". . . and he was a very large man and he had me get inside his garments with him. It was like I was trapped and next to a sweaty, large, smelly body, and it was like I couldn't get away. And he would kiss me on my face and chest and on my mouth and . . . and he would describe other stories about other things he'd done to other girls while doing this. He had . . . things he had done when he was in school, sleeping with other men's wives. He would go into detail about running out of the house at the last minute when the husband came home. He . . . let's see, he kind of made me feel like a prostitute where he would buy me something if I would do this for him and he . . . that was pretty much all of it that I can remember."

Jeremiah explained that he couldn't find a way to tell his parents that the Sunday school teacher they were taking care of in order to be better Mormons in the eyes of God was sodomizing him. As a boy, he'd been keenly aware that his household was filled with controversy and argument. He had stayed up later and later, watching movies or working on a homework project—anything to keep him from going to bed, until one or the other of his parents sent him upstairs. His head was filled with the stories Frank had told about his colorful past, how he had been in knife fights, killed people, and traveled with gangsters. Clearly this was not someone to be toyed with, even if he was now an old man. Frank Curtis hadn't let Jeremiah out of his sight very often— Jeremiah had accompanied him to the doctor and the drugstore, and helped him in and out of the bathtub, and up and down the stairs. And Brother Curtis had given the boy a new Nintendo game, a television, and other special gifts.

Jeremiah was arrested by Detective Springs for molesting the boy in the day care and then released to his mother. Eventually, he was convicted of molestation and sentenced to attend mandatory counseling sessions.

When Stephen English finished with his questions, Jeffrey Kilmer took over. It was already after four o'clock. Kilmer continued the same line of questioning that English had followed concerning Jeremiah and his family's living situation. Kilmer wanted to know how upset Jeremiah had been by his parents' separation, the family's various moves, and having to switch from homeschool to public school. All of these events could have contributed to his emotional harm. Kilmer probed Jeremiah about dating. Was he a virgin? Yes. Would he consider himself a heterosexual or homosexual? Heterosexual. Had he been sexually excited by touching the boy? He had been thinking about a girl.

Then he moved on to the events with Frank Curtis. What, Kilmer asked, had Jeremiah done to try to stop the old man from abusing him? Why hadn't he told his parents? Why didn't he just tell them that the sleeping arrangements weren't working out?

Jeremiah described how he had slept on the floor, gone downstairs, and stayed at a friend's house to avoid Brother Curtis. He drew the layout of the blue house for the lawyers in the conference room and showed how Brother Curtis would have had to get up and down a flight of stairs regardless of where he stayed. At ten years old, Jeremiah had not conceived that he could get away from Frank Curtis.

From a legal standpoint, Sandra Scott was a liability in her son's case. The lawyers knew from the beginning that it would be challenging to get a jury to see beyond the fact that she brought a pedophile into her home and, ultimately, into her son's bed. The best strategy was to turn weakness into strength. Her faith in and obedience to Mormon teachings, the theory went, had made her so vulnerable and naïve as to have put her own son in harm's way. Early on, Sandy had been named as a plaintiff in the suit, under the claim that she too had been harmed. But the idea was abandoned after it seemed that it might be more likely to dilute Jeremiah's case than to strengthen it.

Later, Greg Foster's lawyers filed a counter-claim against Sandy Scott, alleging that she was at fault for any harm her son had suffered. This was a legal strategy that would allow a jury to apportion blame between Greg Foster and Sandy Scott, thereby lessening what Foster would have to pay if Jeremiah was found to have been harmed.

The lawyers for the church, and particularly Kilmer, were also interested in Sandy's relationship to the Mormon church, but for an entirely different reason. It was evident from their questions during Sandy's deposition, which began after Jeremiah had been grilled for a day and a half, that they were pursuing the theory that Sandy had talked her son into filing a lawsuit because she was angry with the church over her divorce.

Sandy had left Kent and the church at about the same time, around the end of 1992. Husband and church were so intertwined that it was hard for her to say which one she sought to escape more. Sandy had grown tired of being subservient to her husband and disagreed with tithing as a requirement for religious participation. Sandy also questioned Mormon interpretations of the Bible and the religion's own history, while Kent remained devout.

Sandy had found work at a dry cleaner, followed by a receptionist position in an optometrist's office, and later in a physical therapy office. She and the children had lived in an apartment or two before eventually landing at her parents' house, where she had opened the day care. Of course, Sandy had lost her license when Jeremiah was arrested for touching the boy in her care, and the boy's parents had filed a lawsuit against her. She had taken the children to a nondenominational church and a charismatic Christian church after leaving Mormonism. But neither seemed to stick.

Kent had stayed with his parents for a while and eventually remarried another Mormon woman, with whom he was starting a second family. He had also become a member of the elders quorum in his church ward. The first rung on the Mormon leadership ladder, the quorum is a brotherhood of men who teach and help one another, and assign responsibilities for various tasks within the ward.

Sandy had contacted Kent immediately when the police arrested Jeremiah. After Jeremiah was released on bail, Kent took his son for a walk and tried to reassure him. Sometime after the initial frenzy had calmed, Kent and Sandy contacted Greg Foster, since he had been their bishop in Portland. What followed became the controversial matter at the heart of Jeremiah's legal claim, the direct link to Jeffrey Kilmer's client. Sandy maintained that Greg Foster had told her and Kent that he was sorry for what had happened and that Frank Curtis had molested other children, but he'd repented and promised that he would never again engage in such behavior.

"I dialed Bishop Foster and he answered the phone and I didn't dilly-dally around, I told him, 'This is Sandy Scott'—I'm paraphrasing—'we have a little situation here. I want you to know about Frank Curtis, I think you should know about him, my son has molested a little boy as a result of Frank Curtis molesting him.' And he said he was very sorry, but that he already knew and he cited that he felt Frank Curtis's repentance was sufficient, and Frank Curtis said he wouldn't do it again, so that was enough for him not to tell me or our family about his past pedophile history."

She and Kent were sharing the phone as they talked to Bishop Foster, Sandy told the lawyers, in such a way that they were handing it back and forth. "During the conversation, before the conversation was over, I heard my husband say, 'Why in the hell' or 'Why didn't you let us know?' I heard that."

Despite their differences, Sandy was not willing to disparage her ex-husband. She was emphatic that they both had tried to save their marriage, and that her ex-husband too was angry about what had happened to their son. Kent was an honest person, she said, and he loved their children. When Kilmer asked her, essentially, if Kent would back up her story, Sandy said she did not believe he would lie. (In his own deposition, Kent Scott said that he and Sandy had spoken separately to Bishop Foster after learning of Jeremiah's molestation. But Kent also recalled that Bishop Foster had mentioned that Brother Curtis "had problems with little boys.")

As the afternoon wore on, the tone in the conference room became more hostile. Kilmer could be aggressive, and he was willing to push witnesses to get what he wanted. Sandy became agitated and defensive as Kilmer picked at her about the potential harm to Jeremiah in filing a lawsuit. He made a point of noting that Kent had not been in favor of suing the church.

"And what was the reason?" Kilmer asked Sandy.

"He said, 'You have nothing on the church,'" she answered.

"Wasn't he also very concerned about the fact that the case wouldn't be good for Jeremiah?" Kilmer asked.

"Jeremiah agreed to file."

"He agreed to file at your urging?"

"My urging?"

"Didn't he?"

"Did I urge?" Sandy turned toward her son, who had been allowed in the room during her deposition. "Can I ask him that?"

"No, but I'm going to ask you that," Kilmer said.

Joel Salmi motioned to Sandy that, yes, indeed, she had to answer the question.

"Yeah," Kilmer said. "You're being awfully defensive here and—"

Salmi interrupted Kilmer, trying to protect Sandy. He'd had enough of Kilmer's act for one day. "Hey, for the record," Salmi said. "For the record, Counsel, you can comment—you can ask her questions, you don't need to comment about her testimony. I deny that she's being defensive."

"It shows it on the video," Kilmer said.

"The video speaks for itself," Salmi added.

"Correct."

"Okay."

Kilmer got back on track. "Now, what I want to go on here with, Mrs. Scott, though, is please—"

Sandy, who was still peeved, corrected Kilmer in midsentence. "Ms. Scott."

"Ms. Scott, and answer my questions, okay? Did you encourage your son to file a suit, yes or no?"

"I talked to him about the suit," Sandy said.

"Did you encourage him to file the suit?"

"I kind . . . I kind of just didn't finish, you know, and you . . ."

Salmi told Sandy that she could go ahead.

"I felt like something needed to be done for him," Sandy said. "Something needed to be done for him."

Kilmer was like a dog with a bone at this point. "Okay. So you encouraged him to file the suit?"

"I filed it," Sandy said. This surprised most of the room, and for a minute, neither Kosnoff nor Salmi quite knew what she was saying. Regardless, Kilmer was about to make her out to be profit seeking on top of negligent.

"You filed it in both your names?" Kilmer asked.

"That's right."

"Okay," Kilmer said. "Now, he agreed, but you encouraged it. Isn't that correct?"

"At the time," Sandy said.

"And you also wanted something out of this suit initially. Isn't that correct?"

"What?"

"I don't know, why did you put your name on it?"

"Personally, I didn't care, you know," Sandy said. "I wanted something for my son."

"Did you ever consider the possibility that filing this suit, whatever benefit it might have for him, might carry more detriment than benefit in terms of his well-being and his future development?" Kilmer asked.

"Sir, I think he has suffered enough, you know?"

"Did you ever, then, consider not filing the suit because there's no need to impose additional suffering, which a lawsuit definitely carries?"

Salmi interrupted Kilmer's repartee with an objection, but it didn't prevent Sandy from having to answer the question.

"I truly let him make that decision," she said. "I presented it to him. Personally, as a mother, I felt something needed to be done here, okay?"

After the questioning ended that evening, Jeremiah and his mother returned to Seattle. Kosnoff and Salmi stayed behind to review with

Gary Rhoades and Jim Hillas what had happened during the previous two days. It wasn't over yet.

Because of scheduling issues among the lawyers, Sandy's deposition resumed a few weeks later in Salmi's office in Bellevue. English questioned Sandy about some of the issues around Jeremiah's counseling. In the months following his arrest and sentencing for molesting the little boy in day care, Jeremiah had been required to attend counseling. Given his young age at the time, Jeremiah's parents were to participate in part of the counseling as well, only Sandy had stopped going after a few sessions. She'd been uncomfortable with the fact that her son was involved in discussions about sex, which was to a large extent sexual education, with professional counselors instead of at home with his parents.

"What was it about the fact that they talked about sex openly that was troublesome to you?" English asked.

"I would have liked to have talked about it with him," Sandy said.

"You would have liked to have talked about sex with Jeremiah?"

"As—yes, the way it should be, with a parent."

"Okay. What was it about the way they were talking about it with him that you felt wasn't appropriate?" English continued.

"I'm not saying it was inappropriate," Sandy said. "I felt robbed."

Kilmer didn't ask a question. He seemed decidedly disinterested in Sandy Scott now, certainly by comparison to his assertive performance in the earlier session. In fact, Kosnoff would later recount to Hillas that Kilmer was reading a magazine during part of Sandy's deposition.

Despite his years in the criminal courts, Kosnoff was disgusted by the stories of abuse that seemed to exist everywhere he turned, and the blind faith of mostly poor people in a church that, as far as he could tell, did nothing to help them. And he was tired of the church's arrogant lawyers who always seemed to treat him like a second-string player because he was not from Portland, not part of their club. At the same time, he was consumed by the Scott case. He talked about nothing else, at work and socially. He needed to know more, to find every piece of evidence, however small, that would make a jury see what he saw, make them yearn like he did to punish this church for allowing Frank Curtis, whom he had come to conclude was an obvious textbook-case serial pedophile, access to children he would likely molest.

Kosnoff continued his Mormon education during periodic phone conversations with Linda Walker, who was an eager listener and teacher and who kept track of the church's abuse cases, many of which she'd worked on at some point. Kosnoff loved history, especially war history. Researching the Mormon church's legal moves was like studying battle strategy, and he approached it much the same way, analyzing what led to one or another course of events.

By this point, Kosnoff had worn the patience of his fellow lawyers with his obsession for learning more about their opponent. So he and Linda shared and rehashed the details of the similar past horrors they'd discovered.

Linda was proving particularly good at finding people. She had a knack for digging up entire populations that had shared a ward or neighborhood. She described to Kosnoff certain patterns that she'd seen on other cases. There was rarely one isolated incidence of sexual abuse in a Mormon ward, she'd found. Once it was known that a boy or girl had been molested, it was worth looking for other people who were about the same age and attended the same ward during the same time period, to see if there were other victims of the same pedophile. If an abuser had moved, it was likely because he'd been caught by someone in the previous ward. There was always a trail of victims. Linda could go off on one tangent or another about the polygamy and violence in Mormon history. Sometimes Kosnoff wondered if she wasn't spewing outrageous conspiracy theories. But, increasingly, he found that what she'd told him was, in fact, true.

As the months went by, Kosnoff also spent a great deal of time making phone calls. With considerable downtime in the court action while the paperwork fight over access to Frank Curtis's church records wore on, he'd turned his attention to earlier unfinished business in the case. He and Salmi both wanted to revisit the matter of Raquel Saban, the ex-wife of Frank Curtis. They'd told the investigators to back off this trail initially because, at the time, they hadn't been certain just what would be needed from other people in Frank Curtis's past. Given all they'd learned about Frank Curtis's growing number of victims, however, Raquel Saban was now an important witness.

Problem was, she'd disappeared. Kosnoff finally tracked down Raquel's daughter in Portland and talked to her at length about Frank Curtis and the Jeremiah Scott case. She had a lot to say about Frank Curtis, most of it bad. It quickly become clear that this daughter had pretty much hated Frank. More important, she mentioned that her brother Manny had accused Frank of molesting him. They'd teased him about it. Raquel's daughter gave Kosnoff a number to reach her mother, who was living with another daughter.

Kosnoff left phone messages for Raquel Saban with no response. But he wasn't interested in waiting around to hear a second version of this story. He'd managed to gather enough information to track down her son Stanley Jr. He lived in Arizona, where his father had lived before his recent death.

Kosnoff reached Manny Saban in Humboldt, just outside of Prescott. He was reluctant to talk but listened to Kosnoff's story about Jeremiah Scott and the lawsuit and Frank Curtis. Manny hadn't wanted to discuss Frank Curtis. When Kosnoff had asked Manny if he'd been sexually abused by the old man, and Manny had ended the conversation, Kosnoff took it to mean that, more than likely, Manny Saban had indeed been abused. Kosnoff figured that they could get a subpoena to make him testify if he wasn't willing to cooperate.

And then two weeks later, Manny Saban called Tim Kosnoff back. He'd obviously ruminated on the subject long enough that he'd found the confidence or trust necessary to talk to the lawyer. Or maybe he was just curious. No matter, Kosnoff was thrilled to have him cooperating again. Manny told Kosnoff about the neighborhood in southeast Portland where his family had lived and about the Mormons and how he'd met Frank Curtis at the church, some of which Kosnoff had already heard about from Manny's sister. Frank had molested him, Manny confirmed, estimating the time period to have been around the late 1970s, which Kosnoff figured to be about fifteen years before Jeremiah was molested.

There were more phone calls. Manny told Kosnoff about a handful of other kids who'd lived in the neighborhood and used to hang around Frank. Manny had suspected that Frank was up to something with some of his friends, he said, but they'd never talked about it. He gave Kosnoff names of the other boys, and told him approximately where they'd lived when they were kids, but he didn't know anything about them now. He hadn't lived in Portland in years. Manny told Kosnoff that he'd told his mother that Frank "had messed with me" and that she hadn't believed him. Kosnoff didn't push for more details of what happened between Frank and Manny. He was afraid that he'd lose this man again, and besides, he was already pretty sure that they'd want to depose him. It was better, he thought, to capture the story fresh in testimony. Manny confirmed something else that his sister had alluded to when she talked to Kosnoff earlier. Raquel Saban had found Frank in the bathtub with another boy from the neighborhood. And, Manny added, his mother had told the bishop about it.

This was the biggest break they'd had in the case in a long time. The isolated bits and pieces of this story were starting to come together. And if this was all correct, it meant that the church had known about Frank Curtis molesting boys even before the episode in 1983 with David Johnson and his friend, and all of it was long before Jeremiah Scott ever met Frank Curtis in the Mormon ward in Portland.

Kosnoff called Joel Salmi the minute he got off the phone with Manny Saban, and then spread the word to Gary Rhoades and Jim

Hillas. He searched through public records and news accounts to see if he could find any of the boys Manny had named, though it was a long shot. And then he got an idea. Kosnoff called Linda Walker and told her everything he'd learned about the boys who lived in southeast Portland more than two decades before and might have been part of a Mormon ward there. Could she help find them?

Joel Salmi had two homes. He lived part of the time in Seattle, close to his office and his daughter, whose custody he shared with his ex-wife. He spent the rest of his time in a small farmhouse near Eugene, Oregon, with his present wife and her children. Salmi's wife, a school administrator, shared custody of her children with their father in Oregon. The custody arrangements had left Salmi and his wife tied to their respective states. So, for more than a decade, Joel commuted between Oregon and Washington.

Joel did much of his work on the Scott case at the farmhouse in Eugene. It was closer to Portland and the court where the lawsuit was filed. He'd moved a wooden desk into a guest room to create an office, and that was where Joel particularly liked to dictate big briefs. He could smell the pigs, hear the chickens, and see the horses out in the pasture. If a car came down the street more than twice a day, it was an event. The farmhouse was peaceful while everyone else was at school. He could focus. Salmi worked on a laptop computer but wasn't at all technically savvy. Sending and opening documents through email was often challenging. He preferred to dictate briefs into a handheld recorder and then send the tapes to Dunn, Carney for transcribing. By now, the Scott team had established a routine in which Jim Hillas or Joel Salmi would start a first draft, Tim Kosnoff and Gary Rhoades would weigh in on it, and then they'd bounce the brief back and forth until it was perfected, landing at Dunn, Carney, where it was generally Jim Hillas's job to file the final versions with the court in Portland.

As the conflict over the church records heated up, Salmi devoted his attention to crafting the extensive written responses to the Mormon church's interminable motions. Of the many legal issues that this case had grown to include, Salmi most enjoyed the intellectual exercise of religion versus the law. High-concept issues didn't come along very often—so much of his practice was negotiating cost and risk—and Salmi was genuinely pleased by the opportunity to engage in significant debate. Digging into the law was a welcome distraction from the long hours and the mounting debt that had come to characterize the Scott case.

The argument around the Mormon church's membership and discipline records had its own evolution inside the lawsuit. The church had first argued that producing records would be impossible, owing to the size of the Mormon membership. Its lawyers told the court that there were eleven million members divided into more than twenty thousand wards, each of which was headed by a part-time volunteer bishop. Issues such as child abuse are handled by individual bishops. "The International Church does not become involved in such situations," church lawyers had written to the court. But then the church's own designated expert on the process, Dr. Lloyd Hale, said in his deposition that a report of the outcome of a church disciplinary hearing was forwarded to Mormon headquarters. Theoretically, anyway, those reports were all in one place: Temple Square in Salt Lake City. The church argued that it would take an unreasonable number of hours and millions of dollars to comb through every membership record looking for all the people who'd been disciplined for molesting children. The Scott team had compromised, with Judge Ceniceros's blessing. Their revised request was for records of all members disciplined for molesting children in the greater Portland area, and the lawsuits that had been filed against the church over molestation. The church had produced some forty-two lawsuits involving sexual abuse in which it had been named a defendant, though Kosnoff figured from researching the issue that there were more. Judge Ceniceros had ordered the church to produce Frank

Curtis's membership file but hadn't ruled on the disciplinary records. They remained a matter of legal debate.

The LDS church asserted clergy-penitent privilege over most of the records, arguing that church discipline was an ecclesiastic pursuit and not subject to review in a court case. The clergy-penitent argument had already been the subject of at least four court hearings and, of course, led to the deposition of Dr. Hale to help sort it out.

Two years into the lawsuit, Kosnoff, Salmi, and the other lawyers were still mired in debate over the clergy-penitent argument, while their access to the evidence they needed to make their case remained on hold. Regardless of how the judge ruled on earlier questions, it seemed that every record request and notice of a deposition the Scott team filed, no matter how ordinary, was met with a hefty brief citing case law on how it violated the clergy-penitent privilege statute. The church was relying heavily on a ruling made by the Utah Supreme Court in an earlier lawsuit against the Mormon church over child sexual abuse. Interestingly enough, that case was designed to penetrate the clergy-penitent statute but ended up helping the church. In 1994, a woman who had been abused by her stepfather filed a lawsuit against the church because Mormon officials had known about the abuse years before and did nothing to try to stop it. She was represented by a civil rights lawyer in Salt Lake City named Ross "Rocky" Anderson, who later became the city's mayor. Anderson had challenged a lower court's ruling in favor of the church's clergy-penitent privilege argument by taking it to the state's high court. The Utah Supreme Court justices, a majority of whom were either Mormon or conservative allies, found that not only were the conversations involving the abusive stepfather protected by clergy-penitent privilege, so were any later conversations in which this information was shared with others inside the church. Essentially, the court solidified the clergy-penitent privilege. But the court in the Utah case had not addressed the issue of records, which was what Jeremiah Scott's legal team was seeking. Also, Utah differed from Oregon in that, unlike most other states, Utah did not require conversations to be penitential in nature in order for them to be covered under clergy-penitent privilege. The Oregon court was not likely to give much weight to a Utah case that essentially clarified Utah law. The Scott lawyers had fought back hard using information from the church's own *Handbook of Instructions*, which lays out policy for bishops and stake presidents, and the deposition testimony from Dr. Hale, the church's expert, about the Mormon church's administrative procedures and its record keeping. The records and information they wanted, Salmi argued to Judge Ceniceros, were not religious. They were never intended to be confidential. This did not involve a man's private confession to a bishop; it was about what church officials did when someone else told them Frank Curtis was molesting children.

There was another issue that needed to be addressed now, a conflict that Joel Salmi was wrestling with on the farm. The Mormons' clergy-penitent argument was intertwined with the constitutional Free Exercise issue. In the case of Jeremiah Scott, the arguments revolved around forgiveness. The Church of Jesus Christ of Latter-day Saints teaches that baptism into the church is a complete cleansing, an absolution of all sin. It is the mission of the church to call people to repentance. In his well-known Mormon text, *The Miracle of Forgiveness*, Mormon apostle Spencer W. Kimball discusses the church's belief in repentance and rebaptism: "The effect of the cleansing is beautiful. These troubled souls have found peace. These soiled robes have been cleansed to spotlessness. These people formerly defiled, having been cleansed through their repentance—their washing, their purging, their whitening—are made worthy for constant temple services and to be found before the throne of God associating with divine royalty."

From the moment of baptism or rebaptism, according to LDS belief, the sins of the past are literally washed away and can no longer be acknowledged. The baptized Mormon starts anew with a "clean slate." Mormons who have been excommunicated, as Frank Curtis had been, may work through a period of repentance that ultimately leads to rebaptism and, once again, a clean slate.

Using this line of reasoning, the church argued to the court that it could not consider Frank Curtis's past sexual molestation of children after he'd been rebaptized. It would be a violation of the Mormon faith to consider his history of molesting children prior to rebaptism in any decision to call him to a position within the church.

The church applied its clean-slate argument to nearly every issue in the case. Its lawyers even seemed to be arguing that Jeremiah had somehow accepted the risk of encountering a pedophile in following the Mormon religion. In a motion asking the court to protect the church's records, its lawyers wrote: "Plaintiff, having voluntarily agreed to abide by, and be governed by, church law cannot now challenge the procedure for, and effect of, a fellow member's rebaptism into the church. Because church doctrine holds that a member's past history is essentially wiped clean upon rebaptism, plaintiff should not be permitted to inquire into facts and events which occurred prior to Curtis's rebaptism in October 1984."

The church's lawyers maintained that to examine whether or not its officials knew about Frank Curtis's past would be to examine the Mormon religion itself, which would violate the Free Exercise Clause. The court, they argued, should not allow the Scott team to use any information on Frank Curtis prior to his rebaptism. It should abide by the Mormon belief that Frank Curtis's history of molesting children no longer existed.

The lawyers insisted that "the church member starts with a 'clean slate.' Since the Church doctrine is the belief that a re-baptized individual starts anew with a 'clean slate,' it would be in violation of the First Amendment to allow a civil court to test the credibility or wisdom of that belief by allowing plaintiff to obtain information concerning

Curtis's actions prior to the rebaptism. . . . The First Amendment requires that the court respect the Church's internal procedures and policies, particularly with regards to church membership."

By filing a lawsuit against the church for failing to warn the Scott family about Frank Curtis's history of molesting children, the church's lawyers argued, the Scotts were "most definitely challenging" the wisdom of the Mormon belief that at the time he was rebaptized, Curtis started with a clean slate. The First Amendment prohibited that sort of religious challenge. The LDS church's lawyers quoted the Utah Supreme Court again in briefs they wrote to Judge Ceniceros arguing the First Amendment issue: "It is not the role of the secular court to pass [judgment] on the wisdom of the ecclesiastical decision to forgive, even if that decision allegedly creates negative consequences to third parties."

It was hard to ignore how utterly divorced the words on paper were from the matter at hand, that children had been sexually violated by a trusted member of their religious community. Salmi thought the church's argument on this one was a stretch and probably wouldn't prevail in court, but the Scott team's briefs had to be crafted perfectly in order to get at Frank Curtis's disciplinary records. Judge Ceniceros had already signaled that he was uncomfortable with anything that involved religious practice. Tim Kosnoff had gone on a tirade with Salmi and Gary Rhoades about this issue. To him, the Mormon church seemed to be taking the arrogant position that it had a constitutional right to molest children. At first, they all thought the clean-slate argument sounded like the handiwork of a creative defense lawyer, maybe even a desperate play. But they'd later come to view it more seriously.

The Mormon church has a deeper historical connection to the Constitution than any of the Scott team lawyers had realized. Even Tim Kosnoff, who by now had become the group's resident expert on Mormon culture, didn't fully grasp the importance of the Constitution in Mormonism.

The church teaches that the Constitution of the United States was divinely inspired by men whom God chose as its authors. One Mormon prophet wrote of being visited in a Mormon temple by the Founding Fathers, who instructed him that the church must protect the Constitution. The idea that the Constitution was handed down from God, "by the hands of wise men," is canonized in the Doctrine and Covenants, one of the fundamental works of the church. In 1957, Mormon president J. Reuben Clark Jr., a former undersecretary of state for whom the law school at Brigham Young University is named, gave a well-known address on the Constitution, in which he said: "I declare that the divine sanction thus repeatedly given by the Lord himself to the Constitution of the United States as it came from the hands of the Framers with its coterminous Bill of Rights, makes of the principles of that document an integral part of my religious faith. It is a revelation from the Lord. I believe and reverence its God-inspired provisions. My faith, my knowledge, my testimony of the Restored Gospel, based on the divine principle of continuous revelation, compel me so to believe. Thus has the Lord approved of our political system, an approval, so far as I know, such as he has given to no other political system of any other people in the world since the time of Jesus."

The LDS church is, in many ways, uniquely American. Mormons believe that their prophet, Joseph Smith, found golden tablets in New York that would inspire the Book of Mormon and the beginning of the church. Mormon history tells that, once translated, the tablets told the story of Jesus Christ having appeared in America after his death and resurrection in Jerusalem. Mormons consider this to be a record of God's dealings with ancient inhabitants of the Americas. In 1830, Smith founded the Church of Jesus Christ of Latter-day Saints. Its followers later moved west to Ohio, Missouri, and then Illinois, after their persecution for various beliefs, including the practice of polygamy. Joseph Smith ran for president in 1844 in a campaign that called for the government to do more to secure religious and civil rights.

According to LDS history, Smith and his brother were killed during the campaign by an angry group of citizens who believed the Mormons were guilty of treason.

While Kosnoff schooled himself in theology, Salmi concerned himself with Mormon history in the judicial system. It so happened that the defining case in U.S. law on matters of religious liberty also involves the Church of Jesus Christ of Latter-day Saints. In 1878, a man named George Reynolds was convicted for bigamy in Utah. He challenged that conviction before the U.S. Supreme Court, arguing that it was his constitutionally protected religious duty as a Mormon to marry multiple wives. (Mormon doctrine includes a revelation from God to Joseph Smith that males are to practice polygamy or face "damnation in the life to come.") The Court ruled against Reynolds, noting that the government cannot constitutionally dictate religious belief but can regulate actions. *Reynolds v. United States* set the legal precedent for such matters and has been quoted in lawsuits ever since. The Reynolds case also is well known because in its opinion, the Court quotes Thomas Jefferson's response to advocates of religious freedom after the first session of the first Congress:

"'Believing with you that religion is a matter which lies solely between man and his God; that he owes account to none other for his faith or his worship; that the legislative powers of the government reach actions only, and not opinions, I contemplate with sovereign reverence that act of the whole American people which declared that their legislature should "make no law respecting an establishment of religion or prohibiting the free exercise thereof," thus building a wall of separation between church and State.' . . . Congress was deprived of all legislative power over mere opinion, but was left free to reach actions which were in violation of social duties or subversive of good order."

In its decision, the Court famously wrote, "Can a man excuse his [illegal] practices . . . because of his religious belief? To permit this would be to make the professed doctrines of religious belief superior to the law of the land, and in effect to permit every citizen to become a law unto himself. Government could exist only in name under such circumstances . . ."

Joel Salmi had to admit that he felt inspired by Thomas Jefferson's and the justices' words as he sat at his desk, recorder in hand, papers spread in front of him, and worked on the Scott team's argument over the soft sounds of the farm animals outside. This was not just some routine legal brief. Salmi felt Kosnoff's passion now more than ever. This was the very heart of the law, right here: constitutional freedom. They were strong on this. And Joel Salmi was ready to score a win.

12

Perhaps it was all the gangster references. Or maybe that, everywhere he turned, there were more victims. For whatever reason, Tim Kosnoff began to pick through Frank Curtis's past whenever he had some time. True, Frank wasn't on trial. Frank was dead. But this pursuit bordered on an obsession, driven by Kosnoff's need to learn more. Despite all reasoning to the contrary, Kosnoff couldn't shake the idea that learning more about Frank Curtis would help him turn the case. The man who had actually perpetrated the crimes that had brought about this lawsuit remained largely a mystery, and Tim Kosnoff couldn't leave that alone.

Once the church had been ordered to produce Frank's membership records, even the most basic version of them, Kosnoff had more clues to Frank's life inside the Mormon community. Genealogy is very important in the Mormon religion, mostly because of the Mormon belief in what is known as baptism for the dead. The church teaches that the progression of life extends from prebirth to an eventual eternal state. And there's a chance for salvation all along the way, even after life on earth stops. Mormons believe that dead souls can still be saved through baptism. They research their ancestors and others in order that they may receive a proxy baptism, in which a Mormon in good standing is baptized in the name of someone who is dead. Following this doctrine, Mormons have baptized the Founding Fathers, several former U.S. presidents, and various other famous people, including William Shakespeare, Leo Tolstoy, and the Mexican Catholic martyr Fr. Miguel Pro. (The church got into some trouble for this ritual back in the early 1990s when the families of Jewish Holocaust victims discovered that Mormons had been baptizing their relatives by proxy, and the American Gathering of Jewish Holocaust Survivors and their descendants complained to the head of the Church of Jesus Christ of Latter-day Saints. Church authorities adopted a policy prohibiting members from including Holocaust victims in their posthumous baptismal ceremonies.)

Likely for this reason, Frank's church membership records included information on his parents and siblings, another ex-wife, and the dates and places of all their births and deaths. Kosnoff already had Frank's Social Security number from his death certificate in Oregon. Having made a career of defending the accused, Kosnoff had adopted a certain skepticism about the colorful stories told by criminals, whom he'd found had a habit of inflating their adventures to boost their egos. As a result, Kosnoff harbored serious doubts about the truth behind Frank's tales. But as more details emerged on what the old man had told people, his knack for endearing himself to the kindness of strangers and leaving town when he got in trouble, it seemed plausible that Frank might have actually been in prison somewhere.

Kosnoff began making phone calls and sending off requests to various public agencies to try to find any other records that might reveal anything more. The biggest challenge was that Frank Curtis was already a senior citizen by the time he connected with the church, or at least that's what the records showed. He was born in 1903. Kosnoff was seeking records that were now nearly a century old. On a whim, he'd contacted the Chicago Historical Society and talked to a man there who worked as a sort of curator of the collection of information and records on Al Capone. The man told Kosnoff that, while Franklyn Curtis was not named anywhere in the records there, it was highly likely that he might have been attached to Capone's organization in some way. Big bosses like Capone ultimately controlled most of the illegal business in town during certain eras.

Kosnoff called and begged municipal clerks all over Cook County and the city of Chicago to look up the oldest records they had for anything on Franklyn Richard Curtis. For the most part, this was an exercise in frustration. Somewhere along the way, however, an old conviction turned up, and information connected to it pointed to another conviction in Detroit. Kosnoff turned his attention to Michigan. On the fourth or fifth phone call, he spoke with a woman in the Circuit Court clerk's office in Detroit. Though they would never actually meet, she was a willing recruit into this journey back in time. Kosnoff figured her to be a middle-aged career civil servant, and he worked hard to present the most charming version of himself over the phone. Either she took pity on him or was curious enough to want to find the answer to the riddles that this lawyer from Seattle was trying to solve. Their relationship began with a simple question.

"If you had to find out if someone had been involved in a crime more than fifty years ago, how would you go about it?" Kosnoff asked his new friend. She told him she'd think about it and ask around the office, and instructed him to call her back in a few days. Kosnoff didn't think this would pan out, but she was still the best lead he had, so he called her back. They brainstormed a bit more on the conundrum of finding Frank Curtis's information. A week or so later, Kosnoff called the clerk again and learned that she'd found something. Frank Curtis had been on probation, which meant that he'd been in prison, which meant that there might be a prison record of him. This pattern continued for more than a month. Each time she unearthed a trace of Frank Curtis in the public records, Kosnoff chased it through the prison system or the state archives or some other agency until the trail went cold. And Frank Curtis's trail cooled frequently. Government agencies have set schedules under which bureaucrats are supposed to purge records to limit storage costs. Fortunately for Kosnoff, however, such tasks are often so low on an agency's priority list that they rarely get done on time. Old records often remain warehoused, somewhere, waiting to be destroyed. Or found. Every so often Kosnoff scored a new piece of information that led to another discovery. He called the Michigan Department of Corrections, which oversees the prisons, and a man there told him that records of that age were likely in archives maintained by the state. Kosnoff called the Michigan State Archives and began the hunt there. He also wrote to the Chicago Crime Commission, requesting any information it had on a man with any of the variations of Frank Curtis's name and vital statistics. It was a constant tease, this archival dig, producing just enough to make him want more.

One morning he received a letter in the mail from the clerk of one of the agencies he'd contacted. Kosnoff had become accustomed to standard form letters stating that nothing was found on the information he'd requested. This one turned out to be different. The letter detailed the research findings of one very thorough, conscientious clerk who worked somewhere in Michigan's Department of Corrections, Central Records Division in Lansing. It included a synopsis of the incarceration history of Franklyn R. Curtis, from 1929 to 1980. Much to Kosnoff's frustration, most of the man's prison records had been destroyed in a fire at a federal records facility. Kosnoff called Joel Salmi immediately. He usually called Salmi at the end of a conversation with his clerk pal in Detroit, or when he'd gotten something new in the mail. He had to tell someone, and Salmi was genuinely impressed with the fruits of Kosnoff's labor. It wasn't something he'd ever do himself, but Salmi valued his friend's commitment and found his work ingenious. He was sure it would pay off, somehow, and so he encouraged Kosnoff. More important, Joel Salmi never thought Tim Kosnoff was nuts, while other people involved in the Scott case were beginning to wonder about his obsession. Piece by piece, Tim Kosnoff would soon possess some of the early parts of Frank Curtis's life. His story was one of a troubled youth, an accomplished con, and a serial predator whose best skill was likely survival.

Chicago at the turn of the century, around the time Frank was born, was already well on its way to becoming the nation's industrial epicenter. The South Side was home to the largest livestock yards and meatpacking center in the country, memorialized in Upton Sinclair's famous novel *The Jungle*. Sinclair, a Socialist, brought attention and, ultimately, regulation to the unsanitary, polluted industry and awakened Americans to the squalid working conditions of the immigrant employees who kept the plants running.

At about the same time that Sinclair's tome was published, the banker J. P. Morgan created the U.S. Steel Corp., which gobbled up small mills throughout Illinois and Pennsylvania. By 1910, the company's most productive plants provided a livelihood to nearly twenty thousand workers and their families in southeast Chicago and neighboring Gary, Indiana—less than a hundred miles from where Tim Kosnoff's Russian-Jewish ancestors would later settle. Manufacturing industries grew in the shadow of the giant steel mills. And so did neighborhoods, where wave after wave of immigrants arrived from Ireland, Germany, and Eastern Europe with the promise of steady work. Franklyn Curtis's family was among them.

Frank's grandparents came from Prague, by way of Wisconsin, in the mid-1800s and ultimately settled in a succession of small worker's cottages that filled areas known as "Back of the Yards" and "Bridgeport" on Chicago's South Side. The working-class neighborhoods were populated by Poles, Lithuanians, Czechs, and Slovaks, each area anchored by its own Catholic parish.

Sometime after his arrival, Frank's grandfather Frank Sabatka adopted a new American surname to go with his new home: Shubert. Consequently, the latter of his nine children—including Anna, Frank's mother, who was born on Valentine's Day 1885—were given the last name Shubert.

By the turn of the century, Chicago's Czech population had swollen to the third largest in the world, behind those of Prague and Vienna. But Anna had her eyes on a young British lad. Like so many of his peers, Norman Curtis had left England for the promise of prosperity in the United States, in the end making his way to Chicago to work in the industrial yards. There, in 1902, he met and married seventeen-year-old Anna Shubert. A year later, Anna and Norman had a son, whom they named Franklin. (Later, his name would be spelled "Franklyn" on documents and in his own signature.)

The family's future, however, was over almost before it started. Shortly after his marriage, Norman again left home. This time, though, adventurous pursuit ended his life. Norman Curtis died in Missouri in 1906, when his son, Franklyn, was three years old. The details of his journey and his death remain a mystery. Suddenly widowed, Anna moved with her young son back to the familiar territory of family and the Czech community in south Chicago. She worked in the homes of families who were better off, or in the offices of industrial plants. As the years passed, Frank became less interested in school and increasingly lured by the thrill and financial promise of the streets. Frank stole whatever he could.

By 1916, young people in Chicago were turning criminal faster than schools could keep track of them—some ten thousand young offenders moved through the criminal justice system each year—leading the city to create the first juvenile courts in the country. The convergence of poor and working-class families, low-wage jobs, and abundant liquor, gambling parlors, and dance halls left a growing number of kids to fend largely for themselves. Teenage gangs, organized loosely by ethnicity, terrorized the streets, preying on immigrants, robbing workingmen of their pay, stealing from just about anywhere, and fighting among themselves.

By the time Frank was eight, he'd spent seven months in Parental School, a city institution where young truants and troublemakers were deposited after they were booted from the classroom. From there, he graduated to Correctional School, a tougher version of Parental School, where charges were kept in supervised custody. Frank landed there at least four times for three-month stretches, mostly owing to varying degrees of thievery. Then, at fourteen, he was convicted of larceny for stealing a motorcycle and served eighteen months in the Illinois State Home for Delinquent Boys, about forty-five miles from Chicago.

Built on nine hundred acres of farmland, the institution was designed to house groups of about fifty boys and staff members in cottages equipped with kitchens and living rooms. The idea was to simulate a homelike environment, since the population included delinquents who had not yet reached their sixteenth birthdays as well as boys who'd simply been abandoned or neglected and had nowhere else to go.

The Home for Delinquent Boys aimed to provide both academic and vocational education, with the goal that the boys would gain job skills and go out into the world as productive citizens. The institute also purported to include both religious instruction and, increasingly, military training. While Frank was locked up there, America entered World War I, sending thousands of young men from Chicago off to war in Europe. The war changed the landscape. What had seemed like a nonstop flow of immigrants into the South Side slowed significantly, which in turn spurred the migration of African-American families from the South looking for newly available work in Chicago's industrial plants and factories.

Frank was not concerned with international politics and uninterested in the prospect of military service. When he returned to Chicago, Frank resumed his life on the streets and eventually hooked up with one of the largest gangs in the city, which, among other things, "protected the color line" by regularly warring against members of the growing African-American community.

By then, Chicago was already in the grip of the corrupt officials and organized crime networks that made the city famously lawless during Prohibition. Gangs and politicians were loosely connected through supposed athletic clubs and ethnic community organizations that were fronts for all manner of illegal business operations. Sometime around 1920, after the advent of Prohibition, a powerful gangster named Johnny Torrio introduced his New York protégé, Al Capone, to Chicago. Capone and his family moved into the South Side, within a few miles of Frank's neighborhood. Torrio and Capone set about making their fortune in the bootlegging industry and soon branched out into gambling and prostitution. Business grew with the help of corrupt Mayor William Hale "Big Bill" Thompson Jr. and a police force that was predominantly on the gangsters' payroll. The homicide rate doubled in Chicago in the two decades between 1900 and 1920.

Given Frank's criminal record and his own account of events, it's likely that he was part of a group of low-level underlings who did enforcement and grunt work for Torrio and Capone's operation. He also worked off and on in the kitchens of a few South Side restaurants where the bigger bosses did business. Young men in Frank's position were often faced with the choice of working for the gangsters or being crushed by them.

Frank had the close-set eyes and straight nose of his Bohemian ancestors and, by his late teens, a hardened face. Having spent a good deal of his youth in and out of reform schools, he hadn't had many girlfriends. The exception was a whirlwind romance with a fifteen-year-old from Indiana named Ida. On a September day in 1924, Frank and Ida stood before the giant ornate altar of Holy Name Cathedral in downtown Chicago and promised to love, honor, obey, and cherish each other forever. Seven months later, Ida went home to her family in Indiana and divorced Frank. He later explained the breakup saying that he was gone most of their marriage, "doing the boss's work."

Shortly after Ida left, Frank was convicted for stealing a car in Tulsa, where he'd traveled with some bootleggers, and spent the next three years in the Oklahoma State Penitentiary, located on a fifteen-hundred-acre farm in McAlester—a place that could rightfully be described as the middle of nowhere. The prison raised cattle and other livestock and crops, all of which were fairly foreign to Frank. He returned to Chicago immediately after he was released. While Frank had been doing time in Oklahoma, Johnny Torrio effectively retired and left his Chicago business in the hands of Capone. As the "booze wars" raged in Chicago, Frank apparently reconnected with some of his old gang and found work on the streets. A year later, in 1928, Frank was arrested while robbing a warehouse owned by Polish businessmen on the edge of the city. He spent time in Chicago's Bridewell Prison, an architectural masterpiece built in the 1800s that was by then woefully inadequate to handle the burgeoning criminal population flowing through Chicago's correctional facilities. After Frank had served about ninety days, the charges were dismissed without any real explanation, and he was free to go back to work. But on a February evening in 1929, Frank's luck again ran out, this time in Detroit, where he'd moved from Chicago, likely for some criminal enterprise, about a week before and decided to stay for a while. At first, he'd gotten work busing tables at the Sunnyside Grill, a forgettable diner on Broadway. He quit within days. Frank was arrested in the back of an alley after his third taxicab stickup. It was a well-worn routine. Frank would pick up a young accomplice—usually a teenage boy no older than sixteen, whom he'd find hanging out on the streets, and lure him with the promise of a job and fast money—and hail a cab. Once inside, he would hold his Harrington & Richardson .32 caliber revolver on the boy (and the cabdriver) while the boy took money from the driver, in this case $12. This time, two beat cops came around the corner and gave chase just as Frank was running away with his booty.

Despite his voluminous criminal record, Frank had beaten more raps than he'd done time for. This time, oddly, Frank confessed to killing a man named Jockliski, whom he knew had recently turned up dead in Chicago. It's possible that Frank was betting he'd be extradited back to the more familiar network of graft and patronage in Chicago, where he stood a better chance of freedom. Under those circumstances, the armed robbery charge in Detroit might be delayed or forgotten. Frank even signed a waiver for his extradition, and Chicago police officers dutifully came to Detroit. But they didn't want Frank for the murder. He was sunk.

The Honorable Charles E. Bowles was on his way to political infamy in Detroit when Frank Curtis appeared before him. The judge would later be elected mayor, a position from which he was recalled following allegations of colluding with gangsters and the Ku Klux Klan. When the judge saw Frank Curtis, at twenty-six, he had already filled a criminal résumé that dated back nearly fifteen years. Frank was clearly connected, but not nearly well enough to reach into the judge's world in Detroit. Frank had been caught red-handed in an armed robbery, not to mention with a young boy recruited to help carry out his caper. Bowles got the idea that something wasn't quite right with Franklyn Curtis. He was simple, maybe . . . or something else. Bowles ordered what was, in that era, the equivalent of a psychological evaluation. The resulting report noted that, while legally sane, Frank was mentally equivalent to a twelve-year-old: impulsive, emotionally unstable, egocentric, and not very intelligent. According to the report, "The patient is seriously lacking in insight and, in his thinking and judgments, seems decidedly simple, primitive and childlike."

The examiner found that Frank had another issue: inappropriate sexual behavior with boys, which, Frank told the examiner, had gotten him into some trouble in his earlier locked-up life but had been undocumented before then. Even in this, Frank's most thorough evaluation, the report is so vague it almost seems to have been written in code: In "sexuality, we might add, there is here indication of some degree of maladaptation, in the light of which it is very possible socially objectionable manifestations may occur. We are impressed in this case, too, by notable lack as respects appreciation and regard for social values and requirements and, in general, by marked antisocial quality as concerns attitude and behavior possibility."

The report seemed to be saying, without actually saying, that bad things had happened and would happen again if this young man wasn't locked up. Judge Bowles responded by sending Frank away with a life sentence on March 21, 1929. Frank moved to a cell at the Michigan State Prison at Marquette, on the shores of Lake Superior. It's impossible to know much about his life there, because successive prison riots destroyed most of the inmate records, including those of Frank Curtis. About the only thing known for sure is that he lived for two decades at Marquette, where he worked in the laundry and the kitchen, until he was paroled in 1950 to Benton Harbor, Michigan, about eighty miles from Chicago. Frank was forty-seven years old at the time.

Five months after his release, Frank stole a $49 life insurance dividend check from a man in St. Joseph, Michigan, a few miles from Benton Harbor, and tried to forge his name as the payee. The event landed Frank back in jail, this time in Jackson County, Michigan, then the largest walled prison in the world, with six thousand inmates. Jackson, birthplace of the Republican Party, is a drive-through county near Ann Arbor. Frank stayed there until he was paroled a dozen years later, in 1962. He would return to prison once more before he left the Michigan Department of Corrections for the last time in 1971. By then, Frank was sixty-eight and had been incarcerated for most of his life.

He lived briefly in Pennsylvania and New York before heading back to Chicago, but there he found he couldn't face the city anymore. The Chicago bus terminal was home to seedy panhandlers, young unwed mothers, drug dealers, poor families, and twenty-somethings steeped in irony jostling through a couple of dozen gates into buses going in every direction. A view of the city stretches out from the upstairs windows. Frank didn't leave the terminal. Chicago hadn't been particularly good to him and offered even less promise for an old man. His mother had died about ten years back, and any other family members who might care about him were long gone.

Frank decided to go west. He'd done kitchen work for a short time in the Oregon logging town of Valsetz, a company town for Boise Cascade, years earlier and promised himself he'd get back to the Northwest at some point. Time was running out. Without any apparent plan, Frank got on a bus headed for Salt Lake City.

This trip west would prove the fateful path that connected Frank Curtis to the Mormon church, and from there to the lives of Manny Saban, David Johnson, Steven Penrose, and Jeremiah Scott.

13

When the dust cleared around Tim Kosnoff's rental car near the small town of Humboldt, Arizona, Manny Saban was waiting outside his trailer, looking apprehensive and slightly menacing. He had dark eyes and a shaved head. The men went inside, where Manny introduced his girlfriend, Anita. She held a baby, Manny's son. Manny and Kosnoff sat down and talked about what would happen the next day at Manny's deposition.

Kosnoff figured it was a good time to get Manny's story on the record. The church's lawyers were dragging everything out, so why not? Also, however mundane, this was accomplishing something and Kosnoff needed that; he needed action. Deposing Manny Saban was the best available antidote to the torture of painfully slow legal arguments. The Scott team had had to file a request with the court to take an out-of-state deposition and then danced around with the church's lawyers on scheduling. By the time all of that was finished, in 1999, it was late summer. Hardly ideal in Arizona, but climate was of little concern right now.

Manny was no stranger to court proceedings, having been involved in one or another justice system since his adolescence. Depositions, however, were something new. They don't tend to happen in the prosecution of the sort of felony mischief—car stealing and the like—that had colored Manny's earlier life. Kosnoff wasn't entirely sure how this was going to go. Manny mentioned again that he was still wanted for a theft in Oregon. They both knew the score on this. If Kosnoff wanted Manny to come back to Oregon and testify in his civil case, Kosnoff was going to have to do something about Manny's outstanding criminal warrant.

That evening, Kosnoff wandered around downtown Prescott, the closest city big enough to offer both a hotel and a court reporter. An old mining town and the first capital of the state before the population moved south and established a new capital in Phoenix, Prescott held strong to its wild west roots. Kosnoff walked past storefronts that showcased cowboy gear, gold jewelry, and outdoor supplies, as well as a string of bars and restaurants on what was, for the benefit of tourists, still known as Whiskey Row. A steady stream of country music spilled out from the bars. Kosnoff sat down on a bench next to a water fountain in the center square of downtown to think through his plan for Manny's deposition and watched people walk by for a while. The human landscape here could be easily categorized, Kosnoff thought: old hippies, with their long gray ponytails; denim-clad working folks meeting for a beer or still drinking from the workday's end; and a good number of Native Americans. Kosnoff was intrigued by how many faces had been completely cooked by the sun, their dark-colored skin deeply creased in a way that he hadn't seen before. He wondered if this was Manny's future.

The following morning, Manny and Anita met Kosnoff at a legal services office in Prescott that the Scott team had procured for the event. Stephen English, along with two other church lawyers, arrived shortly thereafter. The Scott team couldn't afford to send anyone but Kosnoff. A court reporter and videographer set up their machines facing Manny, who was polite and responsive, despite being tremendously uncomfortable.

Kosnoff led Manny through his personal history, how his parents had broken up and he and his brother and sisters had landed with their mother in Portland, and how the Mormon missionaries had come to the door in Felony Flats, and they'd all gone off to church. Kosnoff focused on the era of Frank Curtis, in the late 1970s. Manny described Frank's apartment in the veterinary clinic. It was small, he told the lawyers, but had a living room, kitchen, eating area, and a bedroom with a small bathroom attached. "It was almost, reminded me of an old dog pound because there was chain link fence all around," he said. "It was really secure, you know, you couldn't get in or out." He added that there were dead-bolt locks that required a key on the inside of all the doors, and bars on the windows.

Kosnoff asked Manny if Frank took the boys anywhere else.

"Bus rides to downtown . . . uh . . . buy us shoes and clothes some-times just . . . uh . . . a lot of souvenirs at the hockey games . . . um . . . just like a dad just . . ."

Manny had a tendency to slip into a childlike cadence when he was talking, almost like whining. Kosnoff thought it was odd. These mannerisms seemed to be part of an overall and sudden outbreak of immaturity. He'd bring his hands up and let them fall hard against his sides as he struggled to string together parts of his story. Manny recounted the sleepover in Frank's apartment with several other boys from church and the neighborhood. He explained how Frank had per-suaded Manny's mother, Raquel, that it would be good for her to have a break from the kids, an idea that was appealing, and that the boys would have a good time. Raquel dropped Manny and his brother at Frank's place in the back of the animal clinic. The four or five boys who'd gathered at Frank's had been about eight to twelve years old and bouncing with energy. Manny remembered the water fight they'd engaged in with large syringes from the animal clinic. He told the lawyers how the boys were soaked afterward and Frank had the boys strip down to their underwear while they continued to run around. Occasionally, Frank would catch one of the boys and put a finger inside his anus, Manny said.

"I thought it was some kind of thing that he knew how to uh—make you hurt, like, your brother giving you a charley horse or giving you a brownie or a wedgie, what they call it, or flicking you on the head. I thought it was just a way for him to make us hurt for squirting him."

The boys, Manny continued, had taken turns in the shower of Frank's tiny bathroom before putting on their pajamas and nestling in front of the television in the living room. Manny had been the last one to shower. Frank shut the door behind him. Kosnoff was surprised by how emotional Manny was getting, this many years later, when he talked about Frank Curtis. Every so often he sniffed hard and wiped away tears that seemed to keep welling up and leaking out. Manny was as demonstrative as Jeremiah had been emotionless. And his struggle here was genuinely painful to watch. This wasn't the first time that Manny had told anyone what happened with Frank in the back of the animal clinic, but it was the first time he'd described the details. Before Kosnoff called him, Manny had never intended to discuss it again. Now he was deep into a narrative about the slumber party.

"Well, well, after everybody else had got their shower and dressed, they were all tucked into bed watching TV and when he called me into the bathroom, he shut the bedroom door, then. He didn't on the other ones. And I was already in his big yellow robe that he had me put on. It was like everybody wore the robe before they went into the shower and . . . um . . . he was a really big guy, and I was really small for my age." Manny went on to describe how Frank Curtis had fondled him, and then masturbated and ejaculated on him on the bed while the other boys slept and watched television in the other room, and how he'd awakened his eight-year-old brother and tried to tell him what happened. Manny's brother hadn't understood.

"I was frantic," he said. "I was crying so bad. He probably . . . I probably couldn't talk right. So I called my mother and . . . uh . . . begged her to come and get us, but because I wouldn't tell her why she didn't come. So I sat up all night scared thinking that he, it, was going to happen again just pretty much with my back up against the wall and stayed up all night and waited for my mom to pick me up the next morning."

Manny was falling apart, but Kosnoff had to get this part of the story on the record for a jury to hear later. He asked Manny what happened the following morning, when Raquel had come to pick them up.

"We just got our stuff to leave and in the car on the way home I told her what had happened and she didn't believe me. She pretty much said I was making it up."

Manny continued verbally trudging through the shame and confusion that followed his encounter with Frank: "I just felt like a different person. I felt ashamed . . . um . . . guilt, and I stayed in my room for days, maybe, even as close to a month or more just crying and I wouldn't go to school no more because I just felt ashamed. And it just made me think that everybody in the whole world knew what happened and it was all my fault."

Of course, all the lawyers knew that Raquel later married Frank Curtis, making him Manny's stepfather. If Kosnoff's opponents were worried that Manny's story might hurt their clients, they didn't let on. Stephen English, in particular, maintained a poker face. He seemed pleasant and professional throughout the examination.

As the day headed from morning into afternoon, Kosnoff guided Manny through the events that took place after Frank married Raquel. No one asked him this, but Manny remembered the last time he'd seen Brother Curtis. It was after he'd come back to Portland from Las Vegas. He was walking down the street and saw Brother Curtis a block or so ahead, at the bus stop in front of the Deseret Thrift Store. Manny yelled at him and ran. Brother Curtis was getting on the bus. Manny caught up just as it was pulling away. He banged on the side of the bus and yelled again, "You pervert. I'll kill you. You pervert."

Manny Saban represented how the church had, however unwittingly, been a coconspirator to Frank Curtis. Manny had been swept up by Mormon missionaries into a church where he would meet Frank Curtis. Manny had also provided the earliest notice to the church that Kosnoff was aware of. He'd told his mother what Frank did to him. While she may not have believed him initially, eventually Raquel had told her Mormon bishop what Frank Curtis did to young boys, but to no avail. All of this had taken place some *fifteen years* before Jeremiah Scott was abused by the same man, whom he'd met in the same Mormon church.

Manny recounted that they'd moved to another house around the block and that he had hidden in a shed in the backyard, or ridden his bike or the bus around town. Kosnoff asked Manny to talk about the apartment attached to the junkyard, a place that Kosnoff had by now seen up close and considered to be distinctly creepy. Manny said that a man whom Brother Curtis knew from church lived across the street. He'd been there, Manny remembered, on the day back in 1978 when Raquel had taken her sons over to Brother Curtis's apartment. For some reason that Manny could not recall, the boys were in trouble. Manny remembered Brother Curtis's friend having removed his belt, as if to administer some corporal punishment, but all Manny saw was a man standing near Brother Curtis removing his clothes. Manny was terrified. That's about when Raquel came back.

"There was a knock on the door and it was my mom because we had forgotten our clothes and when the door opened I, we, ran out. And we ran out to the street and Frank and my mom came out there, and I tried to tell my mom what they were going to do to us and Frank started slapping me across the face, probably, six to ten times to where I really couldn't see, you know?"

"And what happened then?" Kosnoff asked.

"The bag that I had my clothes in had an iron in it, and I was holding it in my hand and when he got done slapping me, telling my mom that I was lying, I proceeded to hit him in the head with it, my bag, and then I ran."

Manny remembered that his mother had gone after him in the Pontiac that day. They went down the street that way for a while, son walking determinedly down the sidewalk and mother driving along next to him, until Manny finally got in the car.

After Kosnoff established that Manny never saw Frank Curtis again because he'd been sent to Las Vegas to live with their father, he stopped the questions. Manny had nothing else to give and the whole exercise was becoming too grueling. Neither Steve English nor any of the other lawyers asked much more, other than to clarify that Manny had not told anyone else about Frank's abuse.

Everyone in the office packed up and shook hands. Manny later recalled that one or the other of the defendants' lawyers made a point of expressing concern for his well-being and wished him well. Kosnoff had a few hours before he had to be at the Phoenix airport, so he and Manny and Anita got something to eat and sat down on a bench in the shade. Manny was a mess, shaken and upset. Kosnoff tried to console him, repeating that he'd done a good job and reminding him that it was important that he told the story.

The strangeness of the whole interlude was not lost on Tim Kosnoff, and he continued to ponder this on the drive back to Phoenix. Manny had been so different from Jeremiah. Jeremiah was inscrutable. He could coldly recount events in a very clinical, dispassionate way. Manny had been more compelling. It was excruciatingly evident that this tough man with the outstanding warrants and the girlfriend living in the smoke-filled trailer in the desert remained, on some level, a wounded child. He possessed something similar to the deep sadness in David Johnson, who'd been molested while Frank Curtis was supposedly teaching him religious lessons. Kosnoff had to consider the fact that it might be his client who was different. Then again, none of them shared the explosive anger of Steven Penrose.

The landscape along the highway gradually turned from barren desert back into the mosaic of tiled roofs and traffic as Kosnoff neared the airport. He was excited about the narrative that had been captured in Manny's deposition, and it made him all the more eager to get this into the courtroom. At the same time, Kosnoff possessed a nagging awareness of what he'd done here, that he'd blown into town, stirred up a nest of emotional pain, and taken off again. Linda Walker had begun to call Kosnoff "the angel of pain" because he was usually the one who first spoke to most of Frank Curtis's victims, many of whom had never revealed the secrets of their abuse. It was the job. What else could he do? He had to press on.

Kosnoff was also preoccupied by what had happened to the other boys who had been Manny's friends in the neighborhood. He and Linda had worked hard at finding these men, with mixed results. They'd located Bobby and Jimmy Goodall, who'd grown up with Manny. Relatively speaking, they'd been easy to find since both had long criminal histories. Jim Goodall was incarcerated in Washington, which was familiar territory for Kosnoff, the former criminal defense lawyer. The others remained largely a mystery. He'd have to get back on this task, Kosnoff thought. This is what he knew so far:

FRANK CURTIS TIME LINE OF VICTIMS

1977–1978	Manny Saban, Bobby Goodall, and Jimmy Goodall	Portland (not Chicago)
1982–1983	David Johnson and Steven Penrose	Portland
1991	Jeremiah Scott	Portland

Depositions continued throughout the first half of 2000. Most took place in the conference room at Dunn, Carney, though a few were conducted in the offices of Bullivant, Houser, Bailey, the church's lawyers. The two firms' offices were a block apart in downtown Portland. And while the players shifted depending on which attorneys were available and versed on the subject, Tim Kosnoff and David Ernst from Bullivant, Houser, Bailey were up against each other most of the time. The two men sparred through a dozen or so depositions of former bishops, stake presidents, and other church leaders who had interacted with Frank Curtis.

Underneath the questions about who knew what and how he'd learned it, another story unfolded, one that had nothing to do with the legal issues. The truth was that most of these men had no idea what to do with the shocking information that one of their brethren had molested children. They were untrained in professional counseling and could barely keep up with their gargantuan responsibilities. They all had full-time jobs and large families of their own, on top of which they'd been called into a volunteer position leading hundreds of people. One day they might be helping someone who faced eviction and the next they faced a dying mother or a child who needed special help. Given the insular nature of the Mormon community, most bishops didn't know anything about sex crimes, certainly not enough to understand a serial pedophile.

In each deposition, Ernst or one of his associates refused to allow the Mormons to answer question after question by claiming clergy-penitent privilege. As before, the church's position was that anything that came out of a conversation between a church leader and a church member was subject to protection and remained confidential. Kosnoff dodged and circled in his arguments, and often forced witnesses to explain their reason for claiming the privilege, since most of the bishops clearly didn't understand the law. Much of this quarreling was the trademark of practiced lawyers, but the two men seemed to do their best to get under each other's skin. It was clear that the animosity between Tim Kosnoff and David Ernst grew with each passing deposition.

What bothered Kosnoff more than anything else is that he thought the church's lawyers were obstructing the process. To him, it was an issue of fairness and access. The church was stretching the clergy-penitent argument and then running up the bills fighting about it. The Scott team didn't have the resources to keep battling the objections in court and then redoing depositions.

"If you have to make a financial calculation, then you're priced out of the system, and that's not fair," Kosnoff said years later. It was one thing to lose because you couldn't prove your case; it was another to lose because you couldn't afford to keep up.

On one particular morning in January 2000, Kosnoff deposed Frank Curtis's last Mormon bishop, Melvin Merrell. The man had been contacted by Sandy Scott after she'd learned that Jeremiah had been molested. He'd also been interviewed by the detective from the Redmond, Washington, police department who investigated the case. Ultimately, the bishop had referred the matter for a discipline hearing with the stake president and that hearing resulted in Frank Curtis's final excommunication from the church.

During the bishop's deposition, Kosnoff questioned him about whether or not he'd told the police what he'd learned from Frank Curtis. Ernst had advised the bishop not to answer questions about what the men had talked about on the grounds that it was covered by the clergy-penitent privilege. The morning had been one long debate over what Ernst would not allow the bishop to answer for the same reason. In this case, however, if the privilege had been broken by an earlier disclosure, the bishop's conversation with Frank Curtis could be fair game in court.

"Are you saying that you're sure that it would breach the privilege to disclose that information to me here today, but it would not have breached the privilege for you to disclose it to the police or civil authorities back when it happened?" Kosnoff asked.

Ernst jumped in. "That's argumentative and you're putting words in his mouth I think unfairly. Let's take a break for a moment."

"There's a question pending," Kosnoff said. Lawyers are usually not permitted to counsel with witnesses while there is a question pending for them to answer.

"Well, then, I'd like you to—"

Kosnoff interrupted. "The question will stand, Dave."

"I don't appreciate your attitude," Ernst said. "It's getting a little hostile."

"No, it's not."

"It is, and I don't appreciate it."

"It's not intended to be, David."

"Well, I'm telling you that I feel that you're getting hostile and I think this witness has those feelings and so—"

"I'm really not, David. I think the record will show, and everybody in here will say, that I'm speaking with a very soft voice; my gestures are not pointed or aggressive. This witness has not displayed any kind of fear or reaction. He seems to be listening very carefully to my questions."

"He's trying to do that."

"I'm attempting, in turn, to probe his answers, as I'm entitled to. And so for that reason I'm a little bit troubled at this point because I think you are perhaps, through your speaking objections, attempting to coach this witness and that troubles me a little bit. So what I'm going to ask for you to do, David, is to just allow the court reporter to read back that last question to him and allow him to answer and then we can take a break."

"Very good. Thank you very much for that enlightening information. I appreciate it."

Merrell said that he couldn't remember what he had thought about when he decided to talk to the police in 1993. The group took a break. When they began again, the privilege issues continued, until the Scott lawyers decided to officially put the deposition on hold until the issues were resolved by the judge.

By far the most combative deposition to date was that of Gordon Checketts, who'd been the bishop of the ward where the Johnson and Penrose families and Frank Curtis had attended in the early 1980s. He was deposed in January 2000, in what became quite a scene in the Bullivant, Houser, Bailey conference room.

Gary Rhoades was there with Kosnoff. Stephen English represented the church and Gordon Checketts. Another attorney from Jeff Kilmer's firm was at the table representing Greg Foster.

Bishop Checketts made it clear from the start that he wasn't giving up any information. He either claimed that he couldn't remember or refused to answer most of Kosnoff's questions. About the only information he provided was about his own background. He'd graduated from college in Utah and worked for the Internal Revenue Service before eventually establishing his own accounting firm. He and his wife had three sons. He'd been a member of the Church of Jesus Christ of Latter-day Saints since childhood and had served in a variety of positions for the church, including those of bishop and home teacher. He also had been president of the elders quorum, a higher-ranking group of men within a ward. Gordon Checketts had participated in at least ten church disciplinary hearings that resulted in excommunicating members for adultery, fornication, and various other crimes, but he couldn't recall any involving child sexual abuse.

Bishop Checketts remembered Frank Curtis as an elderly man with limited means. Checketts had once put Frank Curtis to work doing yard maintenance at his home when the old man needed money. Kosnoff asked Checketts if Frank Curtis had ever babysat any of the

Checketts boys, but he could not recall. That's about all Kosnoff had gotten. Gordon Checketts refused to answer anything about any conversation he'd had with anyone about anything while he was bishop, citing the clergy-penitent privilege statute in Oregon. Checketts was under the impression that the law allowed him to refuse to provide any information he thought should be kept confidential, which was not correct. He alternately stated "clergy-penitent privilege," "clergy-member privilege," "bishop-client privilege," or "bishop-member privilege" when Kosnoff asked a question about something that occurred while Checketts was bishop of the ward. The atmosphere deteriorated quickly.

"I believe all my conversations with members of my ward would be clergy-member privilege," Checketts said.

"Let me try and understand and clarify your position," Kosnoff responded. "Is it your position that by virtue of the fact that you were called and placed in the role of bishop, that any conversation you had with any member while you were bishop is privileged?"

"Yes," Checketts said.

The reason the Scott lawyers had subpoenaed Checketts in the first place was to get at a key fact in the case: Joanne Penrose had said during her deposition that she'd gone to Bishop Checketts when she'd learned that her son Steven and his friend David Johnson had been abused by Frank Curtis. She'd also said that the bishop told her that he was going to contact the police. There was no confession involved. It wasn't even a conversation with a penitent. It was, instead, a church member alleging to her bishop that someone else had committed a crime against her son. If Joanne Penrose was telling the truth, and Kosnoff believed that she was, Bishop Gordon Checketts had been alerted to Frank Curtis's behavior and neither reported this to the authorities nor warned other parents in the ward long before Frank Curtis met Jeremiah Scott in Sunday school, moved in with his family, and molested him.

Another eruption occurred on the morning of the deposition,

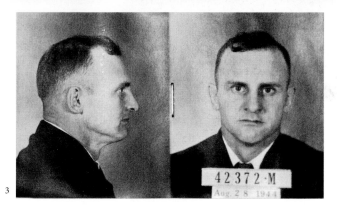

Frank Curtis, as shown in sequential mug shots (March 30, 1929; April 2, 1938; August 28, 1944), for crimes committed in Michigan. The early part of his life was marked by patterns of criminal behavior; by the age of eight he had spent seven months in a home for truants and troublemakers. In 1929, at age twenty-six, Frank filled a criminal résumé that dated back fifteen years. Later in life, Frank liked to tell young boys tales of his past, involving gangsters and Al Capone.

No.	4739	Received	Mar 30-29 3:3 P				58

Name — Franklyn R. Curtis — Alias
County — Wayne — Sentenced — Mar 21-29
Not to Exceed — — Crime — Robbery armed
Not Less than — Life
Recommended — — By Judge — Brulee
Ref. — — F.P.C.

BERTILLON MEASUREMENTS

Height	7.3 IM. 2		L. Foot	26 -
Eng. Height	5 - 8⅞		L. Mid. F.	12
Outs. A.	84 IM. 0		L. Lit. F.	8 -
Trunk	90 - 5		L. Fore A.	49
Head, Length	19 - 5		Beard	D.k
Head, Width	15 - 2		Lips	M.
Cheek, Width	11 - 5		Chin	P.t
R. Ear	5 - 9		Weight	125
			Height, Shoes	5 - 9

GENERAL DESCRIPTION

Age — 30 — Born — Chicago Ill — b. Mar 31-1899 — Nationality — Amer — Religion — Catholic
Complexion — M Sal — Hair — Chest — Forehead — R.c — Eyes — Hazel — Nose — Str
Mouth — M — Lips — M. — Chin — P.t — Build — Med
Home Residence — — Yrs. in Mich. — — Yrs. in U. S.
Occupation — Baker — Yrs. Residence Outside State — — Where? — Ill & Okla.
Parents Born Where? Mother — — Father

RELATIVES

Divorced
Parents Deceased
Bros. Norman Curtis
Aunt Miss Mary Schubert 2317 So Sawyer Chicago
Gdmother Mrs. Eliz. " 2644 "

MARKS AND SCARS

I. Vac: cic. at 4½ & 6½ below Pt of Sho. outs.
Three faint cut cic on fore arm outs.

III. Series of Sm. pit cic on face.
Cut cic 6' long extending from R side of forehead over top of head.

VI. Append. Oper. scar.

Minor Children		Where cared for		Yrs. at School	8	Grade Reached	8
Owner of Real Estate		What?		Where?			
Drink?	No	Smoke?	Yes	Chew?	No	Dope?	No	Venereal?	No
Paroled		Discharged		Remarks			

4

Details from Frank Curtis's 1929 prison records. Tim Kosnoff turned up the records after an exhaustive search. The documents included notes from a psychological evaluation, which stated that Frank exhibited inappropriate sexual behavior with boys that had gotten him into some trouble in his earlier, locked-up life.

While living in Portland, Frank came to know ten-year-old Manny Saban, shown here on his bike in front of his family's house. Barely visible behind him, two of Frank's other victims, Bobby and Jim Goodall, walk toward their house. Manny Saban provided the earliest notice of abuse to the church that Kosnoff was able to determine.

5

Frank Curtis lived in a series of small apartments in southeast Portland. He is shown here attending ceremonies at the Mormon Temple in Salt Lake City, Utah, in the late 1970s.

6

7

The Saban family met Frank Curtis at their Mormon ward in southeast Portland. He appeared to be a kind, grandfatherly type and offered to help the family by watching the kids.

Frank Curtis kept an apartment attached to a junkyard in Portland (shown here in 2009), where he abused his numerous victims. It was here that Raquel Saban caught Frank Curtis in the bathtub with a neighbor boy.

8

Frank Curtis made dogs out of yarn, which he often gave to children.

9

10

Frank Curtis worked at the Southgate Animal Clinic in the late 1970s (shown here in 2009), and lived in a small apartment that was attached to the building. It was here that he would host some of the boys from the church and the neighborhood for sleepovers.

Frank Curtis, shown here in a professional portrait, moved to Grand Rapids, Michigan, some time around 1984. Despite his advancing age, he continued to prey on young boys.

11

The Scott family took Frank Curtis into their home (shown here in 2009). The events that occurred inside this house triggered the entire case of *Jeremiah Scott v. Gregory Lee Foster, The Church of Jesus Christ of Latter-day Saints, et al.*

12

THE CHURCH OF
JESUS CHRIST
OF LATTER-DAY SAINTS

Report of Church Disciplinary Action

Send to:
OFFICE OF THE FIRST PRESIDENCY
47 E SOUTH TEMPLE ST
SALT LAKE CITY UT 84150-1010

ER-691

Instructions

Use this form to report the proceedings and action of a disciplinary council resulting in (1) disfellowshipment, (2) excommunication, (3) reinstatement after disfellowshipment, or (4) readmission after excommunication. This form should also be used to report formal probation or termination of formal probation involving conduct that threatens the well-being of other persons or of the Church (see *Church Handbook of Instructions, Book 1*, 129). If the decision of the council is formal probation for conduct that does not threaten the well-being of other persons or of the Church, complete this form but do not send it to the Office of the First Presidency. In such cases, the stake or mission should keep the form until it is no longer needed (see *Church Handbook of Instructions, Book 1*, 104).

A disciplinary council must be held when evidence suggests that a member may have committed child abuse or certain other serious transgressions (see *Church Handbook of Instructions, Book 1*, 95–96). If a person is disfellowshipped or excommunicated for child abuse or certain other serious transgressions, the approval of the First Presidency is required before he or she may be reinstated or readmitted (see *Church Handbook of Instructions, Book 1*, 105–6).

All presiding officers should be familiar with section 10, "Church Discipline," in the *Church Handbook of Instructions, Book 1: Stake Presidencies and Bishoprics* (1998).

Presiding Officer of the Disciplinary Council

1. Review this completed form and supporting documents.
2. Deliver the following to the stake or mission president:

☐ This form (completed and signed by you and the clerk)
☐ A copy of the letter notifying the person of the council (include certification of delivery)
☐ A copy of the letter informing the person of the council's decision
☐ A copy of the person's membership record
☐ If readmission does not require First Presidency approval, include a copy of the Baptism Record and the Confirmation Record/Baptism and Confirmation Certificate.
☐ If readmission or reinstatement requires First Presidency approval, include the completed Application to the First Presidency form and all required supporting documents (see instructions on the form).
☐ Other supporting documents (if any)

Stake or Mission President

1. Review the completed form(s) and supporting documents
2. Sign the completed form(s).
3. Send the form(s) and supporting documents to the Office of the First Presidency at the address above (except as noted in the first paragraph of these instructions).

The presiding officer should destroy all paper and electronic records related to a disciplinary action after the ward or branch receives an updated membership record or other notification of action on the record

---

Individual Information Complete all blanks that apply.

Full name (last, first, middle, maiden)		Membership record number	Birth date	Sex ☐ Male ☐ Female
Priesthood office held	Date endowed	Temple where endowed	Marital status at the time of transgression ☐ Married ☐ Single ☐ Divorced	
Current ward or branch	Unit number	Current stake or mission		Unit number

Disciplinary Council Information Complete all blanks that apply.

Date of council	Type of council ☐ Ward ☐ Stake ☐ Mission	Did the person attend? ☐ Yes ☐ No	Was the person criminally convicted as a result of the transgression? ☐ Yes ☐ No ☐ Action pending
Were other Church members involved in the misconduct? ☐ Yes ☐ No		Were the bishops of other involved members advised about the misconduct? ☐ Yes ☐ No	
Was the person involved in sexual misconduct with anyone under the age of 18? ☐ Yes ☐ No		Did the person embezzle Church funds? ☐ Yes ☐ No If yes, amount ____	
Reported misconduct		Person's response to the reported misconduct ☐ Voluntary confession ☐ Admission of guilt when confronted ☐ Denial of guilt	
At the time of the misconduct, the person was: ☐ Temple president ☐ Mission president ☐ Stake president ☐ Patriarch ☐ Bishop ☐ Missionary ☐ None of these			
Decision of disciplinary council ☐ Formal probation ☐ Disfellowshipment ☐ Excommunication ☐ Termination of probation ☐ Reinstatement ☐ Readmission			
Was consent given by the excommunicated person for the Church to maintain contact? If yes, and if the person moves, inform the new bishop or branch president ☐ Yes ☐ No			
Presiding officer of the disciplinary council		Position of presiding officer	

Signatures

Signature of presiding officer of the disciplinary council	Signature of clerk
Signature of stake or mission president (if not presiding officer of the council)	Date of stake or mission president's review

4/99. Printed in the USA. 33493

The LDS church fought for years to keep its records on sex abusers out of the courtroom. Judge Ellen Rosenblum of the Multnomah County Circuit Court reviewed a blank version of the LDS Report of Church Disciplinary Action and determined that the church had to produce its records on Frank Curtis and other Portland abusers who had been disciplined between 1970 and 1995.

By 2001, Seattle attorney Tim Kosnoff, who represented Jeremiah Scott in his lawsuit against the Church of Jesus Christ of Latter-day Saints, had spent four years of his life working tirelessly on the case.

14

15

Questions for Mrs. [   ]

1) After you learned that Frank Curtis had molested your sons, did you tell [   ] about it?

2) What did [   ] say he would do about the incident?

3) Did [   ] or any other priesthood leader or bishop or stake president ever say anything about taking any action against Curtis for what he had done to your sons? If so, what was said in that respect.

4) What is the source of the payment of your lawyer's legal fees in connection with his representation of you in this matter?

5) Is it your understanding that the Mormon Church is paying Matt Flynn's legal fees?

6) Who asked, suggested or told you that Mr. Flynn would be acting as your attorney?

The protracted legal battle between Jeremiah Scott and the Church of Jesus Christ of Latter-day Saints arced over four years and three states and centered on freedom-of-religion issues—in particular, the church's unwillingness to reveal its disciplinary process. During a battle over a deposition with the church, Wisconsin judge Emmanuel Vuvunas of the Racine County Circuit Court instructed Tim Kosnoff to write a list of six questions he needed answered in order for the case to proceed. The exhibit has been redacted here to protect its subjects' privacy.

16

17

Frank Curtis returned to Portland in his later years. He died there in 1995, at age 92. Initially buried in the Portland Memorial Mausoleum, his remains were eventually moved to Michigan. His grave is unmarked and never visited.

Manny Saban was living in Arizona when Tim Kosnoff found him in 1999. Although initially unwilling to become involved in the legal battle, he courageously came forward and shared his story.

18

Tim Kosnoff, Sandra Scott, Jeff Anderson, and David Slader spoke at a press conference in Temple Square, Salt Lake City, Utah. Jeremiah Scott received the largest reported individual settlement in a sex abuse case involving a religious institution to date. By settling the lawsuit, the church avoided facing discovery of its assets. The Scott lawyers, however, remained determined to pursue the church and filed a second lawsuit on behalf of victims of Frank Curtis who were identified during the Scott case, which ended in multiple settlements.

when Steve English directed Gordon Checketts not to answer questions about what he'd told the investigator. Earlier, Checketts had said that "an imposter researcher came to my office and posed that she was representing a researcher in Washington somewhere for purposes of studying pedophiles."

Gordon Checketts was referring to Ginger Goforth, of course. The church's lawyers still had motions pending with the court asking that the information she'd uncovered be banned from the case.

"It is clear on its face from these interview notes that she misrepresented who she was . . . ," English had said, "and once this information was received by Mr. Salmi, he understood that the information had been obtained under false pretenses."

Gary Rhoades had been particularly upset about English accusing Joel Salmi of unethical conduct in the middle of a deposition, which is memorialized in a permanent record. Deposition transcripts are often used as evidence in other cases, and this sort of allegation could haunt a lawyer forever.

"What is your evidence in this case?" Rhoades challenged. "Because you are making a very serious charge against a member of this court and a member of this bar *pro hac vice* [for this occasion only], and if you are saying that we will assume that the statements of an imposter or a fraudulent investigator are true and therefore we will impute Mr. Salmi's motives and that in fact he indeed had the state of mind that she describes, then I think we need to have that on the record, Steve, because you're making a real serious charge."

"I understand that," English replied.

Kosnoff, Gordon Checketts, and Greg Foster's lawyer had become spectators. Kosnoff was concerned with what he hadn't gotten from Checketts. The deposition had been scheduled to end by noon because English was flying to London on another case that afternoon, a fact that Kosnoff hadn't known about until they all sat down. This was typical, he'd thought. It took forever to get Checketts's deposition scheduled, with all the motions over the investigator and clergy-penitent privilege claims, and then they walk in and announce that things have to wrap up by noon because the lawyer has to catch a plane. Now English had successfully hijacked the deposition. Kosnoff had tried to turn the focus back onto Checketts. He asked English what legal authority he was relying on to bolster his position that Checketts didn't have to answer his questions.

"I believe there is authority that allows a person who is the recipient of inappropriately obtained information not to allow the other side to benefit by that," English said. "I also believe that it is not appropriate that a lawyer, once receiving information which he knows has been improperly obtained, can get the benefit of that. And these questions seek to get the benefit of that by creating an impeachment situation for Bishop Checketts."

Rhoades seemed genuinely furious at English for this attack. "Your argument, your characterizations and your conclusions and your opinions are noted. Now, for the record, because you said that there was unethical conduct by Mr. Salmi who is an officer of this court . . . if you have facts, show us. If you don't, I want the record to show that this is Steve English's opinion, your conjecture, and your conclusion. And if that's what it is, fine."

They argued more. Time ticked away. English was not going to allow Kosnoff to question Gordon Checketts about what he'd said in that interview. He was working on getting the information thrown out of the case altogether.

Gary Rhoades was still going: "You're precluding the witness from answering because you think that the only way that Mr. Kosnoff could possibly formulate an intelligent question is to rely upon the unethical conduct and the fraud of an investigator," Rhoades said. As much as Tim Kosnoff was enjoying watching Gary Rhoades defend Salmi's honor, he still had a witness to depose. He jumped in and addressed Checketts.

"Next question, did you ever file a police report regarding Frank Curtis or make a police report?"

If it was true that Gordon Checketts had been told by the Penrose and Johnson parents that their boys were abused—and Kosnoff had little doubt that it was—Kosnoff had established that Gordon Checketts hadn't reported Frank Curtis's crimes.

What Tim Kosnoff suspected was that Gordon Checketts had learned the truth about Frank Curtis and had turned a blind eye to the old man's escape on a bus out of town. But he didn't get any confirmation on that theory from Checketts's deposition.

In an attempt to get at more of the inner workings of the corporate side of the church, and ultimately show responsibility, the Scott lawyers had subpoenaed a couple of high-ranking employees of the church's corporate headquarters in Salt Lake City, including the head of its risk management division and a man who had, at various times, overseen both the church's welfare and family services operations. Both men arrived accompanied by David Ernst and a lawyer named Randy Austin from the church's chief legal representative, the law firm of Kirton & McConkie in Salt Lake City. Austin was one of two partners there known for directing the church's representation in matters of religious freedom and the First Amendment, which in the LDS church included sex abuse claims.

The law offices of Kirton & McConkie are located a few hundred feet from Temple Square in Salt Lake City. The geographic relationship is no accident. Kirton & McConkie's roots stem from Wilford W. "Bill" Kirton Jr., who was general counsel for the Church of Jesus Christ of Latter-day Saints for more than three decades, and Oscar McConkie Jr., the direct descendant of an important Mormon apostle. McConkie's son later took the firm's reins. During its half-century existence, the firm had grown into a legal powerhouse of more than a hundred attorneys who practice all manner of law, including intellectual property, international business, and real estate. Nonetheless, Kirton & McConkie's oldest, largest, and best-known client is the Mormon church.

The Scott team had heard about the firm from other lawyers who'd been involved in lawsuits against the church. Plaintiffs' lawyers had been known to refer to the firm as the "Mormon Death Star."

By now, everyone in the Scott case had figured that, for all their competence and reputation, Stephen English and David Ernst were working under the close direction of Kirton & McConkie lawyers. All too often, agreements made with the court or even among the lawyers had to go through Salt Lake City. Randy Austin or someone else from his firm had begun showing up at some of the more important court hearings. And the Scott lawyers began to speculate that part of the reason their opponents seemed to drag things out so long was that they were passing everything through the Utah lawyers.

The church's risk manager testified that all allegations of sexual abuse are handled by Kirton & McConkie directly or with the LDS church's general counsel. As in most religious organizations, the Mormon church, he confirmed, does not screen anyone who works with children because such a position is based on religious tenets—a calling. In several states, including Oregon, church leaders had a legal obligation to report suspected child abuse, and willfully ignoring that obligation was a criminal violation. The exception was when the information is received in a way that it is protected under the clergy-penitent privilege. Kosnoff intended to show that the Mormon leaders routinely followed church law and ignored civil law.

Most of the bishops who were deposed stated that they believed they should, and would, report an incident of child sexual abuse if they were able to do so without breaking the responsibility of confidentiality. And yet none of them had reported Frank Curtis, despite how they had learned about his abuse.

With few exceptions, the witnesses had been contacted by someone from Kirton & McConkie years earlier. Kosnoff also learned that there had been another investigator, this one apparently working for the church, who had interviewed the people around Frank Curtis, in some cases before the lawsuit was even filed. All of the active Mormons who were deposed came represented by the church's lawyers. Ernst refused to allow his clients to answer Kosnoff's questions about who was paying their legal bills, claiming that it was a matter of attorney-client privilege. But it was obvious that none of these individuals could afford the likes of David Ernst or Stephen English, who certainly billed several hundred dollars an hour, and surely more than anyone on the Scott side of things. Kosnoff and Hillas observed that, given the number of witnesses and the amount of time from the Bullivant, Houser, Bailey lawyers, not to mention whoever was now involved from Kirton & McConkie, the church was sinking a fortune into defending this case, certainly hundreds of thousands of dollars, and the costs were still climbing.

Kosnoff also deposed a few people who'd befriended Frank Curtis over the years. One man lived down the street from the junkyard apartment where Frank had lived after he left the veterinary clinic in the late 1970s. The man had given Frank rides to church and to medical appointments, and they'd stayed in touch until Frank Curtis died. The man testified in deposition that he'd learned through ward meetings (men in each level of Mormon hierarchy meet regularly as part of the practice of their religion) that Frank Curtis had been excommunicated, and he'd heard rumors that it was because Frank had molested boys. There were more rumors later, the man said, and at one point he'd asked Brother Curtis about it. Frank had dismissed the question with some vague answer, he said. This man also testified that he'd been told by a Mormon church leader in another state that Frank Curtis was excommunicated "back east" and again "on the north side" for molesting children.

It had been a difficult path to deposition for Frank's friend. Since he'd first talked to the investigators, he had learned that his own son, who was now an adult, had been molested by Frank Curtis on occasions when Frank babysat him. Kosnoff later deposed the son as well. He had been married and divorced twice and was in counseling for anger management after having hit one of his children. His childhood story was eerily similar to that of Frank Curtis's other victims. As a boy, his family was poor. He had grown up near the junkyard apartment where Frank Curtis sometimes stayed in Portland in the late 1970s. Frank had bought him a bicycle and taken him places. Frank had also scared the boy with tales of his shadowy adventures in the mob. In time, Frank Curtis had kissed and fondled the boy and offered him a new BB gun in exchange for anal sex. During one final attempt at sexual activity, the boy ran out of Frank's apartment and never saw him again. He'd been too afraid and ashamed to tell anyone, he said, including his father. Now he felt guilty for not coming forward sooner, perhaps preventing Frank Curtis from harming other kids.

Kosnoff never ceased to be moved by how wounded these people were. They'd all handled it differently—some were angry, some were sobbing basket cases, others were just shut down. The depositions were draining. The constant arguments over who could answer questions about what without violating protected areas of religion were tedious and eventually had to be sorted out by the judge in a series of hearings. The Scott team was learning some useful information, to be sure, not the least of which was the growing number of people within the Mormon church who knew of, or had heard something about, Frank Curtis having molested children before Jeremiah Scott. But the lawyers found it hard to get much traction. They seemed to be going around in circles. Of course, from the defense's view, that was the point.

Joel Salmi and Jim Hillas began to wonder aloud about the need to keep questioning everyone. The church's lawyers had made it clear that they were going to argue the clergy-penitent privilege at every deposition and, regardless of how much of a legal stretch that was, it was expensive to fight the issue all the time. The fact of the matter was that the Scott lawyers were winning most of these skirmishes, but at what cost? Again and again they debated the wisdom of taking on these fights. But Tim Kosnoff remained adamant, driven by a mix of insecurity about his inexperience in civil law and his own perfectionism. He insisted that they leave nothing unexamined. Years later, he would look back on those decisions. "I was ready to buy everything to make sure we had it all. I wanted to order everything on the menu."

Some weeks later, Tim Kosnoff banged on the door of a run-down apartment in Portland. It was about three in the afternoon, and the sun had broken through the clouds. Kosnoff was aware that one or more of the neighbors were peeking out of windows to assess what he might be doing. He was wearing casual slacks and a pullover shirt but looked unmistakably professional, especially in a neighborhood where people routinely strolled outside in pajamas and slippers. For the previous twenty minutes, Kosnoff had started and stopped several episodes of banging, during which he called for Raquel Saban, Manny's mother. She'd been hard to find in the first place and, once located, harder to keep track of, for she tended to move frequently from one crummy apartment to the next. Kosnoff had driven three hours from Seattle on this quest and he wasn't about to go home empty-handed.

Finally, a disheveled Raquel opened the door, looking to Kosnoff like she'd just awakened from a long coma. She was a tiny woman, with long, graying hair. She seemed to know nothing about anything involving Kosnoff until he reminded her who he was and mentioned that they had, in fact, talked on the phone before.

Ginger Goforth had initially interviewed Raquel in front of her daughter's house in the Portland suburb of Gladstone. And then Raquel had recounted to Kosnoff on the phone that when she'd met Frank she'd been busy trying to look after her children and juggle classes at the local college. She'd confirmed her son's story about how the Mormon missionaries brought them into the church, where they'd met Frank Curtis, and added more detail. Back then, Raquel, recently divorced from her second husband, was depressed and overwhelmed with basic survival. She had first tried to find spiritual comfort at a nearby Catholic church, the only religion she'd known up to that point, but the building was locked up. Eventually, she found her way to the local Mormon ward, where she was able to speak to someone who took down her name and address. That's likely why the missionaries had come to see her in Felony Flats. Connecting to the church community was supposed to provide her children with a positive environment and someplace to go. Their father was in Las Vegas at the time and didn't see them often.

Raquel had lived a hard life, having moved up from abject poverty to working poor and then back into poverty. Opportunity came with men. She'd been married twice before Frank Curtis and went on to marry Manny's father a second time after Frank. And there had been the pressure of her newfound religion. Mormon faith involves great emphasis on marriage, child bearing, and uniting close relatives through baptism and other ceremonies. A single mother at forty-seven, Raquel was considered to be in need of a husband and a father for her children, not to mention a companion in the afterlife. Brother Curtis, alone and aging, was in need of a family. She thought of him as a sort of counselor, and he was nice to her children. They'd talk for hours about their lives, and he paid her a lot of attention. He was charming and had a hardy laugh. Brother Curtis complimented the way she'd raised her children. He read the Bible and the Book of Mormon.

Raquel described the situation as little more than a friendship. They went to church together. He worked at the LDS church's Deseret Thrift Store and brought food home from the Bishop's Storehouse. She worked and went to school. Brother Curtis cooked sometimes too, which was a relief. Raquel was tired of cooking. She also told Kosnoff that she and Frank, who was thirty years her senior, had never consummated their marriage. Frank had even maintained another small apartment in southeast Portland.

After they married, Brother Curtis had a hard time with Saban's children. They didn't like him and were defiant. Raquel had always been the one who disciplined her children.

Kosnoff still wanted to know more about Frank's past, and he'd hoped that Raquel could provide clues that would fill in some of the holes that remained in his research. But he quickly learned that she knew surprisingly little about the man who'd once been her husband. Raquel told Kosnoff that Frank had been a bodyguard for mobsters in Chicago a long time ago and had sometimes used the name Frank Black. She said that his Social Security check never came to their house, and she hadn't ever known much about where his money was; she thought, for some reason, that he had a stash somewhere. He always carried a briefcase with paperwork in it. Frank, she said, was very secretive. He'd once introduced her to a man who he said was his cousin, visiting from the Midwest, but that was the only connection to family or personal history. Toward the end of the marriage, Brother Curtis had discovered that Raquel was still smoking cigarettes, usually in the bathroom, after she'd been baptized into the church, and he'd threatened to divorce her over it. Once again, Raquel relayed how she had gone to Frank's apartment one day while they were still married to drop off her son. Inside, she'd found Frank in the bathtub with another boy from the neighborhood. She'd ended any pretense of a relationship with Frank on the spot, she said. Manny had accused Frank of molesting him sometime earlier, but Raquel hadn't paid much attention. She'd disciplined him for lying, in fact. The boys were having a hard time adjusting to life without their father and they'd been acting out, and Frank was the last person she'd have thought would do something like that.

As compelling as Raquel's story was, Kosnoff was holding out for a specific piece of information. Raquel had said earlier that she'd written a letter to her then bishop, a man named Dennis Dalling, whom she'd always liked. When Kosnoff had deposed Dalling, he'd only vaguely remembered Raquel Saban and didn't remember her children at all. He had no recollection of receiving the letter that Raquel claimed to have written. The former bishop, who by this time had served in numerous other positions in the church, some at the stake level, did remember Brother Curtis, however. He recalled Brother Curtis as a favorite teacher of a group of boys that included his son, and he considered the man "a wonderful, grandfatherly-type person."

Kosnoff had come to see Raquel Saban to assess her story. He didn't like surprises and had to know if she was telling the truth or not. Now she elaborated on the letter she had sent, saying that she had told Dalling that "Frank was a pervert" and told him what had happened with the boys in the neighborhood. Kosnoff believed her. She seemed very clear about writing to the bishop. Her account of what happened didn't waver. And she would sign a sworn affidavit saying as much.

Raquel told Kosnoff that she'd never heard back from the bishop, but then again, she hadn't spent much time waiting. Manny was already in Las Vegas with his father, and without Frank, Raquel was alone again with three children to look after. Shortly after she left Frank, she took the children and moved to Las Vegas, leaving the Mormon church behind. Frank had been the one who filed for divorce, mostly because Raquel hadn't bothered. Perhaps he feared Raquel would run up some debt that he'd be on the hook for as her legal husband, or maybe he had some idea about looking for a new family. In any event, Frank Curtis had gotten himself to a free legal aid clinic that had helped him file paperwork divorcing Raquel Saban. Some years later, she remarried Stanley Saban, Manny's father, and they all moved back to Portland together. Stanley bounced around the West following jobs until his death in Arizona in 1997. Raquel had mostly lived with one or another of Manny's siblings. She worked in care homes cooking and taking care of the disabled. Other than writing to the bishop, Raquel had never told anyone else in the church about Brother Curtis and the boys. "Who would have believed me?" she once said. "Who would have believed that an elder in this church was doing something like that if I had told them?"

Kosnoff left Raquel and drove his Peugeot around to various addresses he'd dug up looking for people or places where Frank Curtis had been. This had become a habit whenever he was in Portland and had the time. Sometimes he got out and talked to neighbors. Sometimes he took pictures. He shot a lot of photos at the junkyard apartment where Frank Curtis had been found in the bathtub so many years before. The place seemed like it hadn't been touched in decades. It was unquestionably creepy. There were certain things that Tim Kosnoff absorbed from looking at the houses, from driving around the neighborhood, which were impossible to quantify or to explain even to the other lawyers on the team. The meager houses and scrappy yards, the fast-food joints and the convenience stores, the faces of the residents in the neighborhood all contributed to his understanding of the people involved. Taken together, the landscape offered a look into the economic marginality of its inhabitants and the edge they lived on, giving way to both danger and despair.

He would never be able to understand Frank Curtis, and he didn't really want to. It burned him the way this strange, religious brotherhood seemed to have turned away from the very people who needed help the most.

Kosnoff parked his car and got out to stretch. He wasn't sure what he was looking for here. Something, anything, that would help him explain the injustice to a jury. Another thing about driving around these places, what he'd come to consider crime scenes, was that he inevitably picked up random tidbits of information that were not particularly important but interesting enough to find a permanent home in his brain, waiting to be retrieved later when they became relevant. One such observation: The blue house that Jeremiah Scott had lived in as a child, where he'd been molested night after night by Frank Curtis, was only a short distance, a few blocks in some cases, from the places where Frank Curtis had lived when he was married to Raquel Saban, when he had molested her son and other children, some fifteen years earlier. The Mormon ward boundaries had changed over the years, sure, but as Kosnoff understood it, church members were generally herded into wards by geography, which meant that there might be people who knew Frank Curtis from the 1970s, when he had been active in the Scotts' ward. But why would Frank come back here? There had to be some reason that Frank Curtis thought it was safe to return to the same neighborhood where he'd molested children before.

It was late in the day by the time Kosnoff crossed the bridge out of Oregon heading back home to Seattle. The Peugeot had logged so many miles on this case that he used to joke that the car could drive itself to Portland on command. He had a weakness for European cars, which inevitably cost him a lot of money in maintenance and repairs. The Peugeot was no exception; as the mileage grew, so did the repair bills. And he still hadn't made a dime on this case, despite its having become a full-time job. His fixation on taking the lawsuit into court crowded out most practical concerns, even as he remained blissfully naïve about what it would take to get there.

14

After more than a dozen years locked up, Bobby Goodall had wanted nothing more than to be in the woods. It's where he came closest to finding peace. When the phone rang, Bobby lay stretched across the bed in the double-wide trailer that he'd put on five acres in southwest Washington, outside of Shelton, a logging town on Puget Sound. He'd built a home cradled in the lush, wet green of the fir and hemlock, and married his new bride only a few months earlier on a wooden dock he'd built over the lake where he fished for trout and bass. In some ways, he figured, this was his reward; survival and success had blurred together. Bobby had done the prison-release work, building and painting for the government, but ultimately he'd gone back to what he knew best and did most proficiently. His small estate here was built with drug money.

Bobby's wife handed him the phone with a look and a shrug that told him the caller was unfamiliar, which meant suspicious.

"Yeah," he said into the phone.

"Is this Bobby Goodall?"

"Yeah."

"Are you the Bobby Goodall who grew up in southeast Portland in the late 1970s?"

"Yeah."

"Bobby, my name is Tim Kosnoff. I'm a lawyer in Seattle and I represent a young man named Jeremiah Scott who is suing the Mormon church. Can I ask you some questions?"

"Okay."

The Mormons. Bobby started thinking but was distracted by the next question.

"Do you know Manny Saban?"

"Yeah."

Bobby hadn't seen Manny in years. He hadn't seen anyone from the neighborhood in at least a decade, and even then it was only when he randomly ran into someone's sister somewhere. His mind started to drift back to Manny's house and the park and the Dairy Queen and his friends. Then Kosnoff dropped a bomb, and it was like someone had changed the channel in Bobby's brain.

"Bobby," the lawyer said, "did you know a man named Frank Curtis?"

Bobby stared at the ceiling, his mind racing, trying to absorb all that was coming at it—an impossible task. Frank Curtis. Brother Curtis. So many years ago. What the hell could this be?

"Yeah," he said. "I knew Frank Curtis."

The two men talked more about people and places in Portland. Kosnoff asked Bobby where he'd first met Frank Curtis, and Bobby told him about the Duke Street neighborhood, the veterinary clinic, and then the junkyard apartment. Bobby sensed that he'd passed some test, that he'd convinced Kosnoff that he knew enough to be regarded as an insider. At some point he'd realized what it was that Kosnoff wanted to know, and eventually he had told him about the sexual abuse.

Bobby hung up the phone and looked at his wife, who searched his face for information. He told her simply that the call had to do with a lawsuit about something that happened when he was a kid, and then he grabbed the keys to his truck, walked out of the house, and took off down the road to the bar.

Emotion surrounded Bobby like some kind of poisonous gas. He had to get away from it. He sat down at a table and ordered a beer and a shot. The waitress paused. She questioned him, just to be sure she understood, and gave Bobby a long, sideways glance.

This was Bobby's place. It may as well have been his office, he did so much business here, meeting clients, making deals, delivering drugs. Everyone knew Bobby, and everyone knew that he neither drank on the job nor used his own product. It was his version of professionalism, however perverted, a line that separated him from the junkies and the recreational users with whom he associated. He ran a prosperous business when he remained sober, and had a history that proved things would end badly if he didn't. But this, here and now, was triage. Bobby had never planned on talking about Brother Curtis again. And he had to stop the sensation that seemed to be spreading from his brain into his internal organs, moving through his body like the booze and drugs he hoped would chase it away.

Brother Curtis had done unspeakable things to Bobby's young body for years. Those wounds had healed, but the emotional scars were permanent. The truth was that for all his abuse, Brother Curtis had taken care of Bobby. Brother Curtis had taken him fishing and pretty much everywhere else there was for a kid to go. Brother Curtis paid attention to him when no one else did. Brother Curtis introduced Bobby to God.

They'd had a relationship, he and this older man. And then Brother Curtis left him without explanation. In later years, Bobby Goodall had realized that Frank Curtis was a master manipulator. He'd come to call the old man "the chicken hawk" because of the way he'd preyed on Bobby and his friends. But his hatred for all the other things that Brother Curtis did to him remained tangled up with the rest of his emotions. The memories came, and so did the pain.

People close to Bobby knew that he was a "blackout drunk." When he drank excessively, he slipped into periods in which he could neither control nor later recall what happened. So, much of the following few months would forever remain a mystery. What is known is that things fell apart pretty fast. He dropped from a postprison-fitness weight of about 210 pounds down to about 160. He got sloppy with business. Talked to people he shouldn't. Skirted his own rules. It wasn't long before he was arrested again and went back to prison for violating parole. Soon his house, his car, and his new wife were gone.

Kosnoff continued to work with Linda Walker on finding the rest of Curtis's victims. With Bobby Goodall and his brother, Jim, whom Kosnoff had talked to in a Washington prison, and the Sabans accounted for, Linda turned her attention to the remaining boys who hung around with them and, therefore, around Frank Curtis. As she'd told Kosnoff long ago, it had been her experience that pedophiles like Frank Curtis had multiple victims. They were out there, she believed. They were still out there.

Linda Walker rarely walked away from a research challenge empty-handed. She knocked on doors, called friends, and asked anyone she could find about the boys who'd lived in Felony Flats. Sometimes there were relatives still in town who could reach them. Other times neighbors knew where they'd moved to. She asked Kosnoff about placing an ad in the newspaper. It was a long shot, but he saw no harm. Sure enough, the week after a small square advertisement appeared in a Portland newspaper, a relative of one of the missing boys called to say that the family had moved to Buffalo, New York. Linda called every phone listing for the family name in the area until she was on the line with the boy's stepfather. They talked, and before the conversation ended, he told Linda that his stepson had attempted suicide. He was not sure that bringing up the past was a good idea. Linda found another man from the neighborhood back in Portland, working at a grocery store. Two more lived in Michigan. These were hard conversations. They'd all been abused. They'd never told anyone. One set of brothers had never even told each other, let alone anyone else. Linda was on the phone for hours. She came to know their stories, their families, and their wives. She and Kosnoff had developed a routine in which she would find out what happened and then hand the victims off to him for a follow-up interview. Kosnoff would summarize the information for the rest of the team and they'd assess who needed to be deposed and so on. The number of witnesses was growing by the day, and keeping track of them and where they were and what they'd said was getting to be a full-time job.

As the fight over releasing Frank Curtis's church disciplinary records was coming to a head, the Scott team was caught off guard by an event in the Multnomah County Courthouse. Judge Ceniceros retired. Initially, there was a loose arrangement for him to continue to work on the Scott case, effectively easing into retirement as the case progressed. But in the end, perhaps owing to the county's budgetary woes, Judge Ceniceros left the bench for good. *Jeremiah Scott v. Gregory Lee Foster and The Church of Jesus Christ of Latter-day Saints, et al.* was reassigned to the courtroom of the Honorable Ellen F. Rosenblum. Other than the inevitable delay involved in trying to bring a new judge up to speed on what had become increasingly complicated issues, not the least of which involved wading through religious liberty and the Bill of Rights, the assignment to Judge Rosenblum seemed to be good news for the Scott team. She'd received mostly favorable reviews from other lawyers at Dunn, Carney. Judge Rosenblum was known to nearly everyone in town, not just because of her five or so years on the bench but also because she was active in the Oregon Bar Association. Her Honor also was married to the publisher of the *Willamette Week*, a popular alternative paper in Portland, and had two children. Before her appointment to the bench, Ellen Rosenblum had worked as a federal prosecutor and had done some plaintiff's law in private practice. Most notably, she'd represented author Ken Kesey in a lawsuit he filed against the producers of the film adaptation of his book *One Flew Over the Cuckoo's Nest*, alleging that they had reneged on a contract with him, and won an undisclosed settlement.

Jim Hillas and Lisa Thomas, the paralegal at Dunn, Carney who'd been working on the Scott case for months, set about the task of digging up whatever they could find on this new judge. They reported to Kosnoff and Salmi that while Judge Rosenblum might be socially liberal, she was not always judicially liberal. The attorneys Hillas had spoken with said that the judge liked orderly proceedings and respected intellect. Glibness, they warned, did not go far in her courtroom. Judge Rosenblum was known for being well prepared and decisive, and had sanctioned lawyers who failed to move their cases along.

The first thing she faced in the Scott case concerned the private detective Ginger Goforth. Issues around the work of investigators that Joel Salmi and Tim Kosnoff had hired three years earlier had returned yet again. It was obvious that the church's lawyers were intent on proving that Kosnoff and Salmi had acted nefariously. They'd filed more briefs with the court, the latest round of which included a request to depose Ginger Goforth, the one who had actually talked to the former bishops Gordon Checketts and Greg Foster. Everyone on the Scott side of things was both dumbfounded and annoyed by this whole business. They'd already filed affidavits with the court, swearing to what they had and hadn't done. They'd even turned over the investigator's notes, which everyone had thought was highly unusual and, frankly, a respectable gesture, given that it was traditionally considered to be part of the Scott side's private work product. Still, the church wasn't satisfied. Now its lawyers wanted to grill Ginger in a deposition. There was no doubt that this was a strategic move in the war of attrition being waged by the church—another deposition and more briefs all ate up more time and money. But did anyone seriously think there was some conspiracy at work here? Certainly the church wanted to get rid of any more evidence that its people had known that Frank Curtis molested children before he met Jeremiah, but it had already been established that the man had been excommunicated. In her first ruling in the case, Judge Rosenblum determined that Ginger must answer questions, but only about the notes she'd taken that had been produced earlier.

Ginger and the lawyers convened at Dunn, Carney on a June morning in 2000. Joel Salmi had driven from his farm in Eugene. Jim Hillas joined him in the conference room, along with Stephen English and three other lawyers collectively representing the church and Greg Foster.

Ginger Goforth had gotten married since the case began and was now known as Ginger Simmons. She'd also left the Alexander Christian investigations firm and was, ironically, working for the new state agency that had been created to license and regulate private investigators.

Ginger had shoulder-length brown hair and a slightly crooked face, owing to a tumor near her cheekbone that had been removed when she was a child, followed by a failed dental surgery. She had majored in English at the University of Washington but drifted into the health-care field after graduation, eventually landing a position as a cardiac monitor technician at a Portland hospital. Ginger also possessed a life-long love of detective novels. She had devoured all of Sara Paretsky's tales about gumshoe V. I. Warshawski, and followed the adventures of detective Kinsey Millhone through Sue Grafton's alphabet murder series. She'd also watched nearly every episode of *The Rockford Files* and *Magnum, P.I.*

At some point, the combination of boredom and curiosity hit critical mass and Ginger decided to enter a world she had known only through fiction. She was prepared to devote herself to searching for the truth, solving mysteries, perhaps even righting wrongs. In any case, she figured, detective work would be infinitely more interesting than following the heart rhythms of sick people. Back then, in 1994, Bill Anton was active in a professional association formed with his brethren in the investigations game, and had branched out from his Alexander Christian Agency to offer training. Ginger enrolled in his Anton Pacific Investigations School in Oregon City, Oregon. She was an impressive student, and Anton hired her to work in his firm.

It wasn't long before Ginger was both disillusioned and disappointed, which seemed inevitable in retrospect. The real world of private investigations was far from glamorous. There were no murder mysteries and very little actual sleuthing. Instead, the job involved a lot of sitting around waiting for people. In the real, off-screen world, private investigators do things like secretly watch people to see if they get around well while claiming to be disabled. They find people so that they can be sued. And they talk to potential witnesses to find out what they know before anyone else does.

Most troubling to Ginger, however, was that it was difficult to assign good and bad, right and wrong. There was mostly just the gray area in between. She'd dreamed of seeking truth and justice, and instead she hunted for information that attorneys needed to file legal briefs. The fact that many of the agency's cases involved sex abuse further dampened her enthusiasm for the job. Anton's firm did business with civil tort lawyers who handled, among other cases, numerous sex abuse lawsuits. A few rungs down the food chain, Ginger Simmons was soon steeped in the messy details of the awful things that people do to each other and their children, which is not at all where she wanted to be.

In 1998, when the Oregon State Legislature passed a law requiring private investigators to be licensed, it also birthed a state agency to oversee the licensing and regulating involved. Ginger took the opportunity to work for the state and leave the actual investigating to others. That's not to say her new career was less stressful—investigators were not all happy with the new oversight that came with the respectability of a license, and the phone rang nonstop. She'd been in the midst of sorting out this new world when her former boss, Bill Anton, called and told her they'd been subpoenaed. Both were bemused by a court order that reached into what they considered to be private work product. No matter, Ginger had been summoned to answer questions.

At nine in the morning, she took a seat in the conference room. Steve English began asking Ginger about her personal background. She answered his questions but also shot a look over to Hillas and Salmi, figuring they should object pretty soon. And indeed they did. Salmi soon announced to the room that he would object to all questions outside the scope of Judge Rosenblum's order that Ginger be deposed only to clarify the notes that she'd been made to produce, and that he'd instruct Ginger not to answer English's questions. She'd learned in an earlier meeting with the Scott lawyers that they were exasperated about her being deposed in the first place, since it intruded into their private work in preparing for trial, so she assumed they weren't going to let anything that even came close to crossing the boundaries of what was ordered get past. And she was correct. English asked and Salmi objected for the next four hours. Every word, sentence, and scribble on the notes that Ginger had been made to produce was scrutinized. There was some confusion about the firm's use of the word "we," as in "we conducted an interview . . ." As it turned out, Ginger conducted interviews alone and Bill Anton presented the information to the lawyers. The "we" was really more of a majestic plural, the "royal we." Things devolved into absurdity from there.

"Did you type the word 'He,' capital 'H,' for the last two words of Page 3?" English asked.

"It appears that I did, yes," Ginger said.

"And then you typed the word 'stated'?"

"It appears that I did, yes."

"And what's the grammatical designation after the word 'stated'?"

"Comma."

"And is it your best recollection that something was originally typed after the comma?"

Salmi jumped in. "I'll object as asked and answered. She already testified she didn't know if anything was typed," he said.

"I will ask the question," English said. "I don't think I've asked that specific question. Is it your best recollection that you did originally type something after the word, 'He stated,' comma?"

"I don't know," Ginger said.

"In any of the other documents you'd prepared . . . for the Jeremiah Scott investigation, did you end any sentences in a comma?"

"No."

English was likely looking for an opportunity to show that Ginger, Anton, Kosnoff, Salmi, or someone had fudged the investigation. They were picking nits because Stephen English wasn't allowed to get at what he really wanted. Ginger Simmons had interviewed the Penrose and Johnson families and former bishops Greg Foster and Gordon Checketts before they'd talked to lawyers or anyone else in the case. She'd talked to them before they knew anyone was suing their church.

Ginger hated using tricks to get people to give up information. She had disliked lying, shading the truth, making up some reason to talk to people. Eventually, she categorized this as one more reason to get out of the PI racket. Sometimes she'd say she was conducting research, sometimes it would be conducting a poll for some upcoming event. This time, Ginger had said that she was doing research for Joel Salmi and Tim Kosnoff in Washington State.

She'd interviewed Gordon Checketts at his accounting office in Clackamas, a suburb of Portland. He'd been arrogant, she thought, and intimidating. He was a big man, the way she remembered him, leaning back in his chair, rocking back and forth, peering over the wooden desk at Ginger. Checketts was likely the most crucial interview in the bunch, despite Greg Foster having been named as defendant. It was apparent that he'd known about Frank Curtis early, back when the Penrose and

Johnson boys were molested, years before the Scott family ever met Frank. Ginger remembered that Checketts had stopped talking when she made notes, so she stopped taking notes. When they were done, she'd left the building, driven out of the parking lot, and then pulled over to commit everything to paper while it was still fresh. She'd sat by the side of the road in her red Ford Escort and written down everything she could remember about the conversation and the scene and the feel of the whole office.

Back in the conference room, Stephen English questioned Ginger about her interview with Greg Foster. She'd attempted to contact him at least twice before they actually talked, but Foster was either evasive or too busy. So she'd finally ended up talking to him on the phone.

"Did you tape-record any portion of your interview with Mr. Foster?" English asked.

"I'll object," Salmi said, "and direct the witness not to answer. It's beyond the scope of the court's order."

Salmi gave Ginger some brief instruction on navigating this.

"Did you tape-record . . ." English began, and then stopped. "The record should reflect there was a pause before that answer—before the objection."

"There wasn't an answer," Salmi said.

"The record should reflect that there was a pause before the objection—" English began.

"The objection—" Salmi interrupted.

"—was made," English said.

"There was a pause before the objection," Salmi said, looking for clarification.

"Yeah," English said, and then he continued talking to Ginger.

"Did you tape-record any interview with anyone that you have talked about today that you have notes on in Exhibits 2 through 10?"

"Same objection, same direction," Salmi said.

English ignored him and continued. "Does Alexander Christian have tape-recording equipment which allows it to tape-record telephone conversations?"

"Same objection, same direction," Salmi said.

English moved on. "Is it a fair statement that the quote on Exhibit 10 in Paragraph 1 is not a verbatim quote of what Mr. Foster told you?"

"Yes," Ginger said.

"Is it a fair statement that the quote indicated in Paragraph 2 of Exhibit 10, the one that begins, 'Foster continued, comma, quote, right after his divorce,' is not a verbatim characterization of what he said?"

"It is not."

The report that the investigators had produced for Salmi and Kosnoff noted that Bishop Foster had remembered hearing that Frank Curtis had married a woman with several children and had molested them. Years before he became a bishop, Foster had been in the same ward with Frank Curtis in southeast Portland, but they hadn't known each other. The Scott lawyers had estimated that it was in the late 1970s, about the time Frank was married to Raquel Saban.

English finished up his questions at about four o'clock. Ginger shook hands with Salmi and Jim Hillas, rode the elevator down to the lobby, and walked outside. She couldn't get out of there fast enough. Ginger had thought she'd left this all behind.

15

From his room at the Days Inn in Portland, Tim Kosnoff could see Mt. Hood out the window in the morning. It had been dark when he'd arrived the night before. He awoke early and went downstairs to the room off the lobby where there was continental breakfast. Kosnoff poured a cup of coffee from one of the big thermoses and headed back to his room to prepare for court. The place was beginning to feel frighteningly like a second home.

He liked to get to the courtroom early, to arrange his papers and pens just so on the table. By tradition, the first lawyer to arrive selected which table he'd use. Kosnoff chose the left side of the courtroom, which was closer to the jury box, though there would be no one sitting in the box that morning. They were here for a hearing on a collection of matters vital to the Scott case. There had been other, less important, motions before Judge Rosenblum, but today's hearing would be the lawyers' first real taste of Her Honor's style. She was a petite, sophisticated woman, her bearing enhanced by this particular courtroom, which dated back to 1912 and had been restored to something close to its original state. Dark green marble pillars stood majestically on either side of the room, which was paneled in wood and topped by tall windows. A painting of Thomas Jefferson and John Adams working on the Declaration of Independence hung on the wall behind the jury box. Chief Justice John Marshall, in oil on canvas, looked down upon the proceedings from behind the judge. In this setting, Rosenblum ran her courtroom with decorum and efficiency.

The judge was still coming up to speed with the complicated details of the Scott case. She'd conferred with Judge Ceniceros on many of the issues involved and had read some of the earlier briefs, but there was a lot to absorb. The biggest issue in court this morning was resolving access to church disciplinary records, for few other things could be done without their production, or without establishing that they weren't coming. Joel Salmi, who was the most practiced in constitutional arguments, would lead in the courtroom.

Stephen English, David Ernst, and an associate from Bullivant, Houser, Bailey occupied the table on the other side of the room, along with a lawyer representing Greg Foster. Jeff Kilmer seemed to have handed off much of Foster's defense to two other lawyers in his firm—he rarely showed up at a hearing or deposition anymore.

Salmi began by reviewing the arguments that he and Kosnoff and the Dunn, Carney lawyers had made during the previous two years with Judge Ceniceros. His point this morning was that the matter was, at its core, a simple discovery issue, getting documents from the defendants in order to move the case forward. The Scott team wanted to steer as far away as possible from religion, to keep from getting mired in questions about the courts interfering in religious belief.

"We're entitled to those documents if they're reasonably calculated to lead to admissible evidence, and the defendants failed to meet their burden of establishing that somehow the documents are protected by a privilege," Salmi said.

The issues in the case, he told Rosenblum, were also simple. "The real issue is the church's conduct in failing to inform my client's parents that this man was a pedophile before he came to live in their home, in failing to inform parents of other children who came into direct contact with Frank Curtis as a result of his participation and membership in the Mormon Church. . . . Was that conduct reasonable? And finally, was that conduct consistent with a pattern and practice which shows a reckless and outrageous indifference to an unreasonably high risk of harm?"

Salmi was at ease in front of Rosenblum. He'd litigated many civil hearings. His manner was calm and collegial. When he finished, Stephen English made the church's argument. English was well known, generally operated on a plane above the average lawyer in Portland, and more than held his own against Salmi's competent presentation. The Mormon church was still pursuing multiple arguments about why its discipline records should be off-limits. In the civil justice system, it is perfectly acceptable, if not common, to present competing arguments simultaneously.

As he had argued previously, English told Rosenblum that the church should not be made to produce its discipline records because to do so would require reviewing vast records of the Mormon church, all of which were kept at LDS headquarters in Salt Lake City, which was an unreasonable amount of work. At the same time, the church maintained that its discipline records were not relevant to the case of Jeremiah Scott because it was already known that church officials had excommunicated Frank Curtis for sexually abusing children, and then rebaptized him as part of a repentance process. English again argued that the records were considered confidential under Oregon's clergy-penitent protection laws, even though Judge Ceniceros had already dismissed this theory months before. And then, as it always had, the question came down to an interpretation of the First Amendment's Free Exercise Clause. The discipline records, English argued, were protected from disclosure by the freedom of religion tenets of the Constitution because they were part of the Mormon religion's repentance process.

The church, English told Rosenblum, still viewed the case as one of religious freedom. "When you boil it all down," English said, "what plaintiff is really saying is they think our system is a bad one. They don't like the way we do this. And that's what the whole First Amendment privilege does, it gives us the right to have a proceeding. And maybe they don't like the fact that we fully forgive people, but the last thing in the world that should occur is to have a jury or even, you know, with respect to a judge deciding, 'well this system doesn't make sense in terms of they shouldn't be allowed to forgive people for something like that.' So, that's what really we're getting at."

There was nothing more to say on the subject. They'd been arguing these same points for two years. There were piles of paperwork on both sides citing other cases, examples, explanations, and more argument. Rosenblum had to decide. She'd asked for a sample of a disciplinary action record, to see what information might be included on it. These were one- or two-page reports stating that someone had been the subject of a church hearing for a certain offense, and that an action such as excommunication or other church discipline had been taken as a result.

Salmi argued that because the reports of disciplinary action were forwarded to Mormon headquarters in Salt Lake City, they were not confidential penitent communications.

If it hadn't been clear before, Judge Rosenblum put the lawyers on notice that she wasn't keen on letting these sorts of motions linger, something that Salmi and Kosnoff were happy to hear. "This case is just far too complex and it's been too drawn out I think already, so I'm going to make sure, at least to the extent I'm able to do that, that it doesn't continue to be so drawn out."

But Ellen Rosenblum was also a stickler for proceeding by the book, and she saw a problem with the paperwork. The lawyers had all been arguing about the scope of documents that were or were not, in the case of church disciplinary records, provided through discovery requests filed at the beginning of the Scott case. The judge wanted a motion from Salmi and Kosnoff that addressed specifically what they had not yet received from the church before she would rule on it. Kosnoff found this exasperating, but at least Judge Rosenblum seemed to be listening to their argument.

The other issue scheduled to be addressed was the matter of former bishop Gordon Checketts and the questions he'd refused to answer in his deposition months earlier about what he had and hadn't known and done about Frank Curtis. According to Ginger Simmons's original report, Checketts had said in an interview that he'd confronted Frank Curtis after he learned that the man had abused Steven Penrose and David Johnson, and advised him never to return. The report also stated that Checketts had told investigators that he "red-tagged" Frank Curtis's membership file and sent it to Mormon headquarters in Salt Lake City, and that he had been contacted two or three times over the years by other LDS bishops. Yet, in his deposition, Checketts had said none of those things.

This was Kosnoff's turf, since he was the one who'd taken, or at least attempted to take, Checketts's deposition. He took over from Salmi and addressed Judge Rosenblum.

"Your Honor, Bishop Checketts, there was a remarkable deposition. I took it. Bishop Checketts wouldn't answer any of my questions regarding any communication he had with anybody during the time that he was bishop of the Mormon Church, claimed clergy-penitent privilege to everything. 'Well, Bishop Checketts, somebody—some member of the ward says nice new car, would that be privileged? Yeah.' So, just a blanket assertion of clergy-penitent privilege. This is a man that had communications with two of the victims, David Johnson and Steven Penrose, found out that they had been abused by Frank Curtis, goes to Frank Curtis's apartment, Curtis is packing up getting ready to catch a bus to leave town, has this communication with Curtis in which Curtis admits molesting these boys.

". . . So, there's all these communications which clearly establish that Bishop Checketts knew all about Curtis and what he was doing, and Curtis confessed, and defendants are arguing that, number one, that it's all objectionable because it's all subsumed by the clergy-penitent privilege.

"Clearly none of these communications from these victims, the parents and so forth, are encompassed by the clergy-penitent privilege. Certainly not the kind of thing recognized by our statute. They make a second argument which is a kind of, 'well, it's not fair because the investigator didn't fully disclose that she was actually preparing to file a lawsuit or working on behalf of attorneys who were preparing to file a lawsuit,' and in fact she did disclose that she was an investigator, she was working for Joel Salmi, an attorney from Washington State. Bishop Checketts acknowledged that he was aware there was a possibility of litigation and talked freely with her. And now he doesn't want to talk about that anymore, and the defendants have thrown up these arguments."

Kosnoff ticked off the things that they'd already provided to the other side—investigators' notes and the like. He reminded Judge Rosenblum that they'd "generously allowed" the church to take Ginger Simmons's deposition. Kosnoff also mentioned that the church had accused Joel Salmi of unethical conduct. And that all of the arguments surrounding this issue had been rejected by Judge Ceniceros.

Kosnoff's years of defense work in criminal courtrooms was on display here now. He was smooth, if a bit cocky. He risked coming across as flip to Judge Rosenblum, however, and that could backfire. But at this point, Kosnoff was so far at the end of his rope with what he'd begun referring to as the church's "death by a thousand paper cuts" practice, he couldn't help but impart to Rosenblum how preposterous he thought it all was, how the church's lawyers were wasting all of their time. She seemed to be with him.

"If he wants to deny that he said that to the investigator, he's welcome to do that," Kosnoff said. "If he wants to deny that he told the Penroses and the Johnsons everything that happened between them and Curtis, he's welcome to do that. But he can't just stand mute, refuse to testify. And yet that's what he's being counseled to do by the Church defendants."

Kosnoff was asking Judge Rosenblum to make Gordon Checketts answer the questions. David Ernst responded. He argued that Kosnoff mischaracterized Judge Ceniceros's findings on the issue of Ginger Simmons's conduct. The judge, he said, had called her actions "a ruse" and found that the usual protections afforded to the internal memos, reports, and other work product of attorneys had been violated because of the actions of the investigator.

"This information was provided to Mr. Salmi, there's a fax indication that it went to Mr. Salmi, and for them to stand up and say, well, I was just doing research on pedophiles for Joel Salmi from Washington State, if you were doing research for Steve English from Oregon State, I don't think that would tell anyone that Steve English was an Oregon lawyer and that the results might be published. Well, they were published in terms of a lawsuit that got filed. So, how he can say, stand up and say Judge Ceniceros found no problem with what went on. I don't understand how the lawyer could just say that."

Ernst could be long-winded, which tried the patience of everyone on the Scott team. Rosenblum seemed patient with this, but she would later begin to reel him in. Today was not one of those times, however.

At the end of the hearing, Judge Rosenblum ruled that Gordon Checketts could not be questioned about statements made to him by Frank Curtis, because they were protected by clergy-penitent privilege. As for the rest of the information Kosnoff sought, Gordon Checketts would have to answer under oath. Judge Rosenblum was clearly not pleased by what had happened with the investigators early on, but she also wasn't willing to exempt Checketts from having to testify. In all, it was a good day for Tim Kosnoff and Joel Salmi.

Earlier in the year, Tim Kosnoff had arranged for Linda Walker to talk to Sandra Scott. He'd figured that Linda, who certainly knew more about being a Mormon woman than he or anyone else on the legal team, might get more details that would strengthen their case against what was sure to be a relentless courtroom attack by the other side, assuming they ever got to court. It wasn't that he thought Sandy was being less than straight with them; rather, he sometimes had the feeling she was working so hard on presenting the facts that they might be missing the nuances in the Scott family's relationship with their church that Sandy wouldn't think to add and Kosnoff wouldn't think to ask. The two women chatted on the phone a few times, and then Linda typed up a summary of what she'd learned and sent it off to Kosnoff. There hadn't been anything particularly new or exciting in Linda's report, just some random details about the Scotts' lives and other people in the ward. Sandy had mentioned that she'd heard that the man who had been their home teacher, Don Anderson, had been caught molesting children in a school where he taught some years ago and was sent to prison. At the time, Kosnoff and the other lawyers had noted that someone should follow up on the information, but responding to the church's motions was about all they'd been able to focus on. Chasing down indirect players, like so many other tasks, was relegated to a back burner.

Now Kosnoff had reason to revisit the information. Both he and Linda had been researching legal cases involving child sexual abuse and the LDS church for the pattern and practice argument that the Scott team was going to have to make for punitive damages. They'd have to establish that Jeremiah Scott's situation was part of a larger problem in which the Mormon church had shown a pattern of wrongdoing in order to persuade a jury to punish the church by making it pay out a big award.

Linda Walker had been searching for other LDS molesters from the time she first got involved in the case. This was the sort of thing that Linda did best. The woman was a living library of LDS abuse information, owing to years of working on other projects, and a tenacious researcher. She and Kosnoff had added to their collection the cases noted in the magazine article from Phoenix, plus another batch of lawsuits involving the Boy Scouts of America. (Given that the Mormon church embraced Boy Scouts as its youth program, there was a good chance that a Boy Scout perpetrator operated through the Mormon church as well.) Their database now included more than eighty instances of child sex abuse that involved the Church of Jesus Christ of Latter-day Saints in one way or another. In most instances, church officials had known that a perpetrator had a problem before someone had become a victim.

Every ghastly story made Kosnoff want to dig deeper and fight harder. But even he was unable to explain exactly why this business had captured his attention in such an all-consuming way. Maybe it was his son, Nathan, now the same age as most of Frank Curtis's victims, who drove Kosnoff's passion. Nathan was a daily reminder that these kinds of crimes against nine-, ten-, and eleven-year-old boys were horrific. The victims were compelling. As children they'd been prey to their teachers, their caretakers, their religious leaders. Now many of them had lives filled with failed relationships, crime, drugs, and alcohol. That was hardly new territory to Kosnoff, who had spent his career working with broken people. He had to admit that a certain relief and enthusiasm came from feeling like he was on the right side, the good side. He represented victims here, not criminals. In years of criminal defense work, he'd seen how victims were largely passed over in the system, because the volume was so great; they'd been reduced to material witnesses. In Kosnoff's mind, there were no shades of gray in this work. He was, for once, fighting a genuinely good fight, and it invigorated him.

He and Linda searched newspaper articles for arrests and lawsuits and called the reporters who'd written the stories. Did they know about any others? Linda could get obsessive and Kosnoff would have to rein her in at times, reminding her that they were trying to prove the argument they had, not launch new crusades. But then he too would get caught up in a new piece of information about the church and follow it away from the matters at hand.

Sometimes such revelations were relevant. One day while he was in Portland, Kosnoff took the membership directories they'd finally gotten from the church and cross-referenced the names of the people who seemed likely to have had some interaction with Frank Curtis against criminal records there. Kosnoff was still looking for other people who knew about Frank Curtis's past. In his experience, criminals tended to hang out together. Sure enough, Kosnoff found more than ten people in the LDS directories who had been convicted of molestation, or some other sex crime, which he found astounding. They were supposed to be the ones who cared about children? This morally upright group constantly promoted its profamily image, essentially saying, Kosnoff thought, "We're better than you."

The number of church-related molesters was a matter of simple math, given the number of people arrested for sex offenses and the size of the LDS population in the West, but Kosnoff was nonetheless shocked by how many molesters there were among the wards, cycling through this lay ministry, potentially interacting with children.

Kosnoff's primary task now was to learn more about the situation involving Don Anderson, the Scotts' home teacher. He eventually found the answer, but in another county. Anderson had been convicted in 1981 of sexually abusing two boys who were students at the elementary school where he had been a music teacher. It was evident from the positions he held later in the church that Don Anderson had either not been excommunicated, which would have violated the church's rules on such things, or had been excommunicated and rebaptized, just like Frank Curtis. Don Anderson was an elder in his ward and director of the ward's music program, and of course had been home teacher to the Scotts. The man whose job it had been to bring them religious lessons, hear the family's needs, and act as a sort of liaison between family and church while Frank Curtis was living in their house was also a convicted molester. Kosnoff fired off an email to the rest of the lawyers, laying out the connection. Not only had Bishop Greg Foster not warned the Scotts about Frank Curtis, Bishop Foster sent *another* convicted molester into their home! It seemed that there was no end to the web of abuse. The lawyers immediately agreed that they'd file a notice with the court to depose Don Anderson.

Meanwhile, the attorneys were divided over another issue. Joel Salmi wanted to make an agreement with Stephen English that the Scott lawyers would not pursue Gordon Checketts if the church side would not call Ginger Simmons to testify. He didn't like the idea of having an investigator on the stand, talking about her casework. Salmi feared that Ginger wouldn't hold up well, and that the church lawyers could distract a jury with their "dirty tricks" argument. Further, Salmi reasoned, the Scott team could impeach Gordon Checketts with the deposition testimony of the Penrose and Johnson families. They didn't need to depose him. The risk outweighed what they might gain, Salmi told his colleagues.

Kosnoff was unconvinced. He was afraid that Gordon Checketts wouldn't be honest at trial and that there might be an avalanche of people recanting, denying, or not recalling what they'd said earlier. Kosnoff hadn't witnessed Ginger Simmons's deposition, when Stephen English took her apart, comma by comma, on investigation procedure. Ultimately, Salmi won over the other lawyers on the team and the deal was made. They would drop the bishop and the investigator, at least for now.

On a Saturday afternoon that fall, Tim Kosnoff, Joel Salmi, and Jim Hillas watched through a one-way window as three groups of Portland citizens discussed the case of *Jeremiah Scott v. Gregory Lee*

Foster, The Church of Jesus Christ of Latter-day Saints, et al. The lawyers sipped soda pop and munched on pretzels while they tried to glean every clue they could that might foretell their fate in court. Gary Rhoades recently had surprised everyone by leaving Dunn, Carney to go out on his own. The Scott court work in Oregon was left to Jim Hillas, the young associate still trying to make his way in the firm, along with their trusted paralegal Lisa Thomas and whichever summer interns or associates they could draft into helping.

One of the many tentacles of the legal services industry includes marketing consultants who will convene a mock jury and set up a courtroom for lawyers to hold a pretend trial. The exercise is common practice in civil lawsuits and offers a view into what the lawyers can expect in the real trial. A research firm recruits people to spend a day or two listening to lawyers representing both sides of the case. The fake jurors deliberate, just as a real jury would, and then render a decision on the case. While generally considered a valuable exercise, staging a mock trial is an expensive undertaking. It is a commercial simulation, not actual civic duty, and jury recruits are paid about $100 each for their time. On top of that, there was a fee for the market research firm, which pushed the total cost for a mock trial to several thousand dollars. The Scott legal team had decided that it was worth the investment. They needed a reality check. They'd been steeped in the minutiae of legal motions for more than two years now. It was time to pull back and take a look at the bigger picture and see how the rest of the world viewed their case. With any luck, they'd learn what their chances might be in front of a jury. Collectively, they'd invested tens of thousands of dollars in this case, not counting their time, and everyone was looking for some reassurance that the bill would be paid through a jury award.

The day began early at the market research firm's facility. The largest room was arranged to resemble a courtroom, where mock jurors would watch and listen to the proceedings. With some help from his colleagues, Kosnoff had sketched out screening questions that the recruiters used to whittle down the population of willing participants to a group that closely resembled citizens likely to serve on a Multnomah County jury. There were three groups of twelve people, just in case one simulated jury was unnecessarily swayed by one or two oddballs.

Kosnoff had been cast as the plaintiff's lawyer in this performance. Salmi played for the defense, acting as counsel for both Greg Foster and the church. Jim Hillas, as judge, ruled on their objections and gave the jury its instructions. This casting seemed to make the most sense. Salmi had defended similar civil lawsuits in court, Kosnoff knew the nuances of the Scott case better than anyone else, and Hillas was particularly earnest looking. All three were dressed in their best courtroom suits (Hillas did not wear a robe) and, armed with the scripts and exhibits they'd crafted for the occasion, presented the best version they could to the hired audience. Holding the mock trial offered the added benefit of forcing the lawyers to review all the information they had collected thus far and put together the arguments they'd eventually have to make in court.

Certain factors, however, made this mock trial different from what was likely to happen in front of a real jury. Despite their best acting, it was hard for the lawyers on the Scott team to suspend their view of a case they'd been working on for more than two years. Mostly, this had to do with the passion of Tim Kosnoff. Salmi's admirable performance of what they'd figured the church's lawyers would likely mount as a defense, based on the arguments they'd heard so far and what the church had done in the rare instances when an abuse case had gone to trial, would never match Kosnoff's zeal for going after the defendants. By this point, he'd come to view Mormon church leaders as the architects of child abuse and was perpetually enraged by the smugness and superior attitude of their lawyers. Together, they were the enemy. Even though Hillas tempered Kosnoff, trying hard to mimic what he thought a judge would do in a real court, it did little to hide Kosnoff's inner flame from the mock jurors. His outrage, the other lawyers had to admit, was contagious. It was also way over the top. A real jury probably wouldn't see the same presentation. Joel Salmi, the more seasoned veteran of these courtroom dramas, would likely play the lead role at trial, and a judge would likely cut down considerably what was presented.

Kosnoff had worked on his opening statement fastidiously and chose to immediately address an issue that the lawyers assumed would be the biggest hurdle for a jury: the fact that Sandy and Kent Scott had allowed Frank Curtis to share a bed with their son. Kosnoff and the rest of the team had concluded that the best way to handle the matter was to bring it up right from the beginning and offer the explanation that, he hoped, would satisfy the jurors.

"Because of a rearrangement of living conditions, the only place for this elderly man to sleep was in Jeremiah's room," Kosnoff told the mock jurors. "To Jeremiah's parents, it never occurred to them that Curtis posed any kind of threat staying in Jeremiah's room. Curtis was eighty-seven years old, had difficulty walking. His health was fragile at best."

Kosnoff had found his rhythm.

"Beyond that, Curtis was a High Priest," he said, "a kind of holy man ordained by the Mormon Church, a position reserved for those who had demonstrated moral worthiness and commitment to living the principles of the gospel and power to confer baptism and officiate the highest ordinances of the church."

This was a key point, and Kosnoff had written and rewritten this part of his opening trying to get it right. A jury would have to grasp the trust in, dependence on, and respect for hierarchy demanded by the Mormon religion or Jeremiah didn't stand a chance.

"More important," Kosnoff told his jurors, "the Scotts had been taught to place their trust in the bishop, the *father of the ward* as he is known—to trust and obey the word of their ward bishop. Sandy and Kent trusted that if there was a problem with Curtis, any problem, then surely Bishop Foster would have warned them. The Scotts trusted that their church and its leaders would not knowingly expose them to harm—but they were wrong."

Pretend court filled the first half of the day. It was a concentrated, reduced version of the Scott case, which likely would take at least a week in real court time. Kosnoff had worked with others on the team, mostly Lisa Thomas, who had the unenviable job of keeping the ever-growing collection of documents and information organized, to create a package of handouts for each of the mock jurors. Inside were copies of their exhibits, including Frank Curtis's church records and the sworn affidavit from Raquel Saban, stating that she'd sent a letter to her bishop after she'd found Frank Curtis in the bathtub with the neighborhood boy. The jurors had finished their catered lunches and now were deliberating the points of the case while the lawyers moved from one room to the next watching and listening from behind the glass. They were fascinated by the discussion. By and large, the jurors were sympathetic to the Scott case. The most immediate surprise was how seriously these people were taking their pretend job. They were unquestionably committed to duty. Some were pretty passionate in arguing their points. And they were universally outraged, which was good for the Scott team.

Predictably, some of the jurors were openly critical of Sandy Scott and talked about how she should have been more cautious about bringing Frank Curtis to live in their home, let alone in her son's room. Others thought that, while Jeremiah had clearly been wronged, the church was not to blame, or that the church shouldn't be sued because its money comes from the tithing of its members. People seemed to be generally uncomfortable with the idea of taking money from the church coffers. The Scott lawyers had not counted on another concern: Some jurors were questioning what would happen to Jeremiah if he were to receive a large amount of money, and if such an award might do more harm than good to someone of his young age. Throwing money at the problem, they seemed to be saying, could make things worse for Jeremiah.

The jurors did not like the fact that Jeremiah had touched a little boy in his mother's day care, which Kosnoff expected more than Salmi, who really thought people would understand that Jeremiah's actions were the direct result of his having been abused by Frank Curtis. Some of the jurors made a point of saying things like, "I wouldn't do something like that, even if I had been molested," which Kosnoff knew was a common sentiment among people who haven't been victims. He also knew that, while every victim of child sexual abuse certainly does not go on to be a perpetrator, nearly every perpetrator has been molested. This fact spoke directly to a point that the lawyers were eventually going to have to figure out how to make a real jury understand. The radius of wreckage involved when child molesting was allowed to perpetuate inside a large institution like the Church of Jesus Christ of Latter-day Saints was staggeringly wide. There is never just one victim of a pedophile; there is only the first victim.

Kosnoff had asked the jury to award punitive damages, because that was where the Scott team was heading in the real court case and the lawyers had wanted to find out how willing a jury might be to assign monetary punishment to the Mormon church. A punitive damages award involves determining not only that an entity, in this case the church, should be punished, but also what sort of monetary award would serve as punishment. In other words, how much would be considered enough of a deterrent? Of course, the real court case hadn't gotten that far, so the lawyers had used their best guess of the church's net worth, based on a variety of earlier research done mostly by journalists. Kosnoff had estimated that the Mormon church took in somewhere between $5 and $7 billion annually in tithing income.

Now, to their great surprise, the Scott lawyers encountered what they started calling "the big piss-off factor" among the jurors. Despite some of the jury recruits' early concerns about taking money from the church, and how this might harm others, they seemed, as a group, more than willing to make the corporate entity of the Church of Jesus Christ of Latter-day Saints pay for placing their faith in Frank Curtis's redemption above the safety of children. Salmi knew the most about jury awards in this group, and he'd shared how, typically, the lowballers in the group will bring an award down more than jurors who want to go high will bring it up.

Now, as the jurors debated their way toward agreement, the lawyers were stunned. The lowest award was $50 million, and they went all the way to $1 billion. Sure, Kosnoff had juiced his performance; they all spent every other day being Jeremiah's advocates, after all.

Despite how angry the Scott team was at them, the church's lawyers were certainly competent. No one doubted that, in the reality of a courtroom, Stephen English could execute a brilliant performance.

But the message here was as clear as the glass the lawyers were looking through. These citizens, the representative jurors of Multnomah County, Oregon, wanted the Mormon church to pay Jeremiah a lot of money. And that was very, very good news for his lawyers.

16

If it hadn't provided anything else, the mock trial had given a much-needed boost to everyone involved. Jeremiah and Sandy Scott needed to see that their lawsuit, now entering its third year, was going somewhere. The mock trial told Kosnoff, Salmi, and the other lawyers that their instincts were right, that a jury would likely see things the way they did. Rhoades and Hillas could show the partners at Dunn, Carney that their investment wasn't going into a black hole. Everyone was up, confident. They were playing for the winning team in the big game.

This sense of imminent victory lasted all of about a month before things slowly started turning sour again. This time the cause was a series of events in the Midwest.

There was a growing subplot in the Frank Curtis story that had started way back in the fall of 1999, shortly after the Scott team received Frank Curtis's membership history from the church, while Kosnoff was poking around in Frank's history. One day, he'd sat at his desk at home, sipped his coffee, and began systematically calling every residence in an apartment building in Grand Rapids, Michigan.

Frank Curtis's membership records showed that he'd lived at an address in Grand Rapids, sometime in the mid-1980s. Kosnoff was determined to investigate every community in which Frank Curtis had ingratiated himself. He'd traced the address to an old brick building of subsidized apartments and then used his latest favorite tool, a software program that acted as a reverse directory in which he could look up residents by address, to sleuth further.

"My name is Tim Kosnoff and I'm a lawyer in Seattle, Washington," he said into the phone again and again. "I'm working on a case for a client of mine and I'm interested in finding out information on a man named Frank Curtis."

Neighbor after neighbor reported that she'd never heard of anyone named Frank Curtis. Until he got hold of Pearly Hankins.

"Yes," she said, she had known Frank Curtis.

Kosnoff was momentarily stunned, but he snapped to and began talking. He quickly learned that Pearly Hankins and Frank Curtis had been more than neighbors; they had also been friends. As Pearly told it, back in the mid-1980s, Frank had lived alone in a small apartment on another floor, but they saw each other around the building. Theirs was the sort of building with an office staff on the first floor and common areas with chairs where residents might linger for a change of scenery and some company. Frank was friendly and charming, but lonely. Pearly lived with her older sister and had a steady stream of family members through the apartment. Frank, whom Pearly and her family came to call "Pop," became a regular at the dinner table.

Frank would have been older than Pearly, Kosnoff deduced. She mentioned that she'd had some health problems that restricted her activities. She and Frank would do quilting together, Pearly said, and sometimes Frank made small dogs out of yarn. Kosnoff remembered Sandy Scott mentioning something about these yarn dogs. It was a weird detail, and now he wondered if this was part of some pattern Frank Curtis used to groom victims. Pearly described how she and Frank used to pass the time together in the lobby. When the weather was nice, they sat on folding chairs out in the parking lot and visited. Frank Curtis had talked about his past and mentioned his gangster days in Chicago but had said nothing about having been in prison. Pearly remembered that he'd attended a Mormon ward in Grand Rapids, and one in the suburb of Wyoming, Michigan. In fact, Pop had been the one who brought the Mormon religion to Pearly. He'd given her a copy of the Book of Mormon and, later, had read it to her when her eyesight turned poor. Kosnoff was briefly distracted trying to grasp this scene. In his impression of Frank Curtis, the man was barely literate. Meanwhile, Pearly was still talking about Pop. Eventually, she said, they'd attended church together. She'd been a Baptist earlier in her life, she explained, but the noise and the spirited commotion of the Baptist services rattled her nerves. She'd found the Mormon church more peaceful.

Kosnoff tried to pinpoint dates for the Frank and Pearly story. It was increasingly evident that the Scott team needed to expand its time line to keep track of Frank Curtis's movements. Preparing for depositions was challenging enough, given the growing number of people and places that they were now managing; a jury would never be able to follow this without some kind of visual aid.

Pearly said that Frank came and went a few times from the apartment building. She knew that he'd traveled to Portland and Chicago because she'd taken him to the bus station when he left, but she wasn't sure when that was. Kosnoff quickly calculated the chronology in his head. Frank Curtis must have gone back to the building in Grand Rapids during the time he went missing from the Scotts' house. That would mean Frank had been in and out of Grand Rapids from around 1984 to as late as 1990.

For a time, Pearly said, Frank was out in Greenville, a suburb of Grand Rapids, helping what she described as a divorced woman with a bunch of children on a farm. Pearly said she'd told Pop that he should steer clear of that, because the woman's marital situation seemed questionable. Besides, he wasn't in any shape to be helping anyone else; his feet used to swell up, which caused him to be unsteady. Pearly didn't know anything more about that woman on the farm.

There was something else, though. Pearly told Kosnoff that one time after Frank Curtis left Grand Rapids—she wasn't clear which time—another woman had come to her door looking for him. The woman was "screaming and hollering" about how he had hurt her kids, and that he'd molested her son. Pearly didn't believe Frank would do anything like that. Her nieces and nephews had come over all the time and Frank never did anything wrong around them. Plus, her next-door neighbor's grandchildren were always all over Frank. Pearly told that woman that if she thought Frank Curtis did those things to her child, she should call the police and report it. Pearly hadn't known where Frank was, anyway.

Kosnoff was elated. This was a major breakthrough. He'd suspected there was more history. If Frank Curtis had molested more children, then more people had known about it before he'd met Jeremiah Scott. The problem was that Pearly Hankins didn't know the name of the woman who'd come to her door that day.

After he hung up with Pearly, Kosnoff fired off an email to Salmi and the rest of the team, giving them the rundown. The information was great, of course. But Kosnoff also felt vindicated. His tedious, incessant digging had again paid off. Now he was all the more driven to find out what happened in Michigan. He contacted seven police departments in Grand Rapids and the surrounding towns, trying to track down information that was now nearly two decades old.

The answer came in the mail a few days later—a brief two-page police report from Wyoming, Michigan. Kosnoff tried to make sense of the thing. The report documented an incident in which Frank Curtis had been babysitting the children of a family in his ward there. The parents had told police that Frank had molested one of their sons. The report listed the names of the people involved and showed that a warrant had been issued for Frank Curtis's arrest. But the rest was sketchy. There was no investigation, certainly none of the sort of information that Kosnoff knew would have had to go before a judge. Finding out more would require significant time and research. He looked for the family in the police report but couldn't find anyone by their name anywhere around Grand Rapids.

Kosnoff called Pearly Hankins back, now that he had a name and some more information, hoping maybe Pearly could help fill in the blanks. She didn't know these people, she said. Finally, Kosnoff got hold of another family, the Evelands, who'd been involved in the same ward with all of these people.

Kosnoff called the Eveland family's home in Grand Rapids and spoke briefly to a man named Jack. Yes, he said, he'd known Frank Curtis. They'd belonged to the same Mormon ward years earlier and his family had fellowshipped Brother Curtis. They'd picked him up for church and had hosted him for meals in their home. Yes, he'd heard something about Brother Curtis having been accused of molesting a child. But really, he said, the one to talk to about that was his wife. He handed her the phone.

Jay Eveland had been marginally involved in the incident with Brother Curtis that was memorialized in the police report from Wyoming. Brother Curtis had babysat for a family by the name of Carter. Jay Eveland was a little skeptical of Tim Kosnoff, but she also was deeply concerned about the boy he represented. She told Kosnoff what she knew.

Sister Carter was going away for a weekend to a temple ceremony in Chicago, maybe, or to visit relatives somewhere, and her husband was working a lot around that time. Brother Curtis stayed with the children—three boys and a girl—to help out. This babysitting arrangement had disturbed Jay from the start. Brother Curtis was too old and not suited to the task, she'd thought, and the whole thing just didn't sit right.

Sister Eveland had been designated as a backup, an emergency contact in case something happened or Brother Curtis needed help. Sure enough, before the weekend was over, one of the Carter boys called and reported that his brother had gotten glass in his foot and that Brother Curtis couldn't see it. Jay Eveland had five children of her own and she didn't like the tone of this boy's voice. She went right over to the house and didn't like the feeling she got there either. The Carters lived in a small house with a pitched roof and a picture window facing the front lawn on a block of houses that looked much the same. But everyone came and went through the side entrance off the driveway. Jay Eveland arrived and found the Carter kids, who were known hellions, sitting as quietly as church mice on the sofa in the living room for no explainable reason. Brother Curtis was in a recliner nearby. Sister Eveland could find nothing that hinted of a glass-related accident in the foot in question. She stayed in the house for a few minutes and chatted, trying to assess the situation. She briefly considered whether the glass story was merely a call for help. Finally, she proposed taking the children home with her but ultimately could persuade only the younger boy and girl. Their older brothers would stay.

Jay Eveland had fed, comforted, and kept a close eye on the two kids she brought home with her, but she hadn't questioned them, nor had they volunteered anything that hinted at trouble. She'd assumed all along that it was the little girl who might be in danger. When the Carters came to collect their children, Jay Eveland told Kosnoff, there had been no mention of any problems, and so she'd thought nothing more of it.

Months, maybe even a year, later, Sister Carter called her, seeking counsel. One of her sons had told a friend that Brother Curtis had molested him. The friend had told his father. The father broke the news to the Carters. Sister Eveland told Sister Carter to call the police. Jay Eveland told Kosnoff that she didn't know whether the family had, in fact, reported Brother Curtis to the police. He was gone from the ward by then. But something else happened during the time between the babysitting incident and when they all learned that Brother Curtis had molested the Carter boy.

Jay Eveland told Kosnoff that she'd received "an inspiration" that Brother Curtis shouldn't be around children. Her feeling wasn't connected to the babysitting incident, because she hadn't yet known anything was amiss there. Brother Curtis used to help out in what's called the Primary, or Sunday school classes for children, at church. He frequently filled in when a regular teacher was gone and generally was always around to lend a hand. She hadn't seen him do anything improper, but Jay Eveland sometimes had feelings about things. God spoke to her that way. At some point, Brother Curtis had been called to be a permanent Primary teacher. Typically, the members of a Mormon ward are asked to vote by a show of hands, to sustain these kinds of placements. When it came time for the members of the ward to confirm Brother Curtis in this role, Sister Eveland had held her tongue and not raised her hand to object, even though she felt it was wrong. It was just too public, she'd thought. Instead, she made a quiet deal with the Lord. If God wanted her to do something about this, she'd reasoned, He would put it in her path. So when she found herself alone in a hallway with the bishop shortly after that church meeting, Jay Eveland had figured it was her cue. She told the bishop that she'd received "a prompting" that Brother Curtis, who had just been sustained as a Primary teacher, shouldn't be around children. The bishop, Jay told Kosnoff, dismissed her concerns. This was particularly irritating in that the Mormon faith teaches reverence toward this sort of personal revelation received by members of the church. Later, Sister Eveland had occasion to speak with her stake president during a routine interview to gain admission into the temple. Again, she said that she'd received an inspiration that Brother Curtis shouldn't be around children. This time, she told Kosnoff, the stake president took her seriously, and he told her the feeling she'd gotten was accurate. He mentioned something about Brother Curtis's file having been flagged, which Jay Eveland didn't fully understand, but Tim Kosnoff recognized immediately was a stunning piece of evidence.

Kosnoff wasn't particularly concerned with the spiritual part of Jay Eveland's story. Kosnoff possessed a focused listening ability, or, as he sometimes joked, "tunnel hearing." His brain listened for certain words and phrases: "I told the bishop" or "I knew that" and the like. Everything else was often screened out. "I don't care if it was the voice of God or someone else," he recalled later. "They were on fucking notice to do something about it." Kosnoff was practically coming out of his seat, making high fives in the air.

Jay Eveland seemed reluctant to provide any contact information for the Carter family. They'd moved away, she said. Kosnoff made more calls to more people. Eventually, someone mentioned that the family had moved to Racine, Wisconsin. It was enough. Tim Kosnoff called every Carter family he could find a number for in the greater Racine and Milwaukee areas.

"Is this the Carter family that used to live in Grand Rapids?" he'd asked, until finally he found Mary Kay Carter.

As Kosnoff remembered it, he told her that he was a lawyer in Seattle and he represented a boy who'd been molested by Frank Curtis in a lawsuit. Mary Kay Carter launched into a diatribe about the police in Grand Rapids. She was angry that nothing had been done. They hadn't even looked for the old man, she said. And he had been in Michigan, she said, adding that she'd come across an odd coincidence a few years before. Her grandmother liked to read the *National Enquirer*, and she'd left one of the papers sitting open on a table. Mary Kay Carter glanced through the stories and saw an article about a man who'd wandered into a police station trying to turn himself in for an old, outstanding warrant and the police wouldn't take him because they didn't have any records showing a reason he should be arrested. The man was Frank Curtis.

Kosnoff didn't quite know what to make of this, but it was damned interesting. Mary Kay Carter thought she'd kept the article, but she didn't know where it would be. She promised to hunt around for it. Her story was pretty much a repeat of what Jay Eveland had said, about Brother Curtis having watched her children and then later having learned through someone else that her son had been molested. Her two older sons were victims. Both boys, who were a year apart and would have been about eight or nine years old at the time, had been molested by Brother Curtis. And the abuse had gone on longer than Kosnoff thought. Mary Kay Carter had initially met Brother Curtis while he was volunteering in her sons' Primary at church, just like Jeremiah Scott's mother. Brother Curtis was in and out of the Carter family's home helping out, babysitting, and acting as part of the family for more than a year. He'd molested the Carter boys regularly during that time. It had gotten worse, though, while the boys' mother was out of town visiting relatives, and their father was at work. Kosnoff later recalled that Mary Kay Carter wondered if her sons had a right to file a lawsuit against the police. He told her that she would have to talk to a Michigan lawyer about any claim she thought her family might have. Of course, from his view, legal liability rested with the church, not with the police department. Kosnoff told Mary Kay Carter that Frank Curtis had sexually abused other children before he babysat for her family and that church officials had known about it. Her response was stunned silence.

Now, long after those phone calls, Kosnoff still hadn't been able to get the Midwest story on the record. He'd tracked down the *National Enquirer* story and sent a copy to Mary Kay Carter. Just as she'd said, the story described how Frank Curtis had shown up at a police station somewhere in Michigan. The police hadn't arrested him because any warrants were too old to be valid. The Scott lawyers had gotten an order from Judge Rosenblum to take out-of-state depositions on two bishops, Pearly Hankins, the Evelands in Grand Rapids, plus the

Carter family in Racine. They'd also had to request an order in the circuit courts in Grand Rapids and Racine. This was typically a routine procedure; out-of-state courts didn't care much about a case that was going on in Oregon. But the Mormon church's lawyers had once again challenged the depositions on the basis that they violated clergy-penitent privilege statutes. In Racine, the church had hired a Wisconsin lawyer to represent the Carter family, and he'd added the argument that the depositions were an unnecessary invasion of privacy.

In both states, the church's lawyers had filed exactly what the Scott team feared but also had come to expect—a substantial volume of paperwork arguing why everything the Scott lawyers asked for was privileged communication, followed by all the requisite exhibits that had been gleaned through hours of research. The Scott lawyers would have to respond in kind, with more time and more money. They were now fighting the same lawsuit in three states—Oregon, Michigan, and Wisconsin—each of which was governed by slightly different laws.

The Scott team's evolving time line of Frank Curtis's actions now included a fourth cluster of abuse cases:

FRANK CURTIS TIME LINE OF VICTIMS

1977	Manny Saban, Bobby Goodall, Jim Goodall, and possibly others	Portland
1979	Son of Frank Curtis's friend in the ward	Portland
1982	David Johnson, Steven Penrose, and his brother	Portland
1986–1987	Two Carter boys	Grand Rapids
1991	Jeremiah Scott	Portland

Kosnoff and, sometimes, Salmi would go to Hillas's office in Portland, where they'd attend a court hearing in Michigan or Wisconsin by telephone and try to make a judge halfway across the country understand the nuances of a lawsuit that had been going on in Oregon for three years. There would be more briefs and more answers to briefs in each of the courts, and then they'd all wait while the judges sorted things out.

Kosnoff and his family had scheduled a trip to visit his in-laws, who lived in Wisconsin, at Christmas (his wife, Mary Ann, was not Jewish) and he'd pushed hard to schedule the depositions to coincide with that so he wouldn't have to pay for another flight east. He'd spent so much time on this case already, he couldn't very well tell his family they weren't going.

Another, short-lived plan would have sent Tim Kosnoff and Joel Salmi to Chicago, from which they would drive alternately to Racine and Grand Rapids during the same week. But that didn't materialize either, because the courts were not in sync and the cases in each state continued to drag on.

In February 2001, the Racine Circuit Court scheduled a telephone hearing on the matter, and it seemed as if the case there might finally move forward. When the Scott team received the paperwork from the phone company confirming the conference, they noticed something odd concerning the lawyer representing the Carter family. They knew he was a well-known Milwaukee attorney from a big firm who had defended the Catholic church in numerous civil lawsuits. But the phone number from which he was scheduled to be calling for the hearing was in neither Milwaukee nor Racine. The number was connected to the law firm of Kirton & McConkie in Salt Lake City. There was no longer any question about who was commanding this legal war. Not only did the church have one of the best-known attorneys in Wisconsin representing a third-party witness in a deposition, now they had him traveling to Salt Lake City, evidently to sit with the church's chief lawyers while he attended a hearing in the state where he worked by telephone. Kosnoff and Salmi decided this was a good sign; it showed a high-level concern over the case. At the same time, though, it was a reminder of the apparently unlimited funds available to their opponents. During the hearing, Jim Hillas and Tim Kosnoff participated on the phone, along with the Wisconsin attorneys from both sides. The Kirton & McConkie lawyers remained silent.

There had been another monkey wrench thrown into the works. The church's lawyers filed court papers essentially stating that Tim Kosnoff had harassed the Carter family by phone, even calling under false pretenses. Mary Kay Carter now claimed that Kosnoff had solicited her as a client. Kosnoff filed a sworn affidavit with the court denying all of the allegations. Now they were arguing this in the hearing as well, along with all the clergy-penitent privilege and privacy issues.

To the Scott team's great relief, the Wisconsin judge dispensed with the church's arguments fairly swiftly. "Counselor, anything that's said to a clergyman is not privilege," he said. The judge went on to note the reasons why he had no intention of quashing the subpoena for the Carter family. They would be deposed.

The following day, the church lawyers filed a petition for review with the Wisconsin Court of Appeals, asking that the higher court overturn the Racine circuit judge's order that Mary Kay Carter be deposed. Kosnoff was both angry and energized. They would win this one battle at a time if they had to, he believed, and they were winning. Joel Salmi was a bit dumbfounded by the depth of the fight on the other side. He was keenly aware of how much money the church was spending on this case, much more than it could have settled with them for about two years earlier. The balance on the credit line that he and Kosnoff had taken out to fund the case was growing each month. Jim Hillas was tired, overwhelmed, and worried. Unlike the other two lawyers on the team, he had to answer to the partners of a law firm where he was employed. And he was still a young associate. He hadn't brought this case in the door, but he was in charge of it now. The firm was paying more and more into this case with no resolution in sight. At the same time, they were all basically stuck. They'd invested too much to turn around. The only hope of digging out was to win a judgment at trial.

Kosnoff's way of dealing with the situation was simply to work more, harder. He'd continued to do defense work in the appellate court to make some money and stay afloat, but for the most part, he was living on savings accounts that were supposed to be for his family's future. No matter, the Scott case had consumed him, and he seemed to feel as though he had to personally fend off every attack from the other side. He would find more evidence, more case history, talk to more experts. He worked unceasingly and, while his passion was infectious, it could also be exasperating to everyone else around him. Early in the case, the Scott team participated in a pointless mediation with the church, in which both sides had been light-years apart in their demands. The case was so young that there was really no motivation to continue. Now the mediator had come back with another try at settlement. The Scott team was obligated to take any offer to Jeremiah for consideration, even one that was significantly less than what they wanted. This time, the mediator was floating a number of $2 million. The offer struck a nerve with Kosnoff, who had, by this time, spent more than half a million dollars in time on the Scott case. He was uninterested in settling for a couple of million dollars and exercised over the thought that anyone else on the legal team might consider such an offer as they were marching toward trial. He fired off a hasty email to the rest of the team:

> The defendants' conduct was and is outrageous and 99 out of 100 juries are going to see it that way too. So it comes down to this—where do each of you stand? I need to know and I need to know now. I need to know now whom I am going in to battle with: Neville Chamberlain or George Patton?
>
> . . . The defendants had their chance to settle this case for a few

million dollars on December 1 and that chance is over. It was a one day sale and the sale is over. I went along with it but I will not agree to an endless mediation and settlement process. I just can't function that way. You cannot pursue war and peace simultaneously. It confuses your troops and sends the enemy the wrong message. Ask any Vietnam vet or General Giap [commander of the Communist People's Army during the Vietnam War].

Drama aside, there was reason to believe the case could be won. The mock jurors had demonstrated a willingness to pay out a big settlement. The Racine Circuit Court had ruled in the Scott team's favor, and within a week the Wisconsin Court of Appeals denied the church's petition for review.

Now they faced another judge in Grand Rapids. The court there had found that it could not determine whether or not the bishops were in fact covered by privilege and therefore did not have to testify until it heard the questions. Of course, the bishops were not likely to actually answer any questions because the church's lawyers would direct them to claim privilege, and then they'd all go back to court for the judge to rule on whether that was allowed. Michigan was going to be challenging.

17

Jim Hillas looked at the package on his desk. As local counsel, he was designated to receive such things involving the lawsuit. Its arrival was not a surprise—everyone had expected this, they'd been told as much by the church's lawyers. The shocking part was its size. The neatly formatted volume, complete with little white index tabs poking out of the side for easy reference, was a good three inches high. Nothing about this case was easy, he thought. Nothing. Now they were going to the Oregon Supreme Court.

A month earlier, in January 2001, Judge Rosenblum had finally ruled on the matter of church discipline records.

At about the same time, another unexpected event occurred. A Mormon family unrelated to any of Frank Curtis's crimes filed a petition to the court arguing that they would be irreparably harmed by disclosure of the disciplinary records. Filing anonymously as "John, Jane, and Mary Doe," the petitioners stated that, years earlier, the father had been excommunicated for having committed incest against his daughter.

"Following a period of professional and church counseling and penitence, John Doe was rebaptized and received restoration of blessings from the church," the petition stated. It went on to note that the family had stayed together, that most family members were unaware of the situation, and that those who did know wanted it to remain confidential. "John Doe is rehabilitated and is forgiven by his daughter, his wife, and their church."

Requiring the Mormon church to release its discipline records in Portland would violate the family's right to confidentiality under the clergy-penitent privilege statute, they argued.

Kosnoff thought the petition was ludicrous. It wasn't so much the argument, which he had to admit made some legal sense—the court would most certainly have to weigh the potential of violating other people's rights in allowing Jeremiah Scott's lawyers to collect evidence. But that problem could be easily resolved by having the victims' names removed, something that the Scott lawyers had half expected the judge to do anyway. No, Kosnoff couldn't believe the church would throw out this bit of dirty laundry as a defense. To his thinking, the Mormon church had just announced that it was harboring more sex offenders. Not for the first time, Tim Kosnoff thought that his opponent was hiding something large and significantly uglier than the case they were litigating.

Judge Rosenblum ruled that the LDS church had to produce all records, including discipline records, pertaining to Frank Curtis. She allowed the church to redact some statements made by Frank Curtis that were covered by the clergy-penitent privilege, even though he was now dead. Judge Rosenblum also required the church to produce all reports of disciplinary action relating to alleged sexual abuse of children by anyone else in the Portland area between 1970 and 1995, and all third-party reports of sexual abuse of children made to any church official or representative in Portland during the same time period.

Later, the judge allowed the church to redact information on the "details and circumstances surrounding the misconduct" and statements made at the discipline hearings. Judge Rosenblum also allowed the church to remove the names of victims of sexual abuse but said that the Scott team could petition for those names to be released.

This development was huge. It was what they'd spent untold hours researching, writing, and arguing about for two years. Only now it was on hold. The church's lawyers had petitioned Oregon's high court to overturn Rosenblum's ruling in a legal maneuver called a writ of mandamus, which essentially asks the court to intervene before a legal case is over because there is a threat of irreparable harm.

During the following two weeks, Jim Hillas, Tim Kosnoff, and Joel Salmi worked on a response to the Oregon Supreme Court. Kosnoff spent much of that time preparing for depositions in Wisconsin and Michigan. Hillas was getting buried responding to filings that seemed to be coming in on all sides. Lisa, his paralegal who had worked on this case since its arrival, was managing the filing deadlines in all three states and negotiating the dates for hearings and meetings. The cast of participants had grown to include more than ten lawyers on both sides, plus numerous associates at Bullivant, Houser, Bailey and some law students working as interns that the Scott team had drafted into service. The brown accordion files brimming with paperwork on the case had taken over nearly nine linear feet in Lisa's office at Dunn, Carney. Colleagues noted that it resembled a products liability case, notoriously huge in scope. Joel Salmi had arranged a deal with the landlord of his office building to temporarily use a small empty office down the hall, which became home to all of his work on the Scott case. Tim Kosnoff had moved everything into his home office about a year earlier to save money. Now he was wondering if he should buy a shed.

Thinking back on it later, Jim Hillas would remember a day when he asked David Ernst to stop. Just stop the paper war. They were on the phone discussing some filing that the church was taking to court. Hillas was worn out. "You have to give me a break," he told Ernst, trying to appeal to a fellow professional. The response would stay with him for years. They couldn't stop filing. Hillas believed he knew what that meant: The church was directing the lawyers to keep the heat on.

The courthouse in Racine had both the look and feel of a bygone era of justice. Its marble pillars, tile floors, and heavy wooden doors all contributed to the unmistakable impression that it had been built decades earlier but remained the most important building in a town that was still considered a pass-through between Milwaukee and Chicago. Tim Kosnoff wandered the seventh floor, poking his head into doorways. He needed help.

Kosnoff had come to Racine to take the depositions of the Carter family, whose children had been molested by Frank Curtis while he was babysitting them in the mid-1980s in Grand Rapids. The family had since moved to Racine, and so that's where their depositions would be taken. After all the delays and the court hearings and the motions, they had finally gathered in this courthouse. Kosnoff was accompanied by the local attorney whom the Scott team had hired to represent them in Wisconsin. On the other side was the church's local counsel and David Ernst, who'd flown in from Portland. Greg Foster's lawyer was participating by phone.

Kosnoff would also question Mary Kay Carter's husband, Ted, and one of their sons about the events of Brother Curtis's abuse and their subsequent reporting of it. Mary Kay Carter was more important to the lawsuit, however. She'd told her stake president in Grand Rapids that Brother Curtis had molested her son, providing yet another notice to the church, the Scott team believed, that Frank Curtis was a threat to children.

They were assigned to a small jury room, sparsely furnished with a plain table and chairs. The window offered a gorgeous view across the church steeples of Racine and out onto Lake Michigan. Inside, things were much less peaceful. Kosnoff was getting hammered by the church's lawyers. They objected constantly and instructed Mary Kay

Carter not to answer any questions about what she'd said to anyone about what happened, on the grounds that it was privileged communication. The lawyers also objected to Kosnoff asking Mary Kay Carter to recount exactly what Frank Curtis had done to her sons, on the grounds that it was invasive and unnecessary. But Kosnoff was singularly focused on getting every detail recorded. He was motivated not by prurient interest or a desire to make Mary Kay uncomfortable, as the church's lawyers seemed to think, but rather by a deep fear of missing something. Kosnoff grew frustrated, but also worried. He believed this was important. After all it had taken to get here, he could not go home empty-handed. So Tim Kosnoff went looking for help.

He found the Honorable Emmanuel Vuvunas in his chambers, feet up on his desk, reading a newspaper. Kosnoff introduced himself and reminded His Honor of the case. They'd arrived here following the judge's earlier rulings, after all. Now Kosnoff asked if His Honor would be willing to rule on some of the objections that were being made during the deposition. Judge Vuvunas, whom everyone knew off the bench as "Butch," was nearing retirement from a long and colorful career. He'd long since lost patience with unnecessary complications in court. He liked things straightforward. And so without much consideration, he directed Kosnoff to move the Carter deposition into the courtroom and announced that he'd referee from the bench.

Judge Vuvunas wasn't particularly tall and he'd grown a bit stout over the years, but he was at all times in command of the courtroom. His behavior was legendary. The judge had fooled attorneys who thought he wasn't paying attention, since he sometimes read the newspaper during a trial. The second he heard something he thought was out of bounds, he'd snap into action and surprise a lawyer with a searing glare and a stern warning. Court clerks liked to tell how His Honor once made everyone in the courtroom remain in place after a hearing until his missing football picks were located. For a time, they also called Judge Vuvunas the "Hanging Judge" in reference to his fondness for tough sentences in criminal court. Court reporters routinely omitted the curse words that peppered his rulings.

After Kosnoff and the other attorneys, the videographer, the court reporter, and the Carter family packed up and moved into the courtroom, Judge Vuvunas appeared on the bench, draped in his black robe.

"All right," he said. "What's going on, gentlemen?"

Kosnoff told the judge that they'd reached an impasse and had the court reporter read back the last few questions that he'd asked Mary Kay Carter, which had been to establish whom she'd told about Frank Curtis's abuse and when. He needed the judge to see that Mary Kay Carter's conversation with the stake president was not privileged. The first person she'd called after learning that Brother Curtis had molested her children was another woman in the ward who had children whom Mary Kay knew Brother Curtis had also supervised. (Later, it would become clear that he'd molested those children as well.) She'd wanted to warn the other mother, she said. Mary Kay Carter had then contacted her ward sister Jay Eveland for advice, and then she'd taken her sons to the police station and filed a report. It was after those contacts that Mary Kay Carter talked to her stake president. Judge Vuvunas was trying to get a handle on the time line while the attorneys continued to make their points. Finally, he began to question Mary Kay Carter directly.

"And the purpose [for talking to the stake president] was what? That you didn't want any other children to be in jeopardy?" Judge Vuvunas asked.

"No. So that if Franklyn Curtis was to call them and . . . call him and say . . ." Mrs. Carter said.

"I didn't do this thing," Vuvunas prompted.

"I didn't do this thing or I had a problem at [the] Carters' house so he was aware of what the problem actually was." Oddly, Mary Kay seemed most concerned with how the church viewed her actions in all of this, that she might not be believed.

From there, they went straight into the clergy-penitent issue. Kosnoff had sized up the judge by now and tried to appeal to what he assumed would be Vuvunas's desire to move forward.

"Your Honor, perhaps I could cut this short and perhaps alleviate some of the stated concerns of counsel. . . . All we really need, Your Honor, is that she told [her stake president] about the abuse. That's it. We don't need to get into the nature of the counseling, her feelings, any of the details of that communication, but simply that she told the bishop what had happened." Kosnoff continued, "And I would suggest to you that despite the years that have passed and the way perhaps that she wishes to think about it now, that really her motivation in going to the stake president was to stop this serial pedophile, to get the church to do something, and that's simply not privileged, Your Honor."

Finally, Judge Vuvunas crafted an unconventional solution, but one designed to keep everyone from having to return to Racine. He directed Kosnoff to write down six questions—the questions that the church thought were barred by clergy-penitent privilege—and the judge would ask Mary Kay Carter the questions privately, in his chambers. His court reporter would record the answers but not transcribe them. Meanwhile, both sides would submit their best arguments in briefs on why the information should or should not remain confidential. If the court found in favor of the Scott team, Judge Vuvunas would release the transcript of Mary Kay Carter's answers. If he found for the church, there would be no record of the answers. Kosnoff sat down at the table and wrote his questions on a piece of lined paper from his tablet and then gave it to the judge. David Ernst tried to continue pressing his point about confidentiality, but the court was clearly done.

"There will be nothing transcribed, counsel," Judge Vuvunas said.

"If this shows up in an Oregon transcript—"

"That means they kidnapped my court reporter and beat her over the head to get it from her."

With that, Vuvunas left the courtroom.

They were done in Racine for now, but Kosnoff knew what was coming. More paperwork. He called Hillas and Salmi to break the news. No one was enthusiastic about knocking their heads against the same wall. They were convinced that their position was absolutely right under the law, but still, there were so many battles. It was all just more of the same. Did they really need Mary Kay Carter's testimony? Didn't they have enough already? Or would they risk losing if they started to walk away?

Later that month, Tim Kosnoff looked out the window of his hotel room in Grand Rapids at the Gerald R. Ford Museum across the street and thought the museum would make for a very dull day. He turned back to preparing for the next day's depositions. He'd be questioning two bishops, one who had learned from Mary Kay Carter that Frank Curtis had molested her sons, and another who had counseled Frank Curtis in anticipation of restoring his membership after he'd been excommunicated for molesting children. Kosnoff also planned to depose Jay Eveland and her husband, who was a former bishop.

Kosnoff didn't sleep well on the road. Earlier, he busied himself reviewing his notes, making sure everything was in place, everything was covered. He read and edited the questions he'd prepared. He couldn't risk what he called an "oh, shit moment"—realizing later that something important had been missed. It was all there. He'd talked to Jim Hillas back in Portland, and Joel Salmi in Seattle. They were battling the big and small legal fires across the country by email, but it wasn't yet a big part of daily communication. A Michigan attorney they'd hired would be at the depositions tomorrow, but he didn't know the case well enough to really help with the questioning. The depositions were on Kosnoff's shoulders, and he felt very alone here. He ate dinner, read through his outlines once more, and then put them in his briefcase and tried to sleep, or at least rest.

The next morning, Kosnoff went to the local attorney's office well before the action was scheduled to begin. The videographer and the court reporter arrived and set up in the conference room. David Ernst had once again come in from Portland. The rest of the lawyers and staff slowly filled the conference room. The witnesses were assembled in the reception area. First up was a man who'd been Frank Curtis's bishop and, later, his home teacher. Despite all the clergy-penitent privilege objections by the church's lawyers, Kosnoff was able to get some answers about the time when he was Frank Curtis's home teacher because it was generally not considered a clergy position. The man said that he'd known about Brother Curtis's history of sexually abusing boys, and that Brother Curtis had told the man that he wasn't doing it anymore. Later, Ted Carter, Mary Kay's husband, had told the man that Brother Curtis had grabbed one of his boys and kissed him on the mouth. During his deposition, the home teacher told Kosnoff that he hadn't told anyone about what Ted Carter had said, because he knew that the stake president and the bishop already knew.

"Everybody knew about it, so I couldn't have done anything that hadn't already been done," the home teacher said. "Everybody who should have known, like the bishop, stake president, those kind of people; those people knew. That's all who needed to know. There was no point in me going on with it because the right people knew, and Ted Carter made that clear to me, so I dropped it right there."

Jay Eveland was different from most of the other witnesses who'd been deposed in the Scott case. She and her husband remained solid in their faith but were no longer active in the church. Mostly, they'd been overwhelmed by meetings and helping people—they had five children and had both held numerous leadership positions in their ward. They'd retreated. It so happened that Jay Eveland was also a school counselor who dealt with all manner of family and adolescent crises. She interacted with people in a world outside the insulated Mormon community in ways that few other ward members did. She was not naïve about things like sexual abuse. She'd advised Sister Carter to report Brother Curtis to the police when she called for help that day back in the mid-1980s.

Jay Eveland also had experience with lawyers and the civil justice system. Years before Tim Kosnoff ever contacted her, Jay had filed a civil lawsuit against the Michigan High School Athletic Association, claiming that the organization inequitably administered girls' sports, ignoring recruiting seasons. Four of the Evelands' children were girls, and athletics was their path to college. The Evelands had already been through plenty of legal mudslinging. They had declined the church's offer to provide them with a lawyer for the deposition.

Jay Eveland informed the lawyers in the room that she knew what both sides likely wanted her to say and she didn't care. She planned to tell the truth and let the chips fall where they may. As Kosnoff questioned her, Jay was transported back to a time when she and her husband had hosted Brother Curtis in their home for Sunday dinners. They'd picked him up at his apartment building downtown, near skid row, and taken him to church meetings and services. They'd brought him groceries and given him leftovers. Brother Curtis had sat at their Thanksgiving table. This wasn't at all remarkable. The Evelands had opened their home to all manner of people over the years—ward members, Mormons visiting from out of town, even recovering drug addicts who needed help. This was the way their family operated.

Jay Eveland remained cool and composed as Kosnoff asked question after question, but the truth was that she was furious about the whole situation. She had never met Jeremiah Scott, but it pained her that this boy's life had been ruined. Jay thought she understood how Jeremiah's mother must feel, how difficult this must be for her. Brother Curtis had betrayed all of them. He'd been in the Evelands' home too. She'd interrogated her grown children for any sign that they'd been victims and was satisfied that nothing had happened. Then again, there hadn't been an opening. Jack Eveland used to joke that his wife was so protective, she'd barely let him supervise their children, let alone leave them with anyone else. Their family was solid, unbroken. They lacked the chaos, the circumstance, and the neediness in which Brother Curtis seemed to find opportunity.

But why hadn't they seen it? Why hadn't they known about Brother Curtis? Jay Eveland couldn't let that go. She should have known, somehow, she thought.

Yet the main reason she was sitting in this deposition today was that she'd come closer to catching on to Brother Curtis's evil deeds than anyone else. She was the one, after all, who'd had an inspiration that Brother Curtis shouldn't be around children. When Kosnoff asked her about talking to the stake president, she told the story of how he had told her that her feelings were accurate and that Brother Curtis's file had been flagged. The minute she said it, Jay could tell that Kosnoff was thrilled, though that wasn't her motive. He seemed to be taking this all sort of personally for a lawyer, she thought.

Jack Eveland approached his legal obligation in much the same way as his wife. He hadn't been the one to interact with the church hierarchy on the matter of Brother Curtis, and he hadn't gone to the Carter family's house that day when he was babysitting there. But he'd had plenty of conversations with Brother Curtis. In Jack Eveland's memory, Brother Curtis was a plump guy with a beak of a nose that made him look like Danny DeVito's portrayal of the Penguin in *Batman Returns*. Only he was charismatic. Not necessarily charming, but an interesting old fellow. Brother Curtis had always been vague about his past when they'd talked, saying simply that he'd done things he wasn't proud of. He certainly hadn't mentioned spending decades in prison.

Years later, Jack reflected on the situation with the same puzzlement. If he'd been asked to pick the child molester out of a hundred people, he noted, Brother Curtis likely would have been about the ninety-seventh choice. He was old, grandfatherly. The Evelands didn't know what a pedophile looked like any more than the Carters, or the

Scotts, or anyone else did, but Brother Curtis had never seemed like he fit the picture.

There was no reason anyone in the ward would have known why Frank Curtis had been excommunicated, or that he had been accused of child sexual abuse, unless they'd been told by someone in the church hierarchy. Brother Curtis was assumed to be the same as the people who trusted him. Mormon culture tends to be insulated, and it was even more so in Grand Rapids, long the stronghold of Dutch Calvinists critical of the LDS church. Ward members turned to each other for help and advice. They acted in service to each other, their brothers and sisters, for the common good of their religious community. They shared a specific belief system and a lifestyle designed to exclude the sins of the outside world. And they accepted on faith that their brothers and sisters had been through the same worthiness tests that they had, believed the same things, had the same standards. Ward members believed that their leaders had been inspired by God when they called people into positions of trust. All of this had made them feel safe.

Pondering Brother Curtis's crimes years after his deposition, Jack Eveland offered a troubling observation: The very things that made their religion a strong spiritual community may well have made them vulnerable to the likes of this serial pedophile. "Frank Curtis in the Mormon Church was like the perfect storm."

After the depositions concluded, Kosnoff drove around Grand Rapids, looking for some of the places he'd been hearing about. His flight didn't leave for a while and he had time to kill. Plus he wanted to get to the bottom of something that bugged him. Kosnoff headed toward the police station in the suburb of Wyoming, with the idea of finding out if there was more of a record on Frank Curtis than he'd gotten in his earlier request. A few miles into the journey, though, he was lost in the suburbs. He drove up and down a few main drags lined with fast-food joints and chain grocery stores, and looked at pitched-roof houses weatherized for the hard winters. It was a gray, cold, miserable

March day. He thought about the people who lived inside these houses and tried to imagine Frank Curtis there. There were a lot of Dutch names and more Protestant churches than he'd ever seen. Finally, he found his way to the police station and talked to an officer behind the desk. She looked for records. There was nothing more on Frank Curtis. No one seemed to know anything about him having wandered in, as the *National Enquirer* story had described. Kosnoff had considered that the tabloid had made the whole thing up, but where would the name Franklyn Curtis have come from? Kosnoff decided the old creep must have come in looking for a meal and a bed. But it seemed he'd never know for sure. Kosnoff didn't have the actual article with him and so had been confused. In fact, it had been Detroit where the *Enquirer* reported that Frank Curtis attempted to turn himself in back in 1992. Empty-handed, Kosnoff left and, this time following directions from the police, drove to the airport for a flight home.

Kosnoff could think of countless leads and pieces of evidence to chase down, relics that might tell the story of the crimes of Frank Curtis. But he had never once considered that he might actually hear Curtis's voice, literally from beyond the grave, an encounter that would soon serve to illustrate just how bizarre this case had become.

18

It had not escaped Tim Kosnoff that Franklyn Curtis, although dead, was still in Portland. He was interred in the Portland Memorial Funeral Home and Mausoleum, which is like a city of the dead. The largest mausoleum in the west, Portland Memorial is home to some 80,000 bodies interred on eight floors of winding marble corridors in a building that stretches across two and a half city blocks.

Unbeknownst to Kosnoff, however, Frank Curtis was moving. At some point during the case, the church's lawyers had subpoenaed Frank Curtis's interment records, perhaps seeking information on relatives. (It might have been possible to assign some shared liability to the estate of Frank Curtis in court.) In any event, the subpoena set off a series of unusual events. As it turned out, Frank Curtis had been obsessively concerned with his final resting place. He'd sent change-of-address notifications and letters outlining his wishes everywhere he went. He'd arranged to be interred in the Portland Mausoleum, and then later exchanged that property with a plot in a cemetery on Lake Michigan. But he'd never made any new funeral or travel arrangements. When Frank Curtis died in Portland, the funeral home there had him interred in the mausoleum according to his original plan. Upon reviewing his records to respond to the subpoena, however, the mausoleum's managers realized that Frank Curtis rightfully belonged in the Michigan cemetery. So, while the civil lawsuit over Frank Curtis's legacy of molestation was going on, his body was disentombed and sent by air freight to the cemetery in Michigan where he was buried, and where he remains, in the ground with no headstone.

The estate of Frank Curtis consisted primarily of a cardboard box of belongings, which had been given to the man who'd lived down the street from him years earlier. There were letters and pictures from a man named Keith Webb in Utah. Kosnoff asked Linda Walker to help him track the man down, and she did. She'd first talked to Keith Webb's wife and later connected directly to him. Linda confirmed that he'd met Brother Curtis in the 1970s, while doing missionary work in Portland. Keith had helped Curtis study LDS teachings in anticipation of his baptism and joining the church. They'd kept in touch over the years, through letters and occasional visits, because Curtis didn't seem to have any family.

It was clear to Linda that these people had no clue about Frank Curtis's brutal behavior toward children, and she found herself in the awkward position of having to educate them on the circumstances surrounding the lawsuit.

Keith Webb had ended up with a collection of random souvenirs from the old man, which he promised Linda he'd search through the garage to find. Some months later, Tim Kosnoff received several snapshots, which he added to a small collection of photos that had come from another friend of Frank Curtis's. There was Frank in front of the Mormon Temple in Salt Lake City. Frank sitting in a lawn chair on someone's porch. Frank standing next to a Christmas tree. Kosnoff studied the pictures. Frank Curtis's gray-white hair had thinned over the years, and he wore glasses. He remained a fat man, though.

There was no doubt about that. The buttons on his shirts were often strained.

Along with the photos, Kosnoff received an unexpected, exceptional artifact. As part of his conversion to Mormonism in 1977, Frank Curtis had made an audiotape in which he told his life story, a version that cloaked as much as it revealed. The intended audience of the tape was unclear, but Kosnoff speculated that its creation had been part of Frank's religious studies to advance in the Mormon church. An audiotape might also have been easier for a man with limited writing skills. Kosnoff found a recorder and fit the cassette tape into it.

My name is Franklyn Richard Curtis. Born March the twenty-first, nineteen oh three. Seventy-four years old. I've been asked to state for this particular recording my conversion into the Church of Jesus Christ of Latter-day Saints . . .

Suddenly, Frank Curtis was in the room. The voice was strong but recognizably that of an older man. Well-worn, but not gravelly. His cadence was slow; he often paused between words for no particular emphasis. The voice was sort of folksy sounding, mumbling, Midwestern. Not booming, as others had described. Then again, Tim Kosnoff wasn't a nine-year-old boy. Manny Saban had never been able to stay in the room when the actor Wilford Brimley was on television because his voice reminded him so much of Frank Curtis.

Born Chicago, Illinois. County of Cook. Lived a tough, hard life. Stole everything I could get my hands on. Stole food to eat when I was hungry. Stole because I enjoyed it. Got a lotta whippin's. . . . I'm not trying to excuse it. No one else's fault. Not my mother's. Not my dad's. Or anyone. I choose to do the things I wish to do.

> . . . I did a lot of things, awful lot of things, which I'm ashamed
> of. It's not very nice to tell people that you was once a gangster . . .
> a thief. But ya know, that was life.

Kosnoff was fascinated. The voice on the tape seemed kind of
moronic, but there was some hidden edge layered in Frank Curtis's
voice. Or maybe Kosnoff was imagining it. In any event, he was entirely
focused on listening to what the late Franklyn Richard Curtis had to
say for himself.

Curtis went on to describe how he'd arrived at the Chicago bus
terminal one day in 1976 from Pennsylvania—"Pensy," he called
it. Kosnoff had done enough research to know that Frank Curtis
must have just been paroled from prison. That's when he'd decided
to head west. Some years before, he'd worked in Valsetz, Oregon,
slinging hash in a restaurant and playing canasta in his off hours,
and had always intended to return. His desire to return to the west
seemingly motivated Frank Curtis to get on a bus going to Salt Lake
City.

Aesthetically, the two cities couldn't be more different. Chicago
was gritty, urban, old, and gray. Salt Lake City was clean, crisp, and scenic, with a view of snow-topped mountains from the middle of downtown. Frank decided to stay awhile.

There was one big predicament, however. He was flat broke. But
he was also enterprising. Shortly after hitting town, as Frank described
it on the tape, he headed to the nearest Catholic church and asked for
work, a plan that must have seemed more likely to succeed than just
asking for a meal. It did. Someone put him to work washing windows.
In payment, he received a voucher at the end of the day for a meal and
a room at a nearby residential hotel.

> I didn't want no charity. I work for what I get. . . . They watched
> me but it didn't do no good to watch me because they didn't have

to. I did the job. They were happy enough for a while. They left me alone.

Frank sounded more proud than defiant. He seemed to want to get across the message that he was a man who did the right thing. He made a point of saying that he'd stayed around and washed every window in the church building.

That's the only thing a man's got that don't cost any money. You must keep your word. If you give a promise, you do exactly what you promised to do. Remember that always.

One evening, he'd left his little room in the run-down hotel to find some dinner. Frank described how he watched the people flowing into Temple Square. The massive Mormon complex, rimmed by flower gardens and a wrought-iron fence, takes up about ten acres in the center of Salt Lake City. To the unknowing, it looks a bit like the castle of Disney's Magic Kingdom, and even more so at night, when its tall, pointed spires are lit up and pop out dramatically against the darkness. Tours of the grounds, which include the immense round Tabernacle, home to the famous Mormon Tabernacle Choir, leave every ten minutes. Adjacent blocks house the church's huge headquarters building, library, genealogy center, bank, bookstores, and so forth. Frank was intrigued. He also didn't want to go back to the dismal hotel room. Instead, he fell in line with a tour group and, as its members wandered in and out of the big, beautiful buildings, listened to the fresh-faced young man at the front of the group talk about the history of the Mormon church, its persecuted prophet Joseph Smith, and the word of God.

I had a lot of time on my hands and didn't want to go back to sleep and was wide awake, so I puffed on, and huffed and puffed on my good old cigar and went on in there. I passed the little house and looked around a minute and then I seen these people who were going to get information. I took the cigar and threw it down. I started over towards the information, and I looked back at that cigar . . . that was a half a cigar. So I scolded myself, I said, "Hey, stupid, that would last you all night tonight." Normally I would have went and picked it back up and crushed it out, but I never made no attempt. It felt good. . . .

. . . So I got on the tail end of this sightseeing tour as I call it. You know, when I went into that building where they usually start in the corner, I had to stop 'cause I got hot from my head to my toes. That warm feeling went through me and I almost passed out. It felt good. So warm. I shook it off and says, "I don't know what's happening, but I guess I better go." And we went from place to place. Then, at times, that feeling would come back on me. Sitting in that seat.

I kept listening to the boy talking, just listening to him talk . . . gosh, he knew what he was talking about. I felt that every word he said was a drop of truth, and my mind started wondering why in the world didn't I get to this religion, why couldn't I find it so I could've studied it and learned it many years ago when I was young. Well, at the end I told the fella that I'd like to have a Book of Mormon. I don't have any money, so there was no use asking for none, but I'd like to have one with a little other information. He give me some more information. He give me some people to contact when I told him come willy-nilly I was going to Portland. I'd take that information and study it over. Well, of course I went on back to my hotel. Couldn't understand it. I kept thinking about what I'd seen on my way to the hotel. Went up there and I read the introductory of the Book of Mormon. Read a couple of the brochures, laid down and went to sleep on the subject.

Kosnoff was somewhat skeptical of this endless cavalcade of remarkable circumstances. He believed that Frank Curtis was a con artist of the first order and had by now dismissed any notion that the man was actually moved by religion.

By definition, Franklyn Richard Curtis was a classic pedophile. According to the American Psychiatric Association, pedophiles are individuals older than sixteen who act on recurring and intense sexually arousing fantasies, urges, or behaviors involving prepubescent children. The disorder tends to be chronic, particularly among those attracted to males. It is common for pedophiles to threaten their victims to prevent disclosure. They often develop complicated techniques for gaining access to children, including winning the trust of the mother, or marrying a woman with an attractive child. Frequently, such an abuser is attentive to the child's needs in order to gain his affection, interest, and loyalty, and to prevent the child from reporting the sexual abuse.

Kosnoff continued to listen to the tape. The next morning, a Monday, Frank washed up and put on clean clothes. He packed up his suitcase and headed to the post office. Frank said he had arranged for what little money he had to be sent in care of general delivery at the postal service, and he needed that money to continue moving west. But the deliveries were delayed. On the tape, Frank described how he headed over to the bus station and sat down for a while, and then was again drawn to the LDS Visitors' Center across the street.

I automatically steered toward the ramp that goes up to the statue of Jesus. Now, I had ducked and dodged kneeling for many years, always used an excuse: I'll get a cramp, my legs hurt, or something. But, you know, I knelt down there and nothing hurt me. No worry about a cramp. No worry about any aches or pains. It didn't hit me until I got up after I prayed. I prayed for understanding.

> I prayed for enlightenment. I prayed Lord that if this was the right
> religion let me know. . . .
>
> . . . As I stepped off the escalator, a tremendous thing, this heat
> wave hit my head and feet at the same time and all the swaying
> like I was going to pass out. Everything went dark in my eyes and
> I stiffened a little and I opened them up again and it was this fella
> walking toward me.

Frank explained that he felt dizzy and that his toes were a little
numb. The same thing had happened the night before when he walked
around on the tour. The Mormon man looked seriously at Frank and
told him that he had been called by the Lord. He'd be happy to explain,
the man said, and invited Frank into an office for a presentation.

> Seemed like no matter what he said, it fit the situation I needed
> to know.

Frank told the man that he'd like to learn more, but he was on his
way to Portland as soon as he got his check from the post office. The
man told him that there were people in Portland who could help Frank
get a good start and gave him the name and number of the stake president there, along with those of a few other active church members. He
also gave Frank some literature, including a book titled *A Marvelous
Work and a Wonder*, by LeGrand Richards, a former church elder who
created much of the gospel outline used by Mormon missionaries.

There was a break in the tape, where Frank had evidently stopped
and started his tale again. He described how the Mormon man in Salt
Lake City had taken him to pick up his check. Frank's envelope was
there, he said, but it contained a bank check for $50, not the cashier's
check he'd expected. Frank, who possessed neither a driver's license nor
a credit card, couldn't cash this.

He sounded both dumbfounded and impressed as he described

how the Mormon man had taken him to the bank, cosigned the check so that Frank could cash it, and then took Frank out to lunch. It was clear that such a gesture had been an exception in Frank Curtis's life. The man was a bishop in Salt Lake City. The title impressed Frank, who had grown up a Catholic. A bishop, in Catholicism, is a fairly high rank, essentially the head of a geographical region of parishes.

The story continued. Their stomachs full, Frank said, the men shook hands, and the bishop pressed $30 into Frank's palm. He'd evidently balked enough to make a show, but accepted. It would get him some food later. The bishop also reminded Frank to contact the Mormon leaders in Portland.

> . . . I says, "I won't waste a minute." Thanked him in a way. On the way to the bus station I looked at what he give me. I think it was two and a half. I'm almost certain now. This was a long time ago but I'm certain it was.

Frank read a little of the book that the bishop had given him on the bus between naps. Given Frank's limited education, this would have required a fair amount of patience and effort. By the time he arrived in Portland, as his story went, Frank was eager to connect more with these generous people.

In Portland, Frank called one or two of the church members from the list the bishop had given him. They connected Frank to a local bishop. The man found Frank a place to sleep and some work cleaning a small diner downtown, for which he received meals.

> I worked and worked all the time. I moved the things slowly and cleaned up and he kept marveling at the fact that I took my time but I progressed fast. . . . Got near noon and they fixed up a lunch for me and man was I hungry. Yeah, I showed him what it was, quit fooling around and eat. I really ate.

Frank spent a few days in the small room of a fairly seedy joint nearby. Seedy was familiar enough, but the smell of stale booze and cigarette smoke and the loud noise bothered him more than it used to, when he was younger. The bishop in Portland connected Frank with what amounted to an LDS employment agency. One thing led to another and, within a few days, Frank was hired as a kennel helper at a Mormon veterinarian's clinic in the southeast part of the city, where there was an apartment for him in the back.

. . . He asked me one strange thing. Are you a man of your word? I says of course I am. That's the only thing a man has is his word. He may never have no money but if he keeps his word he's a man. He says that's fine. He said I have to go home and pray with my wife about this. We'll let you know tomorrow. You call me. I said that's fine.

In his mind's eye, Kosnoff could see this all unfolding. The tape was largely irrelevant to the lawsuit, and Kosnoff thought it was more of a reflection on the church. This had been such a part of Frank Curtis's many seductions, how he'd become accepted, pitied, even liked by the people who'd brought him into their homes. Kosnoff wasn't drawn in by the voice on the tape recorder, but he could imagine how Frank's folksy charm and pseudoshame over his mysterious, dark past could make him seem an interesting, if quirky, character.

After a couple of days in his new home in Portland, Frank said, he received a call from a church elder, wanting to visit. Elders are Mormon men who do particular jobs in the church—in this case, act as a visiting teacher to check in on members of the flock and teach Mormon principles. Frank was lonely and eager for company. This visit would mark the start of Frank's Mormon education, during which a young Keith Webb and a Mormon elder came to the veterinary clinic for an hour or two a few days a week trying to get him to understand the Book of Mormon and connect to the Lord.

> Two wonderful kids [the elders] and they went through their routine. They give me these lessons. I had them there every day that they could come. If they missed a day I worried about it, but they came and they asked me one day, "Are you ready to accept the Lord? Are you ready for baptism?" I says Lord I thought you would never ask. You're driving me crazy taking so long. You coulda' asked me a week ago. Oh, they were happy.

After a few months, Frank was baptized in a ceremony that was, by his choice, performed by the Portland bishop who'd found him a home.

Mormon Doctrine, a classic work on the beliefs of the Church of Jesus Christ of Latter-day Saints, written by elder Bruce McConkie, a longtime member of the governing body of the church, describes the ritual that Frank would undergo: "He has become a new creature of the Holy Ghost: the old creature has been converted or changed into a new one. He has been born again: where once he was spiritually dead, he has been regenerated to a state of spiritual life. In real conversion, which is essential to salvation, the convert not only changes his beliefs, casting off the false traditions of the past and accepting the beauties of revealed religion, but he changes his whole way of life, and the nature and structure of his very being is quickened and changed by the power of the Holy Ghost."

On November 27, 1976, according to his church membership records, Franklyn Curtis was baptized into the Church of Jesus Christ of Latter-day Saints in the Linwood Ward in Portland. Two months later, as his education and conversion continued, Frank received the Mormon priesthood through a sustaining vote of the local ward membership. Technically, as a priesthood holder, Brother Curtis had been given the authority to act in God's name.

Now Frank Curtis talked about how pleased he was to have attained priesthood status. The brotherhood of Mormonism also brought with it friendship, something he'd not known for a long time. He was invited to Thanksgiving dinner at the Portland bishop's house and to Christmas at the vacation home of his boss, the veterinarian, in the LDS enclave of Sandy, Utah.

Shortly after his baptism, Frank Curtis was summoned to the bishop's office. Frank evidently wondered if he'd done something wrong, but he wasn't sure what that might be. He went to the small office in the ward building, which wasn't far from the animal hospital. The bishop seemed to be in a good mood, which he took as a positive sign.

The bishop, Frank said, asked some casual questions about how things were going at the animal clinic, and whether Frank had been able to keep meeting with his religious teachers. And then the bishop told Frank that he'd been called to be a Primary (Sunday school) teacher and a "special interest leader" for adults. The latter merely meant that he would be on hand if they needed to fill in a program in a pinch. The former choice, though, was because the bishop apparently thought Frank would do well with boys.

> . . . He set me apart for the Aaronic priesthood and I thought that was the ultimate of success, the finest thing that could happen to me. Gosh, I was wrong because when I got the Primary call and the special adult call I thought that was a step higher and beautiful.

Things progressed rapidly. Within months, Frank moved on to hold the Melchizedek priesthood, a higher designation typically held by men of a certain age, and then was called to be an elder.

The next thing happened is I got called into the bishop's office and he says, I'm going to recommend you for an elder. A lump jumped in my stomach. I couldn't say nothing for a few seconds. I took a deep breath and I says I sure thank you. He said I gotta ask you some questions personal. And I said you just ask any questions you want. I've got the answers in my heart. He says I feel that you have. So I gave 'em.

Frank Curtis was installed as an elder during a church conference the following week.

. . . They asked all the priests that were there, all the elders and whoever was in the place, they said Franklyn Richard Curtis of the Linwood Ward has been recommended to be an elder. All those of you who can sustain it please raise your hand. And I was scared. I closed my eyes. I held my hand up—they told me I should vote for myself—and then he'd say, "Any against?" and I waited. Nobody was against it. I sat down with a sigh of relief. Rushed back home. Got out of there.

It seemed clear that Frank was insecure about his status in the church. There were moments, Kosnoff thought, where Frank nearly disclosed something and then backed off. A year after he became an elder, Frank Curtis had sat for a worthiness interview and received approval for entrance into the Mormon Temple in Salt Lake City, perhaps the most sacred place in Mormonism.

I said to the bishop, you say you want to interview with me. He says you bet ya. So after Sunday school I went into his little office, we sat down. He says I want you to understand I have to ask these questions. They're serious, they're personal. And I said, "Bishop, there is nothing that you can ask me that I don't have an answer for from the bottom of my heart." He said I believe you sincerely that you do. So he asked me the normal questions which I had the answers because I had been as good as a human being can be.

If I laid none of the major things, might have thought things now and then, but I begged the Lord for forgiveness. But other than that, I done exactly that. I never turned a call down and anything they asked me to do in the church like I was supposed to. I sustained the presidency. I sustained the bishopric. I sustained everybody from the top to the bottom. What could I say that was wrong? So he said, well, you'll have to see the [stake] president and get an interview with him. I says, "Hey, leave that to me, doc." I said, "Give me that little piece of paper that you got there and I'll dash out and take care of it."

Frank Curtis must have been given a Temple Recommend, because on the tape he was talking about having participated in a sacred Mormon Temple ceremony in Salt Lake City with the family of the veterinarian who owned the clinic where Frank lived. Apparently he'd forgotten to pack the special temple garments necessary for this event, and there was some kind of scramble for a replacement, but it was too small. With some help, Frank Curtis stuffed himself into these new garments so as not to miss participating.

Oh, but I wasn't going to miss that for nothing. And I tell you one thing, at the end of all the fine things that was done, I passed through that veil it seemed like I went from the tortured world into tranquillity. Smooth everything felt. No more sick, no nothing. I was at peace with the world. I can't just explain, but that, my friends, I can say was the ultimate in the greatness of things that could happen to me. . . .

. . . It was about the last part of the session there I got sick in my stomach, and I was afraid I was going to vomit, so I had to be very careful. And I got through, and I didn't get to stay for the sealing of their family of children, which, uh, which hurt me. But I was sick, and I was afraid of ruining their rugs. Ah, it's beautiful in there. So I dashed out and changed clothes, but I got out. I got my stomach settled down a little and I wouldn't tell them any more after that, about that one time that I tried to make sure nobody would worry about me. They treat me like their own granddad. That's a wonderful feeling.

19

When Tim Kosnoff walked into the law office of David Slader in the spring of 2001, he came as not just a lawyer but also a salesman. He was there to sell the Scott case.

It had become increasingly evident that Kosnoff, Salmi, and Hillas needed help. *Jeremiah Scott v. Gregory Lee Foster, The Church of Jesus Christ of Latter-day Saints, et al.* appeared finally to be heading to trial. And they were outgunned. Preparing for a trial of this size would require more lawyers, more staff, more money, more everything. Their opponents had a seemingly unlimited budget and at least two major law firms working on the lawsuit. Joel Salmi and Tim Kosnoff were paying interest on a credit line that was nearly $85,000, and that wasn't counting all of Dunn, Carney's investment or anyone's time. They were in this case for several hundred thousand dollars. Kosnoff had sensed fatigue, which in dark moments he interpreted as doubt, from his colleagues.

Another turn of events made it necessary to seek help. Kosnoff had known for a while that Joel Salmi was becoming disabled. They'd been walking back from lunch one day and Kosnoff noticed that his friend was having difficulty making it up the sidewalk, which was odd. A college athlete, Salmi had always been a formidable opponent on the racquetball court when the two men played. Salmi explained that he had a form of muscular dystrophy. He'd watched other family members struggle with this degenerative disease for most of his life with the knowledge that he too would one day lose mobility. The fatigue and the aches had already arrived. Long before the Jeremiah Scott case had consumed the lawyers, Salmi and his wife had planned to take their children on a trip through Europe during the summer. If they didn't go now, Salmi feared, he couldn't go later. He'd told Kosnoff and the rest of the Scott team that he wouldn't be able to take the case into the courtroom. Without Joel Salmi, they didn't have an experienced civil litigator on their side. After some deliberation, they decided to seek a new partner. The logical choice was an experienced trial lawyer from a firm that could bring in resources. And that would no doubt mean selling a hefty part of their interest in the outcome of the lawsuit. As a contingency case, the lawyers would receive a percentage of any award above the actual costs of the lawsuit, which they'd been funding.

Kosnoff had been talking periodically to David Slader and had outlined the case to him over the phone. Slader and another lawyer named Jeffrey Anderson in Minneapolis had litigated a number of civil cases against the Roman Catholic Archdiocese of Portland. Kosnoff thought Slader might be interested because the case was in Portland. He wasn't entirely sure of the odds of Anderson taking the case, however. Anderson was legendary in legal circles for having sued the Catholic church all over the country. He had represented more than four hundred plaintiffs, for whom he'd won close to $50 million in settlements and awards. He was famous for having boldly sued the Vatican, and for bringing the media spotlight onto the Catholic church for harboring and hiding priests with a history of abuse. He and Slader had represented plaintiffs in lawsuits that had recently been rolled up into one big settlement involving forty victims. They were still working on some later cases when Kosnoff contacted Slader, and then Anderson, who suggested they all meet at Slader's office.

Like Kosnoff, David Slader had started as a criminal defense lawyer in Chicago and then moved west to Portland. He'd represented juvenile victims in sexual abuse cases early in his career, and it had stuck. Slader had become an expert in the laws around sexual abuse and remained attached to the work in various ways, regardless of where or what kind of law he was practicing.

Slader's office was located in the former Portland Police Department headquarters, a fact that was memorialized in the brick exterior. The office staff had to regularly reassure clients that there were not, in fact, police there anymore. After the introductions, Kosnoff began his presentation on the Scott case and how it had evolved—what they'd found, how they'd approached it, everything they'd learned in the depositions, how the church had reacted, and so forth. He'd chosen a dark suit for the meeting, which had the effect of making him look stylish and European. Anderson was short and trim, and practically percolated with energy. He was leaning forward in his chair, hanging on Kosnoff's story. Slader had a slower, calmer manner about him. He was a beefier man, his face framed by gray hair and beard, and could look at once disheveled and wise, sort of professorial. He had turned to Anderson in the Catholic cases in much the same way that Kosnoff was now turning to both of them. Slader, who was Jewish, had been accused by critics of being anti-Catholic, which he believed was unwarranted. He liked the idea of representing victims against some other religious institution.

Jeff Anderson liked Tim Kosnoff immediately. Kosnoff reminded Anderson of himself. Anderson also had started his career in criminal defense work and then had taken on civil rights lawsuits. Among other things, he'd handled a lot of police brutality claims. Then, in 1983, a friend referred a young man to him who had been molested by a

Catholic priest in Minneapolis. Anderson agreed to represent the man and blindly walked into a challenging institutional abuse case. And then something completely unexpected happened. Anderson caught a Catholic bishop lying under oath in a deposition. The church offered a large settlement, attached to a confidentiality agreement, but Anderson advised his client that taking it wouldn't do anything toward fixing the problem. To take a confidential settlement, Anderson had reasoned, would perpetuate the secrets. Instead, he called the newspapers. That was the beginning.

Now, listening to Kosnoff, Anderson sensed a kindred spirit. Later, he would refer to Kosnoff as "a pit bull with brains." He was impressed by the depth of Kosnoff's research, with all the information he'd unearthed, with his passion. About ten minutes into the meeting, Jeff Anderson had decided that he wanted to work with this guy.

Anderson had never sued the Church of Jesus Christ of Latter-day Saints, and he didn't know much about the Mormons. There wasn't a big Mormon population in Minnesota. But he'd heard that the Mormon church had sex abuse problems. He'd had calls every now and again about a Mormon complaint, but he'd never been able to participate for one reason or another. Linda Walker had, in fact, talked to Anderson on the phone years earlier, when she was working on other cases. Anderson had read a couple of books about Mormon history. Together with the information that Kosnoff had learned, this intrigued him. The Scott lawsuit easily met Anderson's criteria for jumping in, which was that he believed it could both help the survivors and further the greater cause of stopping institutional abuse. Jeff Anderson no longer got involved in run-of-the-mill lawsuits.

"Yes," he said, after Kosnoff finished. "We'll help you."

Jeff Anderson would forever remember watching Tim Kosnoff physically change in the room that day. Anderson thought Kosnoff looked a bit like he possessed a winning lottery ticket. His excitement and enthusiasm were renewed. Help was on the way.

With Jeff Anderson and David Slader on the plaintiff's side, the feel of the case changed immediately. There still wasn't a balance between the opponents, given the resources of the LDS church, but this was no longer David vs. Goliath.

Anderson was a general. He directed strategy and watched the big picture. He didn't get involved in the groundwork. That was left to Slader and Kosnoff, and to a lesser extent Jim Hillas, who'd been glad to hand over much of the local work to Slader's office. Kosnoff, Salmi, and the Dunn, Carney lawyers had given up a big share of any future award to get Anderson and Slader on board, but everyone agreed it was the smart play.

The first order of business was a complete assessment of the Scott case and where things stood in each state. Anderson and Slader both recognized an eerily familiar path of a scorched-earth defense, though they were surprised by the unrelenting nature of the assault. This defense was more intense than anything they'd seen in Catholic church cases. The Scott team was getting hammered with motions on all sides. The church was making clergy-penitent claims everywhere, and the real legal issues seemed to be clouded by red herrings like the fight over what happened with the investigators, which Anderson paid no mind to, having determined that it was unimportant to the case. He often called clergy-penitent privilege "the shield and the sword of the church," saying that churches had "used and abused the privilege in gross and obscene ways" to keep from having to testify in civil lawsuits. The Mormon situation was different from that of the Catholic church because of its lay, and rotating, clergy. There was less clarity around who was legitimately covered. Also, the Church of Jesus Christ of Latter-day Saints was controlled from its headquarters, whereas each Catholic diocese was its own corporation and answered for itself. The Mormon church was self-insured and therefore under no pressure from an insurance company to handle lawsuits in any particular way.

Anderson's first step was usually to map out an extensive battle plan, but the Scott team had collectively done so much work already that this was largely unnecessary. The new strategy was simple: They must go from being on the run to chasing the other side. The path to changing position was through punitive damages. Moving the request for punitive damages forward was crucial. It was the game changer. It would motivate the church.

There was also a legal issue that needed to be refocused. A seemingly innocuous change would make an enormous impact in fighting the church's First Amendment arguments. As they all knew, legal interpretations of the Free Exercise Clause had established that religious belief was protected by the Constitution, but potentially harmful actions were not. The courts were very particular in how they applied this belief-versus-conduct standard. The LDS church had argued, for instance, that it had a constitutionally protected right to practice redemption—the "clean slate" argument—and in doing so, call a rebaptized Frank Curtis into a leadership position within the church. Legally, it was right. The courts had established that placing someone in an ecclesiastic role was an extension of belief, an internal move done in the exercise of religion, not an action. But doing so was not without responsibility. Once Frank Curtis was placed into the position, the legal argument went, the Mormon church had an obligation to see that he didn't molest more children. The argument that Frank Curtis should not have been called to a position where he had access to children could lose. The better argument was that the church allowed him to molest: The church failed to warn others, failed to supervise Frank Curtis, failed to protect children.

Jeff Anderson also wanted to dismiss Greg Foster as a defendant. This was part of streamlining the lawsuit, something that typically happens as a civil case heads closer to court. Anderson liked having an unambiguous enemy. It was easier for a jury to understand. The message was simple: The church knew that Frank Curtis had molested children, kept records on him, put him in the path of more children, and kept it a secret. The church was responsible. Greg Foster and all the other bishops, he reasoned, were merely pawns in the operation.

In May 2001, Greg Foster was dismissed as a defendant in the lawsuit upon the agreement of both sides.

Slader's Portland office became the new Scott war room. Boxes and boxes of papers arrived from the other lawyers and were stacked around the room. A table in the center of Slader's office was the center of a brief-writing machine designed to force the opposition into responding instead of initiating. Anderson was on the phone with Slader and Kosnoff daily. Slader was on the phone with Hillas. Salmi, too, continued to weigh in on the legal briefs. The Scott team started a small flurry of motions to push the case forward.

The church still had not provided the discipline records that Judge Rosenblum had ordered produced and were attempting to modify the order. The Scott team asked the court to sanction the church, arguing that it was in contempt of court for not following the judge's orders. Small matters were resolved and things kicked into action with hearings and a trial date on the calendar.

As part of a larger campaign to clear up all the outstanding tasks that had been put on hold for lack of manpower, or just because they weren't urgent, the Scott legal team obtained Frank Curtis's patient records from the nursing homes he'd lived in toward the end of his life. Included in these files were medical records from a few times that Curtis had been hospitalized over the years. His medical history contained a surprising, if not downright odd, revelation: He'd had three penile implants.

According to his medical records, Frank Curtis had undergone a cancer-related prostatectomy in 1970. At some point—there was no date noted—he had also undergone an orchiectomy, removing testicles. Doctors routinely performed both procedures simultaneously then, as a precaution to prevent cancer from recurring. The prostatectomy would have likely been the reason for the initial penile implant, usually installed in a surgical procedure within a couple of years of prostate surgery. Since such prostheses were fairly new in the early 1970s, they often ended up needing to be replaced after malfunctioning or because of some medical complication, such as an infection.

The information prompted both shock and minor horror among the Scott legal team. The boys from the Portland neighborhood where Frank Curtis had lived in the 1970s had remembered him having had some urology-related surgery, but that's all anyone had known until now. The implants certainly helped to explain Frank Curtis's continuous sexual activity during his advanced years. Although, based on the victims' testimonies, there had been less evidence of Frank Curtis having achieved erections as he got older. David Johnson, who was molested in the early 1980s, had remembered Brother Curtis achieving erections. He and one or two others had testified that the man had attempted to anally rape them. But Jeremiah, molested in 1991, had distinctly remembered that Brother Curtis had been incapable of an erection. Much of Frank Curtis's sexual activity with boys had involved oral sex, digital penetration, and fondling.

A couple of the boys from the mid-1970s in Portland had remembered visiting Frank Curtis in the hospital about the time that he married Raquel Saban, when Frank indicated to them that he was having some surgery to fix his genitals. That was likely one of the implant surgeries, which meant that two were accounted for. The third remained a mystery. One clue might have been that Frank Curtis had a pacemaker installed in 1987 while he was living in Michigan. Doctors would not likely have undertaken any implant surgery on an eighty-four-year-old patient with a pacemaker, which left a window between 1978 and 1987.

Even early penile prostheses—usually fairly simple bendable silicon devices—were not obvious, certainly not to someone under the age of thirteen. Later devices were more commonly inflatable, involving a reservoir of saline tucked away in the abdomen. These required the user to squeeze a pump in the scrotum to cause an erection, but none of this was readily detectable. There would have been no reason for any of Frank Curtis's victims to know anything about any prosthesis.

From a medical standpoint, the more interesting information was the orchiectomy. Removing the testicles—castration—results in a plunge of testosterone (the point of the surgery is to deprive the prostate cancer cells of testosterone, which fuels their growth) and a decrease in sex drive. Many experts in sex offender therapy argue that castration doesn't stop a pedophile's desire for sexual contact with children, because the behavior is not driven solely by hormones. Frank Curtis seemed to have proved that theory. In any case, the first surgery had erased Frank Curtis's hormonal ability to have sex, while physiologically enhancing that ability. Whatever the psychological mysteries of this paradox, the net effect was to enable Curtis to pursue his victims deep into old age.

The next question was who had paid for all these surgeries. Frank Curtis was a pauper as far as anyone knew. Two theories floated among the Scott team. Either the government, through Medicare, or the church, through its welfare system, had paid for Frank Curtis to get penile implants, they figured. While the latter was an intriguing idea, there was no evidence to support it. More likely, Medicare had paid the bill because all the surgeries had stemmed from the initial cancer treatment and were therefore not likely considered elective. Kosnoff sent off requests for Frank Curtis's Medicare records, but getting anything back was a long shot since the records were now thirty years old. And, in truth, they didn't need this information anyway. The implants were a curiosity, to be sure, but they had nothing to do with the legal issues in their case.

Linda Walker waited in the lobby of her hotel in Portland for the lawyer she'd talked to over the telephone for three years. There had never been enough money to fly Linda to Portland, and so she and

Tim Kosnoff hadn't met until he walked in the front door. Kosnoff was shorter than she'd imagined, and she hadn't put gray hair on him. She was smaller than he'd expected. They were an odd pair, the chatty grandmother and the crusading lawyer, off on an adventure. Kosnoff drove her to Felony Flats, where Manny Saban and Bobby Goodall and the other boys Frank Curtis abused in the 1970s had grown up. They went to the veterinary clinic and the creepy junkyard apartment. They went to the trailer park where Frank Curtis had lived and where he'd molested the Penrose and Johnson boys, and another place, where Frank had lived when he left the Scott family. There, they knocked on doors, looking for anyone who remembered something. Linda was good at this sort of groundwork. She could talk to anyone and usually get a response. It was hard to ignore Linda Walker when she got her mind onto something. She'd spent so many years making calls and walking precincts for politicians that talking to strangers was second nature.

Linda and Kosnoff had another reason for an outdoor adventure that day. After the Scott case had been in the newspapers a couple of times, Kosnoff had received a call from a woman who claimed that she and her sister had been sexually abused years earlier by a man named Manuel Ulibarri, their Mormon home teacher. Her parents said that they had told their bishop about the abuse when they learned about it from the older daughter, but that the bishop had instructed them not to go to the police, saying the church would handle the situation. And then the younger girl was abused. Again, the family had notified their bishop, but nothing happened. More than a decade later, the church finally put a note in Ulibarri's file indicating that he should not be given assignments that put him in contact with children.

Kosnoff thought that he and some of the lawyers on the Scott team might represent the sisters. And then he got an idea to borrow a tactic he'd seen the police use. In his criminal defense practice, Kosnoff had represented a lot of clients engaged in growing and selling marijuana.

Often, they'd gotten busted because they'd basically told the police what they were doing. It worked like this: Police officers would show up at the door, without a warrant, and tell a client that they knew he was growing marijuana inside. They'd ask if they could come in and look around at the operation. Inevitably, the clients would acknowledge their crime and agree to let the police in. There was no need for a warrant.

Kosnoff and Linda went to Manuel Ulibarri's home and knocked on the door. Kosnoff introduced himself and told Ulibarri that they knew he'd molested the girls for many years and that they were filing a lawsuit against the Church of Jesus Christ of Latter-day Saints because church officials knew about the abuse and allowed Ulibarri to continue doing it. Kosnoff told Ulibarri that he was trying to understand how and what the church knew about what he was doing. Sure enough, Ulibarri spilled his whole story, about how he'd molested the girls and had gone through counseling with the church and had repented. Oregon law required only that one party consent to a conversation being tape-recorded, and Linda captured the entire conversation. They managed to conceal how surprised they were at how well this plan worked. Kosnoff was quite pleased with himself for having pulled off an investigation tactic that he'd borrowed from his former opponents.

David Slader's paralegal, a particularly capable woman named Dawn Krantz-Watts, who'd also worked in criminal defense law, functioned as his assistant, chief investigator, and scheduling monitor. She also handled the clients. That was their routine. She would call the clients every week or so to check in on everyone to make sure someone wasn't in crisis or missing, and to keep people on track with appointments. Shortly after talking to Tim Kosnoff about the case, Slader and Dawn drove up to Washington to pick up some files from Joel Salmi's office and meet with Jeremiah Scott.

They met at some nondescript chain restaurant in Bellevue. Jeremiah was accompanied by his girlfriend. Everyone had been skeptical about her motives for no good reason other than the simple fact that Jeremiah was a plaintiff in a civil lawsuit from which he might earn a significant amount of money. Attorneys are all too familiar with the increased popularity that sometimes comes with the promise of an award, and so they tend to be wary of newcomers, whether or not such skepticism is warranted. Jeremiah wore glasses, which aged him slightly, but he still looked significantly younger than his twenty-two years. He and his girlfriend were about to move to California, where he would study photography, an idea that had been met with conflicting emotions by his lawyers. They wanted Jeremiah to succeed, to heal, and to move on with his life. That's what the lawsuit was about. But it would be hard to manage appointments and court appearances with his living so far away. Also, it was apparent that the lawsuit had dragged on so long that Jeremiah was moving on without a legal resolution. He had an increasingly different life now than he'd had when he'd first called Tim Kosnoff four years earlier. The evolution would only speed up with the move to California. He was less attached to the civil suit he'd started.

Slader and Dawn found Jeremiah to be as impassive as they'd heard. He was polite and asked numerous questions about what these new lawyers were bringing into the game and what was going to happen. He seemed concerned with protecting his relationship with his father, who was remarried, had started a new family, and was climbing the ranks in his Mormon ward. Kent Scott continued to oppose the lawsuit.

Dawn thought Jeremiah was working hard to seem confident and later concluded that he was nervous about going to trial. The lawyers had speculated on whether their opponents would make an issue out of Jeremiah's conviction for molesting the boy in his mother's day care at trial. Conventional wisdom dictated that it was risky to attack a victim, because a jury could punish an attorney for harassing a sympathetic victim. Slader thought that, given Jeremiah's young age, a jury would easily see his crime as an extension of his abuse. The Scott lawyers were even prepared to argue that Jeremiah's conviction and the subsequent hell that went along with it was part of the overall harm done by the church.

On the way home, Slader and Dawn talked about how Jeremiah would hold up as the intensity of the lawsuit increased. He was going to have to be evaluated yet again by yet another psychiatrist. It was part of the process that each side was allowed to repeatedly pick apart his emotional state. Jeremiah was obviously wounded and shut down, but would a jury fully understand this pain if he remained stoic on the witness stand? One thing was certain: The plaintiff's side needed to get to trial. Everything weakened with time—memories, emotions, connection to the issues, people's resolve. The church's strategy to drag out the process until there was nothing left of the case might work.

20

In March 2001, the Utah Supreme Court handed down a ruling that prompted a frenzy of emails among the Scott team. The court had reviewed a sexual abuse lawsuit against the Church of Jesus Christ of Latter-day Saints there and upheld a lower court's dismissal of the case because the First Amendment prevented the courts from intruding into the practice of religion. Would this affect the Scott case? Kosnoff was worried. He conferred with Slader, who was less worried. Ultimately, they concurred that Utah was too far afield, even though it was a Supreme Court decision. The complaint in the Utah suit was sufficiently different from their case. But the event served as another reminder that there was no room for error.

The legal standard for punitive damages in the state of Oregon dictated that Jeremiah Scott, through his attorneys, had to prove "a reckless and outrageous indifference to a highly unreasonable risk of harm" and that the LDS church acted "with a conscious indifference to the health, safety, and welfare of others." The Scott attorneys agreed that meeting this standard was a slam dunk. They had plenty of evidence that the church had known that Frank Curtis was a pedophile for more than a decade before he committed heinous acts of sexual abuse against a young Jeremiah. Church officials never warned members that Brother Curtis posed a danger, nor did they ever report him to the police. The Scott lawyers would later write that "in cloaking Frank Curtis with the garb of religious authority," the church held him out as a trusted elder in the ward. Parents invited him into their homes and left their children alone with him because of the high regard that Frank Curtis had enjoyed.

The bigger task at hand was determining how best to present the facts, first to Judge Rosenblum, who would have to rule on whether the Scott team could seek punitive damages, and then to a jury that would have to award them. Negligence was one thing, but the Scott lawyers knew that anger would motivate a jury to punish the church with an award. Anger would come, they believed, from all the evidence that the church had known for decades about Frank Curtis and what he was doing to children.

Since he'd handled nearly every deposition, it made sense for Kosnoff to mine the transcripts for information that they'd need to use in the argument. He also reread his collection of Mormon literature and the bishops' handbook for relevant passages. Despite the newfound motivation that had come with Jeff Anderson and David Slader, Kosnoff couldn't shake his exhaustion. The Scott case had by now taken over nearly his entire legal practice. And in some ways, he joked with friends, this was probably for the best, because if he'd had any other significant cases at this point, they'd likely be in tatters.

He and Linda Walker were talking and emailing. It helped to be able to bounce things off someone who wasn't also consumed with writing a brief. Linda had been working on a lawsuit in California involving a Mormon bishop who was also a doctor. The man had lost his medical license for abusing his female patients, most of whom were members of his ward. Linda had worked for the lawyer of one of the victims, but the case was winding down. With the new funding that came along with his new partnership, Kosnoff had been able to rehire Linda to do work on the Scott case again.

They'd discovered another group of victims in Sheridan, Wyoming, where Frank Curtis had moved after he'd left Portland the first time, when he'd been caught by Raquel Saban. Linda had searched everything she could think of and finally found a contact with archived telephone directories that dated back decades. She'd had the directories searched using an old address for Frank Curtis, one that was on his membership records. A few steps later, they were in the thick of yet another abuse scenario, this one particularly awful.

Frank had moved to Wyoming in the late 1970s, after Raquel Saban caught him in the bathtub with a neighborhood boy. Church leaders there had arranged for Frank Curtis to move in with a large family who lived in a house owned by the bishop and another man in the ward. Brother Curtis had molested three of the children in that family, two of them girls. This was the first time the Scott team had heard of Frank sexually abusing girls. Linda located one of the victims in a Utah prison, where he was serving time for having sexually abused his daughter and a friend of hers. This man's father also had served time for having molested girls in the family.

Yet another victim from the same time period was serving time in an Oregon prison. He'd started doing drugs in the fifth grade and never stopped, and had been convicted on drug-related charges.

Also, in the past few months, Linda Walker had found and Tim Kosnoff had interviewed more of the boys from the neighborhood in Portland where Manny Saban and the Goodall brothers had grown up. Among them were three more victims. The record of Frank Curtis's sexual abuse was growing bigger all the time. By early 2001, with these new victims in the picture, the time line looked like this:

FRANK CURTIS TIME LINE OF VICTIMS

1977–1978	Manny Saban, Bobby Goodall, Jimmy Goodall, and four other boys (including the boy Raquel Saban saw in the bathtub)	Portland
1979	Son of Frank Curtis's friend in the ward	Portland
1980–1981	Two girls and a boy in one family, and another boy in the ward	Sheridan, WY
1982–1983	David Johnson, Steven Penrose and his brother	Portland
1986–1987	Two Carter boys	Grand Rapids
1987–1988	Two children of another family in the ward	Grand Rapids
1991	Jeremiah Scott	Portland

The sexual carnage of Frank Curtis seemed to never end, and Kosnoff was starting to feel something like abuse fatigue. For the most part, it was Linda and Kosnoff who interacted with the victims, and he was swimming in their stories and the wreckage of their lives. This saturation of grief and suffering made him quicker to anger at his opponents. The other lawyers noticed that every time Kosnoff dove into another victim's story, he became more wound up. The reaction was understandable but also made him hard to deal with. Privately, they often wished Kosnoff had a mute button. He was taking every move from the church personally. There was no question that Kosnoff's passion was the horsepower that had driven them this far, particularly through the hellish months of assault. Yet he seemed unable to distinguish the niggling annoyances from strategic hits anymore. The lawsuit had drained his emotional energy and left him raw. He would blow up, cool off, and then blow up again. He was tired, impatient, and irritating to everyone around him. He wanted more, and they just didn't have any more to give.

During his son's break from school, Kosnoff took his family to Disneyland for a few days. In an uncharacteristic move, he did not check email or talk to anyone connected to the Scott case for nearly five days. Everyone was happy for the break, though they knew it would not last.

Jeff Anderson wore his cell phone on a holster. He was on it constantly, talking to lawyers all over the country. He was so used to speaking to the media that he'd developed a habit of spelling the names of everyone he mentioned. He'd come to Portland for a strategy meeting, and he was pacing around Slader's office directing the action. Anderson was an effervescent man with wispy blond hair around a face that had history. He wore crisp shirts that bore his initials and, often, suspenders. People described him as intense only because they couldn't come up with a stronger word. Anderson was a legendary energizer who worked sometimes sixteen hours a day in the thick of a legal case. He also traveled constantly, an unavoidable part of the greater campaign, despite raising six children. A decade earlier, his own daughter had been abused by a therapist who was a former priest. He emerged from the heartbreaking experience with the unique viewpoint that he believed allowed him to relate better to his clients. Anderson rarely started a case anymore; instead, he typically parachuted in to help plaintiff's lawyers who were underwater against big opponents in institutional abuse lawsuits. He liked to say that he'd worked sex abuse cases longer and made more mistakes than anyone else. There was another reason behind Jeff Anderson's willingness to jump into someone else's case, though. Big legal fights over issues of clergy-penitent privilege and First Amendment interpretation tended to be appealed to higher courts. There was always the possibility that a less-experienced, outgunned attorney would lose one of these battles in a higher court where the verdict would set a precedent that would affect similar lawsuits in a way that was harmful to plaintiffs for years to come. So, as much as anything, Jeff Anderson joined lawsuits to protect legal theories and future clients.

He also liked Portland. The weather was significantly better than in Minnesota and the city accommodated his quirky personal schedule. A recovered alcoholic, Anderson regularly attended AA meetings. He'd replaced other addictions with exercise and worked out for an hour or two every day. He didn't sleep much, nor did he often eat lunch. But he read obsessively. In Portland, Anderson could work late, visit Powell's City of Books late into the night, and then jog through the warehouse district around midnight before going back to his hotel.

On a Saturday morning, the entire Scott legal team convened in Slader's office. Tim Kosnoff, Joel Salmi, Jim Hillas, and Jeff Anderson were all there, along with the two paralegals who had managed the operations and the materials and the multitude of other parts of the process. They were facing the biggest court hearing in the case, the arguments over punitive damages.

The Oregon Supreme Court had refused to hear the church's mandamus petition requesting a review of Judge Rosenblum's decision that it must produce the disciplinary records. Rosenblum had agreed to some modifications, such as redacting victims' names, in response to the petitions from other Mormon families concerned with privacy. Finally, facing possible contempt sanctions, the church had produced its Record of Disciplinary Action for Franklyn Richard Curtis, and a similar record of other sex abusers who'd been excommunicated in Portland during the years they'd agreed upon.

The records showed that the church had disciplined Frank Curtis three times, two of them excommunications. After the first excommunication, which occurred in Pennsylvania in 1983, he'd gone through ecclesiastic counseling and was rebaptized in Michigan in 1984. The final excommunication was after he had been convicted of abusing Jeremiah Scott. But there was a surprise in these discipline records: Brother Curtis had been disciplined for "homosexual acts." It had been the sin of sexual activity with another male for which he'd been stripped of his Mormon church membership, not because he'd molested children. On one occasion, the record stated "homosexuality/child molesting," but the words "child molesting" had been crossed out.

No one was quite sure what to make of this. Homosexuality is a grave sin in Mormonism, to be sure. The church devotes immeasurable energy fighting gay rights in political arenas. But surely this notation in the records had to be some sort of administrative shorthand. Who knew? Anderson and Slader were equally perplexed. This was an odd wrinkle. In any event, they figured that a jury would not like the church having apparently been less concerned that Frank Curtis's victims were children. Everyone agreed that the discipline record should be enlarged and used as a prop in the courtroom.

As morning turned to afternoon, the room buzzed with energy. Everyone contributed, regardless of position or pecking order. Papers lay stacked and scattered everywhere. The lawyers wrote thoughts and ideas on a flip chart that stood near the conference table. Various members of the team filled a whiteboard on the wall with lists and tasks. Everyone was assigned responsibilities. Information and theories flowed out of Kosnoff like he was purging some inner poison. He and Slader had butted heads earlier, mostly owing to style conflicts. Slader may have been a bundle of nerves internally, but he operated with a decidedly low-key style that was as annoying to Kosnoff as his demanding drive was to Slader. But not today. Today they were a team. Slader possessed an encyclopedic knowledge of Oregon law as it pertained to abuse. Kosnoff knew the facts of the Scott case better than he knew most anything else. Salmi and Hillas, who had experience on the defense side of civil lawsuits, sharpened the team's arguments. Anderson orchestrated the show and contributed direction. Paralegal Lisa Thomas, who'd kept track of things with military precision during the previous three years, impressed the entire room with her command of the case. Together, they were a formidable force, and it began to feel like they could make the church pay for its sins with Frank Curtis. It began to feel like they could win.

Tim Kosnoff was a news junkie. The sound track of his daily life was an amalgamation of radio, television, and Internet broadcasts. But on the morning of the punitive damages hearing, he drove from his hotel to the courtroom in silence, sipping his Venti Drip from Starbucks. He wanted to avoid any outside distraction, any other information that required processing. His brain was engaged in the case of Jeremiah Scott and nothing else. He arrived early, as always.

David Slader and Dawn Krantz-Watts followed a ritual they'd adopted years before and performed prior to every trial or important hearing. They walked from the office to the courtroom, which was several blocks, in silence, each carrying a briefcase. Anderson came from his hotel, pumped like a prize fighter ready to enter the ring. Hillas and Lisa Thomas walked from their office nearby. Secretaries, assistants, colleagues, and everyone who knew anything about this case had come to watch the hearing on punitive damages. The lawyers exchanged only small talk, and little of that. Intelligent discourse threatened their focus.

Stephen English and David Ernst arrived with Randy Austin and another lawyer by the name of Von Keetch from Kirton & McConkie in Salt Lake City. Keetch was a senior partner at the firm, known for his work on earlier abuse cases against the church. If Kirton & McConkie was the Mormon Death Star to plaintiffs, Keetch was its Darth Vader. He'd graduated from Brigham Young University and its law school, and had clerked for Supreme Court justices Warren Burger and Antonin Scalia. Keetch was the church's constitutional expert. When the case of Jeremiah Scott came across his radar, Keetch had been presenting an argument in support of the Boy Scouts of America's right to exclude homosexuals from its ranks, a matter pending before the U.S. Supreme Court. Keetch took a seat in the back of Rosenblum's historic courtroom.

The Scott team had prepared props for this event. Slader in particular liked to use all kinds of media and exhibits to keep a jury engaged. This fit with his general old-school style of courtroom theatrics. One poster board was a blowup of Frank Curtis's discipline records, which showed that church leaders had held hearings on the subject of his abuse, which ultimately led to his excommunications. Another was a time line of Frank Curtis's activities that included symbols of stop and yield signs along the way to illustrate where the church could have stopped Frank Curtis before he got to Jeremiah Scott. The time line also featured a picture of a young Jeremiah, in backpack and sneakers, looking like he was off to the first day of school. It was a not-so-subtle reminder of the innocent child he'd been. Slader had made a rubber stamp that read "Do Not Allow Unsupervised Conduct with Minors," which he planned to use in trial to illustrate how the church could have kept Frank Curtis away from the children in its wards, even after he'd repented and been rebaptized. This strategy also allowed the Scott lawyers to steer clear of any theological arguments.

Jim Hillas had spent days preparing for his portion of the argument. He'd made an outline, reviewed the bullet points, analyzed what he thought Judge Rosenblum would do, and then reviewed the arguments that they'd crafted in earlier briefs. The Scott case was permanently etched in his brain. He wanted to be short and direct in his presentation. He was nervous but also confident. Everyone on the Scott side thought they had a compelling case. As taxing as it had become, this was the most exciting case Hillas had ever worked on.

If Judge Rosenblum found that the Scott lawyers could seek punitive damages from a jury to punish the church, they believed it would change everything. The church could end up facing a big payout, to be sure. But the lawyers had theorized that there was something more motivating about punitive damages in the Scott case. Oregon law dictates that if a plaintiff is allowed to seek punitive damages, then the plaintiff is also allowed discovery into the defendant's assets to determine what amount would be an appropriate punishment. The church had never opened its books. The assets of the Church of Jesus Christ of Latter-day Saints remained a well-kept secret. Conversely, if the court found against them, the Scott team would have to scramble to get the church to move forward in the case. There would be little reason for the church to offer anything, and the Scott team would have to rethink their entire strategy.

The courtroom was alive with anticipation. And at the same time, the moment seemed almost surreal. There had been so much planning, scheduling, and general buildup to get to this hearing. How strange actually to be sitting in court watching the drama unfold.

Judge Rosenblum entered and things began promptly. She was elegant with a firm hand. One at a time, the Scott lawyers presented the parts of their case. Their points were refined and straightforward: The Mormon church had documented knowledge that Frank Curtis repeatedly raped and sodomized young boys and never made a single report to the police, which would have saved numerous victims from harm; Greg Foster never mentioned that Frank Curtis had a history of sexually abusing children when Sandra Scott conferred with him about bringing Curtis into their home; and the handling of Frank Curtis was consistent with a pattern and practice of failing to report, warn, and otherwise prevent the sexual abuse of children. In an insular religion with tremendous emphasis on worthiness and position, the Mormon church had held these men up as trustworthy. They were, in effect, LDS-approved. But the star of the show was Exhibit A, the poster-size discipline records. Slader reinforced the point with a show of the records of other people whom the church knew to be molesters and who were potentially still working with children.

When they were finished, Stephen English made an impassioned argument about the First Amendment and the Mormons' right to practice their faith and their belief in redemption. It was a similar refrain from earlier hearings.

"They punished him under Church law, he was forgiven, he repented, and he was rebaptized. And the Church believes that when that occurs that he becomes a new person and you start from there. I realize this is hard because intuitively you say, 'Well, gee, you can't do that.' But that's where we talk about the First Amendment. . . . This is how we do it in our religion."

This was about more than just baptism. The argument spoke to the fundamental Mormon belief that people are called into positions in the church through an inspiration that a church leader received from God that such a person is worthy of being there. The unspoken end to the phrase is that someone has been called "by God."

There were no surprises here. The defense's best strategy was attempting to persuade the judge that the entire case was an intrusion into religious belief, that she was being asked to regulate the practice of forgiveness and the cleansing of sin. The more they could keep the case centered upon religion, where constitutional protections existed, the better.

In the lead-up to the hearing, the LDS lawyers had outlined their points in volumes of briefs: "The law does not require churches to abandon the mission of saving sinners or to become mini-police states in order to avoid punitive damages," noted one point. There was no evidence, they argued, that the church had intended to commit harm. These were matters of "ecclesiastical cognizance, not legal issues for the civil courts and juries." The church maintained that Greg Foster did not know Frank Curtis's history of molesting children when he spoke with Sandy Scott about Brother Curtis moving in. A church cannot be held liable for the harm that one of its members visited upon other members, they argued.

The Mormon church had done more than any other organization to prevent child sexual abuse, its lawyers wrote. They pointed out that Mormon religious teachings include a very strict sexual code. "Any form of sexual relations outside marriage is sin of the most severe nature in the sight of God and the Church. Indeed sexual transgressions are considered more serious than all sins with the exception of murder and denying the Holy Ghost, and members who engage in such conduct are subject to Church discipline."

For all of the church's arguments that religion could not be brought into the courtroom, there was a lot of religion in the defense briefs. The lawyers noted the church's hotline for abuse, a resource for bishops dealing with abused victims in their wards. They pointed to the hotline as an example of the Mormon church's commitment to protect children. The Scott team had heard this before and argued that the hotline was an avenue to control lawsuits because calls were directed to the church's lawyers. The church was using the hotline example to counter the absence of any formal training among its leaders, but in so doing, it eloquently articulated the problem in a brief filed before the hearing: "To attempt to train butchers, bakers, doctors, lawyers, accountants, farmers, etc.—all of whom can serve as a bishop—to be experts in dealing with the emotional, psychological, and legal complexities that any instance of abuse presents would be an exercise in futility."

The hearing ran for more than an hour. And when it was over, the Scott team left the courtroom full of promise. They'd done a good job. The law, they thought, was on their side. But Judge Rosenblum hadn't ruled. She'd taken the arguments to ponder. A reporter from the *Oregonian* who'd been in the courtroom asked the lawyers a few questions about the case. Local media and the *Salt Lake Tribune* had reported on the court case earlier, when the court had ruled that the church had to produce its discipline records. Anderson and Slader wanted to increase the media exposure. They'd used the media successfully to keep pressure on the Catholic church in their earlier lawsuits, as well as to find other victims. Both sides held forth in the hallway, pointing out the merits of their case and answering questions until there was no one left but the lawyers.

A couple of months after the punitive damages hearing, Tim Kosnoff was in an ice-cream parlor in Seattle when his cell phone rang. He'd taken his son there for a treat late one June afternoon. Since the hearing, things had been temporarily quiet in the Scott case. The trial was set for August 20, 2001, only two months away. The call was from Slader, with news from the court. Judge Rosenblum was going to rule in favor of their punitive damages motion: They would be able to ask a jury for punitive damages against the church. In one sense, this news was not a surprise. No one could see, legally, how the judge could have ruled against them. But there had been so many unexpected twists in the case that Kosnoff no longer believed anything would happen the way it should. He stood there, elated, still trying to take it in. But there was another aspect to the ruling on punitive damages: The court clerk had signaled that Judge Rosenblum was going to issue an order that was more complicated than just an approval of their motion to amend the complaint. No one knew what this meant.

At the same time, Rosenblum was dealing with another matter. She would seal the church's discipline records, which the Scott team was not at all happy about. They wouldn't be able to focus media attention on what they'd planned to show was a long history of placing children in the path of child molesters. But that was a small loss. The ruling on punitive damages meant their lawsuit had just become very big. Still, as the court proceedings seemed finally to be heading in the direction they'd hoped, the Scott team had no idea just how complicated this case would get.

21

The Columbia River Correctional Institution in Portland is a minimum-security prison. Tim Kosnoff had traveled there for Bobby Goodall's deposition. As a defense lawyer, Kosnoff was certainly familiar with prisons of all kinds. Robert Eugene Goodall was also familiar with prisons. He'd spent the majority of his adult life locked up, after having spent time in Portland's juvenile facilities. At thirty-two, Bobby Goodall had the distinction of having lived in every prison in the state of Oregon. At present, he was housed at the South Fork Forest Camp in Tillamook, a minimum-security arrangement in which inmates worked on state forest and parklands, mostly clearing brush and trees, and cleaning up the riverbeds. Some maintained a fish hatchery. When needed, they fought fires. Bobby had made his way to the outdoors, even in prison. Someone within the Oregon State Corrections Department had wisely realized that Bobby, who had collected some firefighting experience and was a self-taught outdoorsman, was both an asset and a better inmate when he was working outside. Bobby's days passed quickly there. He rose around five o'clock, ate breakfast, and boarded a prison bus for the day's assignment. He and the rest of the inmate workers put chain saws to unhealthy trees, planted new ones, cleared vegetation, and occasionally constructed buildings at campgrounds. At four o'clock in the afternoon, they rode the bus back to the prison, where they cleaned the equipment, ate dinner, and went to sleep.

Years before, Bobby had capped off a career of drug-related crimes with a second-degree-assault conviction that earned him an eight-year minimum sentence. He'd ended up with an extra two years because his psychiatric evaluations had indicated that he was an angry, emotional mess. He'd finally earned release in 1998. Tim Kosnoff had found him during his short time on the outside that followed. That's when they'd first talked on the phone. Afterward, Bobby had been busted for possession of methamphetamine, violating his probation. He was back inside for another two years. He'd been brought to Columbia River for his deposition. Bobby was wearing his prison look. He sometimes called this part of himself "Prison Bob." He wasn't a large man, but he looked somewhat menacing. Cold. Prison Bob had a steely glare behind his glasses. Tim Kosnoff was there when he arrived. The Mormon church was represented by a new, younger lawyer from Bullivant, Houser, Bailey named Scott Brooksby.

Kosnoff led Bobby through his background, the facts about growing up around Duke Street with the rest of the boys from the neighborhood, and his older brother, Jim. Bobby had been among the youngest and most abused of Frank Curtis's victims, and this became more evident as he answered the lawyers' questions. As best he could remember, Bobby was eight years old when Brother Curtis began coming to his house and talking to his mother. The old man would tell Bobby's mother that he was leading a group of boys on one or another church scouting activity, and he persuaded her that it would be good for Bobby to come along. Brother Curtis had remained a fixture in his life, off and on, until he was about thirteen. During his deposition, Bobby had a hard time keeping track of dates and assigning events to them. He had trouble focusing and got confused trying to follow the questioning. It wasn't that he didn't know the answers so much as he couldn't narrate the story in a linear fashion. He remembered fragments of scenes and pieces of information and was still trying to figure out how to put it together. This was working well for Brooksby—the more Bobby Goodall came across as confused and unsure, the less reliable he'd be as a witness. Kosnoff saw it as more evidence of the wreckage.

Bobby had spent time in Brother Curtis's apartment at the veterinary clinic, at the junkyard apartment, and a couple other locations. The last place he'd seen Brother Curtis was in an apartment complex that had a swimming pool. He and some other boys were brought there to swim in the summer. Kosnoff questioned Bobby about having gone to church with Brother Curtis. He remembered going to two different Mormon wards with the old man, and that he'd been in a Sunday school class with other kids there. Kosnoff wanted to get at the fact that people in the Mormon ward would have seen Frank Curtis with Bobby and the other boys.

Brooksby questioned Bobby about the sexual abuse he'd endured. What followed, through broken answers and disconnected dialogue, was an agonizing tale of evil. Brother Curtis had raped, sodomized, and performed all manner of sexual acts on Bobby over a period of about five years. So many times he couldn't keep track, and in so many locations he couldn't remember them all. There had been no way for a little boy's brain to make sense of it. None of the boys had known much about sex to begin with. Curtis would do these things to Bobby one week, maybe for the whole week, but sometimes not again for the rest of the month. Bobby remembered the time at the junkyard apartment when his brother, Jim, went after Brother Curtis with a baseball bat because it had made Bobby start to realize that the things they were doing constituted some dark, sinister act that made him bad. Complicating matters, Brother Curtis had given the boys beer and wine, and

Bobby had been drunk regularly throughout elementary school. Drugs followed soon after.

Brooksby pressed further on the sexual abuse, asking more detailed questions about what happened where and when. Bobby was getting rattled and angry. His answers were less clear and he was frustrated. He'd never talked about these things in such detail.

Kosnoff jumped in. He didn't like Brooksby and thought he'd crossed the line of what was needed, trying to make Bobby blow up. And there was a good chance he might. Kosnoff had had plenty of clients start firing f-bombs and go after a prosecutor. Bobby had demonstrated through his earlier criminal career that he had anger management issues. Kosnoff figured this was sure to end badly. There were two parts to his next course of action. The first was to get in Brooksby's face a bit, stop his questioning, and take the heat off Bobby for a while in hopes that he might regroup. A few minutes earlier, Kosnoff had decided that he was willing to call a halt to the entire deposition and risk whatever court action might follow if the judge ruled against his objections. So Kosnoff objected again and again, making small speeches about how the ugly details of Bobby's sex abuse were irrelevant and Brooksby's approach was causing him undue stress. But Brooksby wasn't backing down, for obvious reasons. Any jury could see that Bobby Goodall had been horribly harmed just from the facts. It could be important to impeach Bobby as a witness, to neutralize his testimony.

"This is a discovery deposition," Brooksby said. "And, you know, unless it's attorney-client privileged, or there's some other legitimate basis for you to instruct the witness not to answer, I think I'm entitled to ask him the questions. And the fact that they're difficult or stressful is not a basis for instructing him not to answer."

"Yes, it is," Kosnoff replied. "Yes, when you're questioning an adult child-sex-abuse victim about events to which he has never discussed in this level of detail, has never received any therapy for, and is at the point where he feels that he cannot sufficiently deal with the questioning by virtue of the emotional and psychological reaction that he's having, then I think that questioning is rising to the level of harassment of the witness . . ."

And so it went back and forth for several minutes.

The second course of action was to take Bobby Goodall out into the hallway and try to calm him down. Years later, Kosnoff would still remember the conversation they had in the prison hallway outside the deposition room.

"He's trying to push your buttons," he said to Bobby. "He's trying to do what they always do, which is to make you feel bad. It's defense lawyer bullshit. He's trying to get your goat. Don't let him. Keep your cool."

Bobby knew Kosnoff was right. He knew how to do court, and this wasn't all that different. They came back into the room and he sat down.

"I'm sorry to get upset," Bobby said.

"How many times do you think he abused you or improperly touched you?" Brooksby continued. "Can you give me an estimate?"

"Hundreds."

The deposition continued on from there.

Jeff Anderson couldn't believe what he was hearing on the phone. Judge Ellen Rosenblum had ruled that the plaintiffs could seek punitive damages against the Church of Jesus Christ of Latter-day Saints, and at the same time, she'd held off on allowing the Scott team to proceed with discovery on the assets of the Mormon church. In the meantime, she had ordered both sides to meet with a specific pair of mediators—Ann Aiken, a federal district court judge, and Lyle Velure, a circuit court judge in Eugene. Judge Aiken had dismissed the same case out of federal district court more than three years earlier because of jurisdiction issues. The coincidence was odd, but then again Judge Aiken had never ruled on any of the substantive issues in the case.

The pair had worked together numerous times before in mediating complicated cases. Not by coincidence, Anderson assumed, they had worked with him and David Slader in crafting their multicase settlement of abuse cases with the Archdiocese of Portland. In that situation, however, Anderson and Slader had chosen the mediators. This was weird. Jeff Anderson had never been ordered into a specific session with court-appointed mediators. He believed that Judge Rosenblum was sending a very clear message: End this case. Clearly, she had followed the law as she saw it in ruling on the punitive damages, but she wanted the case settled before the Scott lawyers started digging into the church's assets. The issues would almost certainly get messy with yet more constitutional questions involving a megacorporation formed around ecclesiastic pursuit. It was hard to imagine that the framers of the Constitution envisioned this situation.

But Kosnoff and Anderson wanted nothing to do with a settlement. They were going to trial. The point was to change the way the church handled sex abusers and their victims, and that would happen, the Scott lawyers believed, only if the truth was revealed in court. Slader and Hillas wanted to get the church into court as well, but they were less interested in a bigger crusade. This was about winning the most they could get for their client.

The Scott team would go to the mediation, of course. They had no choice. But they were not interested in settling *Jeremiah Scott v. Gregory Lee Foster, The Church of Jesus Christ of Latter-day Saints, et al.* Quite the opposite, in fact. In the wake of Judge Rosenblum's ruling, the Scott team amended their complaint to include damages of $1.5 billion. As far as any one of them knew, this was the closest a plaintiff had gotten to forcing the Mormon church to reveal its inner workings and its finances. With the trial date quickly approaching, the Scott lawyers were ready to swing for the fences. They could think of nothing that would keep them away from a jury that would surely be as outraged as they were by the church's actions. It was all about their client now.

22

Eugene, Oregon, is about two hours south of Portland by car, at the end of the lush and fertile Willamette Valley. It is a college town, home to the University of Oregon's nearly three-hundred-acre campus and some twenty thousand students. Eugene is also home to a division of the United States District Court for the District of Oregon, which is where Judge Ellen Rosenblum sent the Scott case for mediation. Specifically, Rosenblum sent the lawyers to Judge Ann Aiken's chambers in the federal courthouse. Jeff Anderson flew to Portland from Minnesota and then drove to Eugene with David Slader and Dawn Krantz-Watts. Jim Hillas also drove from Portland. Joel Salmi and Tim Kosnoff flew in from Seattle. And Jeremiah Scott flew in from his new home in California. He would have to participate and ultimately decide on any settlement, if one was offered.

Everyone spent the night at the Hilton hotel in order to be at the federal courthouse first thing the next morning. There was noticeable stress and nervousness among the Scott team, and Jeff Anderson was increasingly wary of what was to come. The fact that they'd been ordered into a very specific mediation with court-appointed mediators did not sit well. It meant that they'd already lost a measure of control and Anderson fully anticipated that there would be pressure to settle. Slader also was concerned about what was ahead. Lyle Velure, in particular, was a zealous mediator and Slader worried that Velure would come down hard on Jeremiah to take a deal. For his part, Kosnoff was furious. They'd already been through two failed mediations, and the church had been unwilling to offer anything close to what the Scott lawyers thought a jury might award. Now that Judge Rosenblum had ruled to allow punitive damages, that figure had grown. Kosnoff viewed the exercise as a waste of time, another stall tactic. They were too close to trial. After years of slow, torturous paperwork, they would be able to have their chance in the courtroom. They should be preparing their case for the jury.

The day had gotten off to a rough start. Dawn, who had been tasked with the job of driving people the short distance from the hotel to the courthouse, had overslept, which was uncharacteristic of her. She'd called Slader in a panic and there was a scramble to get everyone organized and moving after breakfast. In the courthouse, the men all headed up the stairs except Salmi, who waited for the elevator. Today was not a day that Joel Salmi could climb stairs.

Dawn arrived a short while later and attached herself to Jeremiah. It was her job to stay with the client. That was always her job. She was the hand-holder. She would sit with him, talk to him, and procure water, snacks, or whatever else he needed. Really, she was monitoring Jeremiah for the lawyers, to make sure he wasn't freaking out. The drama of the whole scene, the gaggle of suited lawyers in the federal courthouse with two judges, was often enough to set a client on edge. By now, Dawn and Jeremiah had become friendly acquaintances. She'd called him weekly, even when there wasn't anything new to say.

Jeremiah seemed nervous. As part of mediation, the plaintiff in an abuse case typically has to talk about what happened to him and say what he wants to get out of the lawsuit. After all of the deposition questions and the psychological examinations he'd already been through, Jeremiah would likely have to share, yet again, the details of what happened a decade ago in the blue house with Frank Curtis. Still, whatever sort of examining would happen during this mediation was likely to be significantly less difficult than taking the stand at trial, where he would no doubt be grilled by the church's lawyers in a public courtroom. In some ways, it was a warm-up.

The Scott team was ushered into Aiken's conference room and took seats around a large rectangular wooden table. The walls were lined with bookshelves. There were no windows. The room connected to Judge Aiken's chambers, which was decorated with photographs and awards. Today it would serve as the center of these negotiations. The opposing side occupied a room down the hall. The Scott lawyers didn't know exactly who was in the other room. As the day wore on, it became a kind of sport to add a new name to the list as someone was seen in the courthouse.

Stephen English and a handful of lawyers from Bullivant, Houser, Bailey were there, as were Von Keetch and Randy Austin from Kirton & McConkie. Someone recognized the head of risk management for the church, whom the Scott side had deposed earlier.

The proceeding wasn't the sort of arrangement in which representatives from both sides sit down together at a table and hash things out. Instead, everyone stayed in their respective camps, and the mediators moved from one to the other trying to get each to a point of agreement. Sometimes one or two representatives would be summoned into chambers for a more intense chat. For all the rules of procedure in the civil process, there are virtually none governing mediation, except that what happens must remain confidential. Given the stature and tenure of Aiken and Velure, there was an understanding that the mediators could influence the Scott case with a phone call if one side or the other didn't play ball.

The process starts with a kind of assessment of the strengths and weaknesses by both sides. The Scott team had agreed that the strength of their case was in all of the prior notice that church officials had received about Frank Curtis's proclivity to molest children. They had deposition testimony from three families in Portland and Michigan who had told church leaders, and there were records that showed Frank Curtis had been disciplined for molesting children. No one had warned the Scott family or anyone else. And Frank Curtis had been allowed access to yet more children. The weaknesses in their case included Jeremiah's conviction for fondling the boy in his mother's day care, and the fact that Sandy Scott had moved Frank Curtis into their home, into her son's bedroom, after Bishop Foster told her that he didn't think it was a good idea to have the man live there.

Ann Aiken and Lyle Velure had sort of an odd-couple routine. Aiken came across as an understanding, if disappointed, maternal figure. Velure was bombastic. He was a big man with a big voice and could, by his very presence, be intimidating. He also had a sort of crass good-old-boy style. He was known to tell bad jokes and talk about football during mediation. Lawyers sometimes referred to the pair as "Mom and Dad."

From the start, the mediation was significantly different from Slader and Anderson's negotiations with the Catholic church, over which Aiken and Velure also had presided. To begin with, no one in the Catholic cases had been ordered to be there, and the lawyers had chosen the mediators. Ending the Catholic cases had been more of collaboration and included several conditions aside from the money; victims were allowed to be heard, and the church apologized. There had been a more compassionate focus. This negotiation felt like a hardball business transaction.

The day wore on. Aiken and Velure came and went; they cajoled and threatened. The lawyers easily recognized hyperbole and bluster, but Jeremiah was listening to everything too, and much of the scripting of the mediators was likely for his benefit. Mediators talked of settlement figures in the millions, and the grueling ugliness of a trial.

In the conference room, the lawyers kept up a running sound track of small talk. They discussed current events, gossiped, and told stories about other cases they'd been involved in or had heard about from other lawyers. Jeff Anderson was a bundle of energy. Periodically, he'd walk in the hallway. Kosnoff too was climbing the walls. He didn't like being a hostage in his own case. Every so often, he'd rant about the unfairness of being forced into this situation and threaten to leave. Joel Salmi usually calmed him down and then they all got to talking about something else.

The mood got tenser in the afternoon. The Scott lawyers figured the church didn't want to be subject to an asset examination that came with punitive damages, nor did the church want its discipline records in front of a jury, and that would motivate the defense to make more serious offers. But that was only speculation. Given the church's history of dragging everything on as long as possible, it was also conceivable that the church's lawyers would appeal Judge Rosenblum's ruling on the punitive damages, effectively keeping the Scott case on hold indefinitely.

And then, without warning, a confluence of small events created a storm inside Judge Aiken's chambers. Years later, no one would fully understand what, exactly, happened, only that the entire weird event caught everyone completely by surprise.

Jeremiah left, possibly to go to the bathroom. For no good reason, he ended up in the judge's office, without his attorneys. At the same time, Kosnoff had stepped out of the judge's suite to do something. A few minutes later, Slader and Anderson learned that Jeremiah was in chambers alone with the mediators, panicked, and also went into the judge's chambers. A heated exchange broke out between the lawyers and the mediators. Jeremiah became uncharacteristically visibly upset.

Kosnoff returned to the conference room dumbfounded, learned what was going on, and eventually joined the scene in chambers. There was more arguing among the lawyers and the mediators. And then, in the middle of all of this, Jeremiah said something loud and clear: "Stop."

Jeremiah Scott was done. He didn't want to go to trial. He didn't want this case to go on one more minute. He'd aged, changed, moved, and moved on since the day he opened the phone book and made the call to Tim Kosnoff four years before. Now he just wanted the whole thing to be over. The Church of Jesus Christ of Latter-day Saints was willing to pay him $3 million to end the lawsuit. He wanted to take it and go away. His attorneys explained that there would likely be other, better, offers and that they believed he would win if they went to court. *Jeremiah Scott v. Gregory Lee Foster, The Church of Jesus Christ of Latter-day Saints, et al.* was an important case; it had become so much larger than one victim's compensation. But there was no case without a plaintiff. As much as they were invested in this crusade, the lawyers had to listen to their client. And he was telling them to stop.

The deal had been made. Three million dollars proffered and accepted. The process dictated that a formal settlement document would be prepared in the coming weeks, sent around and signed, and then a check would be sent from the church, through its lawyers, to Jeremiah's attorneys. After the bills were paid, Jeremiah would get his money.

There were no handshakes between sides. In their earlier cases against the Catholic church, Slader and Anderson had been used to some representative from the other side, often a Catholic bishop, coming into the room to talk briefly to the victim, express sympathy for what the victim had endured, despite having been legal opponents up until a few minutes before. But there were no apologies from the Mormon church. Years later, no one on the Scott team could remember even seeing their opponents as they left the courthouse that day.

The LDS church's lawyers wanted a confidentiality agreement as part of the deal, but the Scott team held firm. Jeremiah Scott had won the largest reported individual settlement in a sex abuse case involving a religious institution to date. This fact was part of the victory. The Scott team insisted that the settlement be made public—no secrets or no deal. The lawyers tried their best to put on celebratory faces, for Jeremiah's sake. He had to feel good about this. The outcome was, in fact, good for him. He would be able to get on with his life. And yet it felt like the roof had fallen in on top of them all.

Anderson was deeply disappointed. They'd come so close, he thought. So close to making the church disclose its secrets, and so close to showing how it had placed children at risk over and over again. For years afterward, Anderson would refer to the Scott settlement as "a triumph of darkness" and "a thorn in my heart." They had given it everything. The settlement was good for their client, but they believed it would change nothing.

And yet the church had lost too. It would have to pay a whopping— and public—settlement that would likely influence plaintiffs in lawsuits for years to come. Perhaps more damaging, the church had been made to produce its internal discipline records. The Scott team had penetrated the legal wall surrounding the inner workings of the Mormon church, if only in small measure.

Slader, Anderson, and Dawn drove back to Portland in a quiet car.

Jeremiah got on a plane and went home.

Tim Kosnoff and Joel Salmi went to a bar and tried to make sense of what had just happened. There were so many emotions tangled together, it was hard to isolate any one enough to understand it. Kosnoff had only a vague attachment to his professional life before the Scott case. Now his subsequent life had ended, almost by accident. There hadn't been a trial, but it felt like they'd been beaten, or capitulated. It felt like the church had gotten away with assisting Frank Curtis in his bad deeds. There would be no public examination of what happened. There had been some monetary punishment, but Kosnoff felt like they'd been cheated out of their real reward in the courtroom.

Salmi left his friend in the bar and headed home. He was relieved, and happier than Kosnoff about what had happened. They'd won an impressive award for their client. They could pay off the bank loan and the outstanding bills. They had made some decent money for all their time, even after everyone got his cut. And mostly, it was over. Finally, this case was over.

Kosnoff's flight home wasn't until the next day. He was stuck, alone, in a college town on a Friday night. He called Mary Ann, ate dinner, and drank more. He'd just won a record settlement in his first civil lawsuit, and he was consumed with a sense of loss.

Clarity came later, with perspective. "Jeremiah knew more than I did," Kosnoff would say, reflecting on the settlement. "He knew what to do, and I was too consumed by the case to see that. It was the right thing to do."

Just when the Scott lawyers were getting used to the idea that the case that had consumed them for years had suddenly ended, they received more paperwork and notice of another hearing. Throughout the case, the church's lawyers had fought hard to keep the discipline records secret. Judge Rosenblum had ordered them produced to the plaintiffs, but they'd been produced under a protective order. Now that the case was over, the church wanted its records back. It was not uncommon for records obtained in discovery to be returned at the conclusion of a court case. But the Scott team wanted the discipline records to remain part of the public record. They'd used the blown-up version of Frank Curtis's discipline record, the one showing the excommunication information, in the hearing over punitive damages, meaning it had been introduced in court, which they believed had made it part of the public record. The church was having none of this and in fact argued that the Scott team had violated Judge Rosenblum's protective order over the records.

Both sides were back in court for a final showdown on the records they'd fought over for years in a case that had already been settled. Only this time, they were in front of Hon. Lyle Velure. While he'd acted as mediator in the Scott case, Velure was also a sitting judge in Oregon. Having achieved a settlement in this case, he evidently wanted to make sure it would stick. Velure ordered the plaintiff's team to hand over all of its copies of all of the church discipline records. The evidence of the Mormon church's knowledge of child molesters within its flock was sealed away by the court.

Almost immediately, *Jeremiah Scott v. Gregory Lee Foster, The Church of Jesus Christ of Latter-day Saints, et al.* moved into the media. Jeff Anderson regrouped and arranged two press conferences, one in Portland and another in Salt Lake City. If they couldn't get the church into the courtroom, he reasoned, they'd shine the spotlight on the church. On the morning of September 5, 2001, Anderson addressed the media in Portland. Sandra Scott stood at the microphone and told the gathered press how the church had failed to warn her family about Brother Curtis. Behind her, the Scott team had put up their time line exhibit with the stop and yield signs, showing all the opportunities the church had had to stop this pedophile. The setting was configured in such a way that the picture of a young Jeremiah with his backpack was visible over Sandy Scott's shoulder on camera.

That afternoon, they all flew to Salt Lake City and assembled for a repeat performance, this time in the heart of the Mormon church: Temple Square. It was a gutsy move, but Anderson wasn't about to let the church avoid public scrutiny by writing Jeremiah a check, even a big check.

The Church of Jesus Christ of Latter-day Saints has a public relations machine of its own, which had begun spinning its side of the story as well. Von Keetch from Kirton & McConkie did several interviews with the news media. The church's lawyers characterized the settlement as simply an economic decision to avoid spending more on a trial

defense. Keetch criticized Judge Rosenblum's rulings in the case, calling them a "travesty of justice." The church's lawyers repeated that
Judge Rosenblum had erred in ruling that the church could be held
liable for the actions of one member against another.

"This is a situation that involved two church members. It took place
off church premises, and it wasn't related to a church activity," Stephen English told the *Oregonian*. The lawyers also pointed out that the
church, in settling, had accepted no blame for the situation.

Temple Square, sitting on ten acres in the middle of downtown Salt
Lake City, dominates the landscape. Anderson had decided to bring
nearly the entire team, including Slader, Kosnoff, Slader's paralegal
Dawn, and Linda Walker, plus Sandy Scott. Shortly after arriving, they
were met by LDS security guards, two men in dark suits and crisp
white shirts, who informed Anderson that they were trespassing and
asked them to leave. The line between public and private property at
Temple Square had been the subject of its own lengthy legal saga over
the years. But regardless of the legal consequences, Jeff Anderson knew
that if he was arrested at a news conference in Salt Lake City, it would
only increase media exposure for the case. He had little, if anything,
to lose here. Anderson told the security guards to go talk to Gordon B.
Hinckley, then president of the Church of Jesus Christ of Latter-day
Saints. Hinckley, he said, knew why they were there.

It was a warm day. Threatened thundershowers had not yet mate-
rialized, and lots of people were outside.

More security guards gathered, and so did a number of newspaper
and television reporters. The television camera lights went on and the
security guards backed off, if temporarily, and allowed the press conference to go forward. Anderson wasn't pulling any punches. "This is
the most dangerous place in America for children," he said. He went
on to detail ten instances of prior notice that the church had received
before Frank Curtis got to Jeremiah Scott, and the twenty other victims Frank Curtis had molested along the way. Slader pointed out that

the Mormon church likely possesses the most extensive record-keeping system of any religious organization in America, and yet church officials didn't warn anyone that Frank Curtis was a predator. Kosnoff told the media, "The church had seen Curtis ruin the lives of child after child. But protecting their image is more important than protecting their children."

At the conclusion of the press conference, the LDS security guards, along with Salt Lake City police, told Anderson that he would be cited for trespassing. No citation ever arrived. But the word was out. Newspapers across the country covered the story of the lawsuit and its $3 million settlement, along with Anderson's promise that more lawsuits would be forthcoming. All the local news media in Utah, including the church-owned *Deseret News*, covered the story, as did the *Oregonian*, the *Los Angeles Times*, and news outlets in Michigan. The *New York Times* also ran an article on the case and the settlement.

The phones began to ring at the law offices, as more victims of perpetrators in the church read about the Scott case and wanted something—money, compensation, apologies, some recognition that these horrible things happened to them, too.

PORTLAND

— ⟡ —

2001

23

The metal basketball hoop with the chain hanging down still stood in front of Billy Loyd's old house off Duke Street when Manny Saban returned from Arizona. There was now a big Protestant church across the street on the corner lot where he and Billy and Bobby Goodall and the other boys from the neighborhood used to play. Manny's old house was still there, but it had been painted. Most of the houses in the neighborhood had been fixed up a bit, but they were recognizable. Trees still hung over the alley between where Bobby and Billy had lived. The Dairy Queen remained open for business. Over on King Street, the Southgate Animal Clinic had been remodeled, but it too was still there. So was the Deseret Thrift Store and the Bishop's Storehouse behind it, where Brother Curtis had worked. An apartment complex stood on the old dump site next to the animal clinic now. Brother Curtis's other apartment, the one attached to the junkyard, looked much the same, as if it were frozen in time.

The lawyers had flown Manny and his girlfriend Anita and their son to Portland for a meeting. They walked into the brick building downtown that housed David Slader's office, and Manny talked briefly with the receptionist. Someone was talking behind him in the waiting room.

"Manny?"

He turned around and looked at the man who'd addressed him.

"You don't remember me?"

Manny stared long and hard trying to place the man. He was fairly well dressed, like he worked in an office somewhere. No, Manny did not think he knew this man. Not until he introduced himself, anyway. And then, yes. Slowly, it came together.

Twenty-five years ago, Manny had known the boy this man used to be. He was a scrawny kid living with his mother and his sister and brother in a crappy apartment complex next door to the animal clinic where Brother Curtis lived. They'd ridden skateboards and played basketball and watched television together there. Now, here, in the waiting room, the men shook hands and marveled at how time had aged them. They were both fathers now. Who would have thought this? Behind the laughter and the questions about this sister and that friend, though, awkwardness crept in around them. This really wasn't a chance encounter. There was only one reason both men would be in the waiting room of the law office today. They must have had something else in common too.

Just as that fact was starting to sink in, Dawn Krantz-Watts interrupted their reminiscing and ushered them into a conference room. Slader, Jeff Anderson, and Tim Kosnoff were all there. And so were about six other men, but Manny didn't know any of the others. Toward the end of the Scott case it had become clear that, because the witnesses had been harmed too, there would likely be a second lawsuit. The Scott team had gathered the claims of twelve men: Manny Saban, Bob and Jim Goodall, and four others from Felony Flats, along with David Johnson and Steven Penrose, who'd had Sunday school with Brother Curtis, another man from Portland, and two of Frank Curtis's victims from Wyoming, into one lawsuit against the Church of Jesus Christ of Latter-day Saints. The men, whom the lawyers were now calling "survivors" in the press, lived all over the country; four were in prison.

Now seven of them sat at the table and ate lunch and talked about their pending lawsuit against the LDS church. Slader led the meeting, explaining how things would work now that they were all plaintiffs in the lawsuit that would become known as "Curtis II."

While Slader was talking, Manny looked at his fellow plaintiffs and couldn't quite make sense of what had happened. He couldn't picture these grown men as children, and it seemed unbelievable that they had all been abused by Brother Curtis. Just like him.

The lawyers had convened the group to talk about their lawsuit, but also because the men were good for each other, even if they didn't ever talk again. It was much the same theory behind publicizing lawsuits. Sexual abuse victims can be challenging as clients. Often, they are broken people who wind up in one damaged situation after another. Slader liked to point out that sex abuse victims went through life believing they had no rights, which he called the "I'm a piece of shit theory." They believed that whatever happened was their fault, that they were somehow evil or bad—otherwise, the abuse would never have happened. Finding other victims helped to stabilize everyone, as people began to see that they were not alone.

There was a strategy to bundling the twelve plaintiffs into one lawsuit, besides the fact that they were all victims of the same serial pedophile. The survivors of Frank Curtis were a diverse bunch legally. Some had a stronger case than others, given the statute of limitations and their individual circumstances. Some had been abused once, others repeatedly, a few for several years. Collectively, they created a stronger plaintiff than any one might have been individually. They needed each other.

One morning in early November, Tim Kosnoff stopped by the law office in Bellevue to pick up his mail. The office was really just an address to him at this point. He still shared a secretary who took messages, but that was the extent of his operation there. He'd gotten used to working from home during the early days of the Scott case, and the habit had stuck.

Kosnoff picked through the pile of letters and packages until one envelope in particular caught his attention. It was from the Oregon State Bar. The exterior was marked "Confidential." Kosnoff's stomach sank. This couldn't be good. He opened the envelope and began reading the letter. What the hell? Kosnoff read on, muttered, cursed under his breath, and then walked out of the mailroom and called Joel Salmi.

Stephen English and David Ernst, lawyers for the Church of Jesus Christ of Latter-day Saints, had filed a formal complaint against Tim Kosnoff with the Oregon State Bar, accusing him of unprofessional conduct. Kosnoff was licensed in Washington, of course, but his application to practice law in Oregon was pending. He and Salmi and Jeff Anderson had been admitted temporarily for the purpose of representing Jeremiah Scott with their Oregon co-counsel. But the Scott case was over. A bar complaint would effectively freeze any application to practice law in Oregon while the matter was investigated. If the bar found a violation, Kosnoff could be disciplined or, in an extreme case, lose the ability to practice there, and then have to answer again in Washington.

A complaint necessarily launches an investigation by the bar's own lawyers. It's rare for one lawyer to challenge another's license, generally the sort of thing reserved for egregious behavior, or a truly nasty fight between lawyers.

"You just don't screw with someone's ticket," Kosnoff once said.

He was furious. Joel Salmi was shocked.

The first allegation had to do with Ginger Simmons, the investigator who had interviewed bishops Greg Foster and Gordon Checketts and other witnesses before the Scott case was filed. It was the same issue the lawyers had argued about again and again. The Scott team had thought it was finally over after Ginger Simmons's deposition and after they'd agreed not to call Gordon Checketts to testify. In the bar complaint, English and Ernst asserted that Ginger had misrepresented herself by not revealing that she had been hired by an attorney who was filing a lawsuit against the church. It was not illegal in Oregon for an investigator to shade the true reason for asking questions. The allegation was that Kosnoff had acted unethically in using information that had been obtained through misrepresentation. The complaint alleged that Kosnoff had essentially masterminded the entire thing, that he was involved in hiring the investigators and "developing and reviewing the plan for the investigation." Joel Salmi didn't understand why he hadn't been the subject of this complaint. After all, he had played a bigger role than Kosnoff in hiring the investigations firm. Neither of them had known that Ginger Simmons even existed until the church's lawyers started trying to get Gordon Checketts's conversation with her tossed out of court.

Other allegations in the complaint had to do with Mary Kay Carter and the fight in Wisconsin. The church alleged that Kosnoff had repeatedly contacted Mary Kay Carter and her sons, attempting to solicit them as clients, and that he had told them that he planned to file a class-action lawsuit. Further, they alleged that since he had claimed to be filing a lawsuit when he talked to Mary Kay Carter, Kosnoff had violated an attorney-client privilege by using information he'd learned during their phone conversations.

The church lawyers also alleged that Kosnoff had harassed one of the Carter boys with repeated phone calls and that he'd called anonymously trying to trick the family into giving up information on the whereabouts of one of the boys. Strange as this charge seemed, it was not new. The allegations had first been brought up in Wisconsin when the church was fighting Mary Kay Carter's deposition. Kosnoff had filed a sworn affidavit with the court denying that he'd done the things described. Now this too was back.

Other parts of the complaint alleged that Kosnoff had persuaded Bobby Goodall and others to file a lawsuit against the church, and that he'd violated court orders governing confidential documents. The latter had to do with Frank Curtis's disciplinary records. English and Ernst pointed out that Kosnoff had included the disciplinary records in paperwork that he filed with the court, where it was found by a reporter for the *Oregonian* and included in news coverage of the case. The exhibit was redacted to include only limited information on Frank Curtis, and it was filed before Judge Rosenblum signed a protective order. Nonetheless, the church's lawyers argued that Kosnoff was leaking the records to the press.

There was yet another charge, out of Kosnoff's past. As a criminal defense lawyer in the mid-1990s, before Jeremiah Scott ever called him, Kosnoff had been the subject of a complaint by a prosecuting attorney. The prosecutor had denied Kosnoff's request to have a court reporter present during an interview with a witness. Driven by frustration over not getting what he considered to be a fair shot at information from the prosecutor, Kosnoff had surreptitiously tape-recorded the interview. (Washington law required both parties to consent to tape recording.) He was busted by a low-battery alarm on the recorder, tucked in his briefcase. The prosecutor filed a complaint for unprofessional conduct. Kosnoff responded with case law and legal articles showing that he was allowed to tape witnesses to defend his client. The Washington State Bar issued an admonishment, its least disciplinary action, which is not a part of a lawyer's permanent record. Except the bar's actions were published on an online legal site. Once on the Internet, it was forever available. The church's lawyers had found the old admonishment and worked it into their present complaint by noting that Kosnoff had not revealed the action when he applied to be allowed temporary status to work on the Scott case.

Kosnoff was seething by the time he talked to David Slader and Jeff Anderson, both of whom agreed that the move was an unwarranted low blow, even in the cutthroat world of tort law. Kosnoff at first wanted to file a complaint against Ernst and English for having obstructed and abused the judicial process with frivolous filings, but Slader talked him down. It would seem retaliatory and it wouldn't help his case. Slader himself had once been subject to a complaint for taping—such things tended to happen in criminal defense law—so he didn't think much of that. He referred Kosnoff to a lawyer in Portland who handled this sort of thing and counseled him to take the high road out of it. Kosnoff worried that he might already be at a disadvantage in the investigation. He was an out-of-state lawyer and Stephen English was a prominent member of the Oregon Bar.

Jeff Anderson had lived through all manner of assaults during his years of legal warfare against the Catholic church over the criminal behavior of its priests. But the Mormon church, he observed, played dirtier than the Catholics ever had. The fight was more intense, the paper assault more vigorous. And now this.

The lawyers on the Scott team also saw this move as a way to take Kosnoff out of the game before the second lawsuit. During Gordon Checketts's deposition, Stephen English had complained vehemently about Joel Salmi, accusing him of questionable behavior with the investigators, which had prompted the argument with Gary Rhoades. Tim Kosnoff had been in the same room, mere feet from English, and yet nothing was said about his involvement in the investigators' actions. But now the bar complaint named only Tim Kosnoff. Salmi was not a threat. He had no plans for another plaintiff's case against the church. He and Jim Hillas would resume their business law practice. Slader and Anderson had been just as aggressive with witnesses. And yet neither of them was named. It was Tim Kosnoff whom the Mormon church wanted. He was the engine that had driven the Scott case, the biggest threat. He was also the most vulnerable for a hit like this.

Anderson offered a considered response: "Welcome to the big

leagues," he told Kosnoff. "It's serious. It's personal. Wear it like a badge."

Weeks later, Tim Kosnoff was in Portland conferring with his new lawyer. They had agreed from the start that the best way to approach the bar investigation was to open everything up for inspection: files, notes, emails, calendars, letters, everything. Kosnoff provided whatever the bar investigating attorneys asked to see, and some things they didn't. Now he sat with his lawyer, like so many of his clients had sat with him over the years, for the first of numerous interviews in which investigating attorneys would question him over and over again about what he'd done, what he'd said, and whom he'd talked to during much of the Scott case. Meanwhile, Kosnoff could not represent the survivors of Frank Curtis in their lawsuit against the Church of Jesus Christ of Latter-day Saints in Oregon. That would fall to David Slader.

24

Back in 1998, the Church of Jesus Christ of Latter-day Saints had won a dismissal of the Scott case from federal district court by arguing that the court lacked jurisdiction over the matter. Now the church filed paperwork with the court arguing that the Curtis II case *belonged* in federal district court. Specifically, the church's lawyers argued that this was a constitutional question regarding the First Amendment. Apparently federal court now seemed like a more church-friendly venue. Kosnoff and Slader had worried about this move. They wanted the case to stay in Multnomah County Circuit Court and had encouraged Manny Saban to move back to Oregon to strengthen the circuit court's jurisdiction. The circuit court case was effectively stalled until the federal court held hearings and ruled on the question of jurisdiction.

Meantime, discovery plodded along, which meant revisiting much of the same information used in the Scott case. Months before, Anderson had gone to a prison in Purgatory, Utah, to interview one of the victims from Sheridan, Wyoming, a man who was now doing time for molesting his daughter and her friends. He and two siblings had been sexually abused while Brother Curtis had lived with his family in a home owned by the ward bishop. Ward leaders had arranged for Curtis to move there for a place to stay and to help with the kids. This information opened yet another new trail of victims, including at least one other boy in Sheridan. Jim Goodall, Bobby's older brother, was still in prison in Washington. He hadn't been in court for the earlier lawsuit. The brothers hadn't been out of prison at the same time during the Scott lawsuit, and neither had read the other's deposition. Jim, who had spent much of his child and adolescent years with their father in Yakima, never knew the extent of Bobby's abuse by the old man. Bobby didn't know what happened with Manny Saban. He didn't know that Manny had ever told his mother about it, or that she'd written to the bishop. Before the lawsuit, in fact, none of Frank Curtis's victims knew that the man had molested other boys, unless they'd been there. They certainly didn't know that adults had been aware of what was going on.

Slader resumed work on a handful of abuse cases against the Archdiocese of Portland that were heading into a settlement. He also hired a new attorney by the name of Dayna Christian, a former sex crimes prosecutor in the Multnomah County District Attorney's Office. Christian began work on the Curtis II lawsuit, including more depositions. The church was represented in most of these events by Scott Brooksby. These were not the passionate, hostile fights of the Scott case. Brooksby and Christian were cordial as they traveled all over the country questioning and, in some cases, requestioning men who had been victimized by Brother Curtis.

Manny Saban was deposed again, this time at a hotel in Arizona. He and his lawyers had spent time sorting out a part of his past that was continuing to cause problems for his future as a defendant. Manny still had outstanding warrants in Multnomah County, which he had to deal with before the lawsuit progressed. Years before the Scott case, he'd left Oregon before having completed his sentence on a theft charge. Now he was reluctant to come back to participate in the lawsuit for fear of being locked up.

He'd returned to Arizona within a day or two of the big meeting in Slader's office. Then he became afraid to fly, but not because he was white-knuckled about air travel. After the September 11, 2001, terrorist attack, airport security had become extremely tight. Manny feared that if he attempted to get on an airplane, he'd be caught for the outstanding warrants and sent to jail. On one occasion, he took a Greyhound bus as far as Sacramento, but then decided not to continue and returned to Arizona.

Manny had another problem in the lawsuit besides his outstanding warrants. Oregon law requires that victims file their complaint within three years of being injured. Exactly when the clock starts running was a matter for courtroom debate. Slader and other lawyers interpreted the statute to mean three years from when a victim realizes that he's been harmed. But there was still a problem. Since Manny had talked to his family members earlier about what Brother Curtis had done to him, there was a risk that his claim would be thrown out of court because the statute of limitations had run out.

Years later, Manny would remember Dayna Christian counseling him to remain calm before his second deposition in Arizona. If he got mad, got rattled, he would blow up, which could hurt his credibility. But once the proceedings got under way, the church's lawyers began to probe Manny on why he was after money, why he thought that the church was to blame for whatever harm had befallen him. (He had talked about the money to his siblings, and they'd mentioned it in their depositions.) Manny took offense at these insinuations and things got ugly. He cursed, called the Mormons "faggots," and basically forgot everything his lawyer had told him to do.

"I didn't want the Mormon church to cover it up," he said later. "The money was a nice thing and all, but my thing was shining all this light on the Mormon church to make sure it didn't happen to other kids and be covered up."

Tim Kosnoff was still driving to Portland, but now it was mainly to his attorney's office for interviews with the Bar Association's investigators. With time, tension grew inside the Curtis II lawsuit. Disabled by the bar complaint, Kosnoff was largely stuck on the sidelines, unable to represent the survivors of Frank Curtis's abuse that he'd found and come to know. He couldn't fight the Bullivant, Houser, Bailey lawyers in the courtroom. And yet he possessed the institutional memory of the case. He knew every legal move the Church of Jesus Christ of Latter-day Saints had made through twenty-six volumes of court filings. He knew the church's policies, its rules. He knew where and when Frank Curtis had been during three decades. It was impossible for anyone else to handle the case the way he would have. He called Slader's office constantly, seeking answers and information, impatient and frustrated with the whole situation.

Also, the dynamic had changed within the legal team. Kosnoff and Jeff Anderson meshed well. They had similar styles, both ready to go to the mat, united in a mission. Anderson once said they had no tolerance for injustice and were impatient with people who were patient with it. David Slader could be intense, but he was not on a crusade. He was representing clients and trying to get them the best deal. Despite their differences, David Slader and Jeff Anderson had developed the rhythm of partners after having worked through so many legal fights against the Archdiocese of Portland. They were comfortable working together. But without Anderson, Kosnoff and Slader clashed more.

Linda Walker too was sometimes a point of controversy. She had always worked for Kosnoff, and no one else fully understood the role she played. Like him, Linda had found many of the men who were now clients and, in some cases, she'd been the first one they'd ever talked to about the details of what had happened to them. She'd become attached to these men and was adamant about punishing the church for the abuse they'd suffered. After years of researching the issue, she did not believe the Mormon church would change the way it dealt with sexual abuse without suffering some major financial hit. She was constantly frustrated by the constraints of the legal profession and not shy about sharing her opinions on what ought to be happening. Kosnoff had always defended Linda. He preferred taming zealots to attempting to motivate the apathetic. She'd worked hard. She'd taught him. And she could talk to people like nobody else. Anderson also liked Linda Walker. He admired her commitment. Anderson never walked the middle of the road himself, and he liked eccentric people. But he was gone. Linda didn't fit well in this new arrangement. She wasn't a lawyer. She wasn't a licensed investigator. She was an advocate and a researcher. Also, Linda's zeal was irritating some of the witnesses. No one was really sure what to do with her, and Linda sensed that they didn't trust her.

Dawn Krantz-Watts and Linda, however, got along well. The two women formed a friendship because they spent so much time on the phone discussing one or another of the survivors. Dawn had the job of managing the dozen survivors in the Curtis II case. The men who were not in prison had been offered counseling, but even finding a therapist was its own job. Collectively, they'd struggled with drugs and alcohol and failed relationships. There had been at least three suicide attempts among them. Dawn knew from working on other abuse cases that a female therapist was often the best choice because victims had so many issues with men in authority. It would have to be a woman convenient and willing to see patients outside her work hours or the men wouldn't go. It often took a few tries to find the right person. Every roadblock was potentially lethal to a victim's participation. Managing twelve people's appointments for court, depositions, meetings, and whatever else was going on was equally challenging. As the case dragged on, the plaintiffs moved, changed jobs, broke up and reunited with spouses, and otherwise concerned themselves with the everyday life going on outside of the Curtis II lawsuit.

After a year had passed, it was evident that Tim Kosnoff would have to give up the Curtis II case. He was still under the bar restraint in Oregon and it was impossible to manage the case under the circumstances. He began to concentrate on other pursuits. After the Scott case, Kosnoff had begun hearing from abuse victims with ties to the LDS or another church. Could they have a case too? People tended to come forward whenever they heard or read of an abuse case, which is exactly why Jeff Anderson and David Slader had become so adamant about media coverage. It was good business, to be sure, and it helped their clients to know that they were not alone. That's not to say that everyone who called was a client. Some were opportunists. Some had been the victims of horrible abuse, but for one reason or another, their situations didn't fit within the boundaries of civil law.

Kosnoff and Linda Walker had found one case particularly compelling. It involved the Cavalieri sisters, two women who had been abused by their stepfather. The older sister claimed she had told her Mormon bishop, as well as a Mormon Social Services worker, but no one acted and the stepfather went on to abuse the younger sister. The bishop had not reported the abuse or done anything to protect the children. He had instead counseled the girl not to say anything to anyone else about the abuse. Later, the stepfather was convicted for molestation and sentenced to four years in prison. The Cavalieri sisters lived in Seattle, so Kosnoff could easily work on the case. The church had hired lawyers Tom Frey and Marcus Nash, the first two lawyers Kosnoff and Salmi had met in the Scott case so many years before.

At about the same, Kosnoff and Anderson began what Kosnoff would later come to call "the year of savant filing." Both lawyers were still disgruntled that the Church of Jesus Christ of Latter-day Saints had not been held accountable for its role in the sexual abuse of children within its wards. This was not over, as far as they were concerned. Anderson still had cases against Catholic dioceses in various stages all over the country. But he hadn't liked leaving the Scott lawsuit without a verdict, particularly now that Kosnoff was fighting a bar complaint. So they began pursuing claims in Utah. One of the people who had contacted them after the Scott case was a Mormon woman there who had been molested in the 1970s by a man in her ward. She claimed that she'd told her bishop and had been counseled not to say anything to anyone else. In a strange, heinous turn of events, the woman's son was molested years later by the very same man. Eventually, he'd been convicted for molesting another, unrelated child, for which he was now serving time in prison. Kosnoff and Anderson wanted this case, but it would have to be filed in Utah, which meant that they'd have to find a Utah lawyer to join the team as local counsel. Months went by, and they still had no one. Anderson had approached nearly twenty likely candidates, only four of whom were willing to talk about bringing a lawsuit against the Mormon church. They met but were ultimately turned down. Utah lawyers feared it would hurt their careers. Finally, he and Kosnoff found Mary Corporon, a Salt Lake City criminal defense lawyer who mostly handled death penalty cases. Her firm also did divorce law. She agreed to take the lawsuit.

Immediately, the battle entered the media. Anderson was quoted in an April 2002 *New York Times* article, saying, "We're launching a major assault on the Mormon Church." Kosnoff told the *Deseret News* that "as people perceived that the environment is not hostile to them, that the community is friendly and will not shun them, ridicule them or further victimize them, then I think it is inevitable that more victims will come forward."

The church's lawyers shot back. Von Keetch told the press that the church would "aggressively defend itself and its leaders in cases like these no matter how old they are or how difficult it is to come up with the evidence because we know we're right."

However professionally brave and passionately fueled, the move was not rewarded. In the end, after months of work, the cases went nowhere. Kosnoff and Anderson lost court rulings on motions and couldn't get any traction to move forward. "You just can't sue the shit out of the Mormon church in Utah," Anderson later said. Lesson learned, the two men retreated to more familiar territory. Besides, there was plenty of other work that needed their attention.

25

Manny Saban stood next to Dayna Christian in a Multnomah County courtroom, in front of Judge Ellen Rosenblum. There was no particular reason for Judge Rosenblum to be handling the matter of Manny's unfinished criminal business, but it happened to be on her calendar this morning. Manny and his family had moved from Arizona back to Oregon to participate in the lawsuit. This was the first order of business.

Manny observed that Christian and Judge Rosenblum were friendly toward one another, likely a result of Christian's history as a criminal prosecutor and various Bar Association activities, and figured this could only help his cause. They reviewed Manny's convictions and the status of his sentences and what he was now facing, and worked out a deal in which he would pay a fine and serve much of the remainder of his sentence in weekend lockup, a form of incarceration that took place from eight in the morning until eight at night on Saturdays and Sundays, during which inmates were punished by boredom. The limited-housing arrangement saved the county money and allowed convicts to keep a job on the outside. Returning to Portland had brought other problems for Manny. He reconnected with the drugs that had contributed to his criminal behavior in the first place. Now there was crystal meth, which was harder to come down from than the drugs of earlier years. It made him tired and paranoid. In time, Manny failed to show up for jail. He'd blown his chance to clean up his record.

A few months later, he was dismissed by the court from the lawsuit. Manny fell outside the statute of limitations for filing a claim because he'd talked about how upset he'd been by what happened with Brother Curtis years before. The law, it seemed, rewarded suffering in silence or aggressive litigating. He received a $2,500 check for his time and trouble. David Slader took him to the bank to cash the check, since Manny didn't have an Oregon driver's license. The two men shook hands outside the bank and then went their separate ways. Manny walked down the street, away from an unspectacular end of what had begun twenty-five years earlier, when he'd met Brother Curtis on the lawn at church after the missionaries had come on their bikes to visit his house. Manny had been the first one to speak up about Brother Curtis. In the Scott case, he had represented the first notice to the church. But his own story hadn't fit well under the guidelines of civil law. He was out of the case.

In September 2002, a federal district court judge ruled against the Mormon church's argument for federal jurisdiction. The case would move forward in Multnomah County Circuit Court. Shortly after the federal court's ruling, the church's lawyers called David Slader with an offer for a series of confidential settlements. They began negotiations, and then Slader and Christian met with each of the remaining plaintiffs. The men would get differing amounts, depending on their situation, none of them in the same league as Jeremiah Scott's settlement. One received $140,000, another got more, some less. The lawyers advised the men to take the settlements, and they did.

On March 11, 2003, the Oregon State Bar finally concluded its investigation into the conduct of Timothy D. Kosnoff and found no probable cause to believe that Kosnoff had committed any professional misconduct.

His attorney faxed him the letter from the bar investigators reporting their findings. Kosnoff read it silently, eagerly digesting every sentence. The findings stated that he had not known about or participated in any deception or misrepresentation with the investigators. As for the records that had been revealed, the bar found that there was evidence to support both sides' interpretations of whether or not Frank Curtis's redacted disciplinary records had been wrongly disclosed. Nothing indicated that Kosnoff was any more incorrect in his interpretation than was English. Judge Rosenblum had come to Kosnoff's defense; the report stated that she had told the bar investigators that he had not violated the spirit of her order. Finally, Kosnoff's ordeal was over. He had been cleared by the Oregon State Bar to practice law there again. He was relieved, but it was a bittersweet victory. He'd been kept out of the Curtis II case. He'd spent a year and a half living under suspicion, not to mention paying more than $10,000 in legal fees. This vindication energized him. He put down the letter from the bar and returned to work. He was fighting the Mormon church in the case of the Cavalieri sisters in Washington. Kosnoff was still a formidable opponent. Perhaps more so now.

Years after the fact, Bobby Goodall would decide that it was the smell of the pool that had gotten to him. The scent of chlorine mixed with the dankness in the air and whatever else was around that place. He hadn't remembered the smell to speak of; had he been asked what the place smelled like, he might not have been able to say. And yet it was lodged in his mind, waiting to be called upon. Waiting to come out.

Bobby had put off collecting his settlement money after he got out of prison. It was safer with the lawyers. He'd left prison with some cash, much of which had come from smart card playing. And he'd been able to hustle more here and there. One of his mother's husbands had operated a painting business for a while in Olympia and Bobby had worked for him long enough to gather the skills for a job on a crew. He loved the Washington landscape, but he'd done time in Oregon and had been released there. So he was again a resident of Portland. Bobby didn't entirely know what to do with his portion of the settlement. Money had always passed through Bobby's life. It hadn't ever made enough of a difference that it would be missed when it was gone. But eventually he'd needed to buy things, and he'd gone to collect his funds. David Slader had given what Bobby called the "You know, son, this is a lot of money" speech. Like a father might do, Bobby thought. He responded in kind by saying all the right things about plans and responsibility. But they both basically knew that he was going to blow the money. Bobby bought a car and some other goods, gave some to his mother and sister. Bobby's brother, Jim, was still in prison in Washington. They'd never talked about the lawsuit in which they were both plaintiffs. Just like they'd never talked about what happened. Bobby invested the rest of his money into the methamphetamine business.

For whatever reason, Bobby Goodall was a fairly good businessman in his field. He made and sold with a decent profit. He was professional, dealt fairly with people, and had a loyal customer base. He'd done enough prison time that no one messed with him.

Toward the end of a July day in 2006, Bobby was delivering drugs to a customer who lived in an apartment complex on Killingsworth Street near the airport. The neighborhood was home to low-income housing complexes, bars in strip malls, and a couple of churches that had moved into formerly run-down buildings. Despite a constant state of gentrifying, the area could never quite become someplace better. Bobby had done a lot of business in the trailer park next door, but today was the first time he'd delivered in this complex. He headed down the walkway and looked for the apartment number. That's when the smell hit him. He found the right apartment and was ushered inside. The smell was still there. The apartment was right in front of the pool. He knew this place. He knew that it always smelled like the pool inside. Yes. The little sitting room. The kitchen. Bobby could see the bedroom from the kitchen. The bedroom. The smell. This was Brother Curtis's apartment. He'd been here twenty years before. Brother Curtis had done things to Bobby here, so many times. In this bedroom. In this apartment.

Bobby turned from distracted to disoriented. He tried to keep himself together long enough to finish the deal and get out, but he wasn't making sense. He had to get the hell out of there. He told the customers to meet him later and went immediately to a bar down the street called the Red Apple, a place where he often did business. He needed to medicate. First the booze, then the needles. He hadn't done this in years, shoot up. Now he couldn't get enough. It seemed like nothing could make his pain go away. There would never be enough booze, or drugs, or money to erase the memory of Brother Curtis.

EPILOGUE

Six days after Jeremiah Scott's lawyers stood in Temple Square to announce his settlement and less than a month after what was to be the start of the trial, terrorists attacked the World Trade Center and the Pentagon. Thousands of people died, and everything changed. Studies done afterward showed that the event so shifted everyday life and thought that it skewed jury verdicts downward for months. Had it not settled, *Jeremiah Scott v. Gregory Lee Foster, The Church of Jesus Christ of Latter-day Saints, et al.* would likely have been in trial at the time of the 9/11 attack, perhaps in the jury deliberation phase. Tim Kosnoff and the other lawyers came to believe that Jeremiah might have come away with significantly less if he'd gone to trial.

After the Scott case, Kosnoff devoted his career entirely to representing sexual abuse victims, which he continues to do today from his office high atop downtown Seattle. In 2005, the case of the Cavalieri sisters, which began while the Curtis II case was going on in Oregon, went to trial in King County, Washington, after years of discovery fights. The Church of Jesus Christ of Latter-day Saints was represented in the lawsuit by Tom Frey and Marcus Nash, Tim Kosnoff and Joel Salmi's original adversaries. The jury awarded Kosnoff's clients $4.2 million. It was the first award of intentional infliction of emotional distress against a religious institution in the United States. An appellate court later dismissed a portion of the judgment against the church, but upheld the intentional infliction verdict and ruled that the church still owed more than $1.2 million.

Kosnoff has since represented abuse victims in several states against the Mormon church and numerous other institutions, including Boy Scouts of America, Jehovah's Witnesses, the Salvation Army, and various Catholic archdioceses. In 2006, he and law partner Michael Pfau represented numerous sexual abuse victims in lawsuits against the Roman Catholic Archdiocese of Spokane, Washington. The $46 million settlement negotiated with the Catholic church included certain nonfinancial provisions rare to abuse cases. Among them: Diocese officials must refer to the plaintiffs as "victims" and not "alleged victims," plaintiffs must be allowed a full page in the diocesan newspaper each month for three years to write about their stories if they choose, and the bishop must go to every parish where an abuse incident occurred and inform the congregation. The Spokane diocese filed for bankruptcy in the wake of lawsuits over child sexual abuse.

Jeremiah Scott graduated from college in California and became a professional photographer. His work has been published in numerous national magazines. Shortly after leaving the Curtis II lawsuit, Manny Saban was arrested on an unrelated charge and served his entire outstanding sentence in Multnomah County Jail. Manny lives with his girlfriend in Portland, where he works as a cabinet finisher and is raising his son.

Bob Goodall is incarcerated in Oregon. In 2009, he returned to the South Fork Forest Camp to perform reforesting work. He has since been transferred to another facility. Jim Goodall remains incarcerated in Washington.

Jeffrey Anderson continues to work on institutional child sex abuse lawsuits around the world. In 2006, the government of Mexico issued a five-year exclusion order banning him from the country because of lawsuits against the Catholic church and after Anderson accused a prominent cardinal of protecting a sex-abusing priest. In a lawsuit in which Anderson represented the plaintiff, the U.S. Ninth Circuit Court of Appeals ruled that the Vatican could be sued as the employer of abusing Catholic priests and bishops. The Holy See had claimed immunity from U.S. law and appealed the ruling. In 2010, the U.S. Supreme Court refused to hear the case. Anderson continued to pursue the Vatican and has said he intends to pursue testimony from Pope Benedict XVI. Anderson has not handled another case against the Church of Jesus Christ of Latter-day Saints.

Joel Salmi practices law in Washington. He is no longer able to walk and relies mainly on a scooter for mobility. He continues to travel, however. Salmi has not sued or defended another religious institution since the Scott case. Most insurance carriers have stopped writing policies that cover church organizations for liability of that nature.

Jim Hillas became a partner at Dunn, Carney, then left to form his own law firm in 2010. He continues to practice business law in Portland.

After completing settlements in the Curtis II case and all of the lawsuits against the Archdiocese of Portland, David Slader retired. He lives in Portland.

Dayna Christian left Slader's office and accepted a position with Bullivant, Houser, Bailey, the law firm that represented the Church of Jesus Christ of Latter-day Saints, where she is now a partner.

Linda Walker is semiretired but continues to work for the Child Protection Project and work part-time as a researcher for lawyers all over the country.

Dawn Krantz-Watts opened her own legal services business in

Portland. She continues to work with attorneys on numerous lawsuits regarding sexual abuse against the Church of Jesus Christ of Latter-day Saints and other religious institutions.

Stephen English and David Ernst continue to practice law at Bullivant, Houser. The firm has represented the LDS church in other sexual abuse lawsuits that followed the Scott case. English represented the church in a later suit in Oregon in which a jury ordered the Boy Scouts of America to pay $1.4 million to an abuse victim of Timur Dykes, who had been the subject of numerous earlier lawsuits against the church. In this case, the church settled for $350,000. In 2008, English won a $36 million verdict against a venture capital fund broker and the now-defunct Arthur Andersen accounting corporation for fraud, negligence, and misrepresentation. Von Keetch and Randy Austin are senior partners at Kirton & McConkie, where they continue to direct the church's legal defense in numerous lawsuits, including sexual abuse cases. In 2005, Keetch was named to the Appellate Court Nominating Commission charged with reviewing applications for candidates to the Utah Supreme Court. He continues to write on religious freedom issues and religious land-use issues, and has authored several briefs filed in the U.S. Supreme Court on the issue.

In 2005, the Honorable Ellen Rosenblum was appointed to the Oregon Court of Appeals, where she remains on the bench.

In 2007, the Honorable Ann Aiken presided over a lawsuit against the federal government filed by Brandon Mayfield, who had been falsely detained after the 2004 Madrid train bombings. The case and the judge received national attention when Aiken struck down as unconstitutional certain provisions of the USA Patriot Act that pertained to government surveillance without a warrant. In 2009, Aiken became the first woman named chief justice of the U.S. Federal District Court in Oregon.

The Church of Jesus Christ of Latter-day Saints has settled numerous lawsuits over child sexual abuse. It has not faced a jury in a sexual abuse case since the Cavalieri sisters' case, which marked its third time in court on such a matter. (The first was in the early 1990s, in a Los Angeles case involving molestation by a camp counselor; the second was the late 1998 case over Charles Blome's crimes in Texas.) In March 1999, the church announced that it would require that all adults called to participate in scouting must first be certified by the Boy Scouts of America. The church also continues to operate a twenty-four-hour help line staffed with professional LDS counselors to advise local ward leaders on how to handle allegations of sexual abuse. (And critics continue to characterize this as a direct line to the church's lawyers to assess liability.)

Franklyn Richard Curtis lies beneath the grass in an unmarked grave in a Michigan cemetery on the eastern shore of Lake Michigan, about one hundred miles from Chicago, where he was born more than a century ago. There is no headstone, no ornamental urn, no planted flowers, nothing to note his life or his death. As far as is known, he has not received any visitors.

ACKNOWLEDGMENTS

In researching this book, I learned about twenty survivors of Frank Curtis, including some who were not part of any lawsuit against the LDS church. Given what I know of Frank Curtis's history, I suspect that there are more. While perhaps extreme in ways, Curtis operated in the manner of a classic, serial pedophile. An unrestrained predator, he was aided by those who knew his propensity to harm and failed to protect the most vulnerable in his path.

No one can truly know the psychological and physical trauma suffered by the men and women in this book. I am thankful for the opportunity to tell their stories.

I can't imagine how difficult it must be to relive the time and events involved, which makes me all the more grateful for the recollections shared by Stanley Saban Jr., Robert Goodall, James Goodall, Christopher Bischoff, and Jeremiah Scott. Each of them made it abundantly clear that his primary motive in cooperating was to prevent similar abuse from happening to more victims.

Circumstances prevented Christopher Bischoff from speaking to me until the book was going to press. Though his story is not included, it is significant. Like so many other children harmed by Frank Curtis, he survived unfathomable pain and near-constant fear. Chris provided valuable confirmation and detail that was helpful at the end of the process.

This book could not have been written without the cooperation of Tim Kosnoff. He was remarkably generous with his time, patient with years of my incessant questions and requests, and honest in his reflections. I am profoundly grateful for all of it. Likewise, Joel Salmi endured years of questioning with patience and good humor. In addition, he taught me a great deal about the law, for which I also am thankful.

Jeffrey Anderson, James Hillas, and David Slader gave me hours of valuable time. Their reflections on the case, the issues, and the law informed and improved my work immeasurably. I also benefited tremendously from the knowledge and memory of Linda Walker and Dawn Krantz-Watts, both of whom were driven by their commitment to seeing justice for the victims of Frank Curtis. Linda Walker, in particular, put up with years of my information quests and never turned me down. Lisa Thomas, another paralegal who worked on this case, was also helpful.

Sandra Scott shared with me significant information regarding some particularly painful parts of her life, for which I am grateful. I am also thankful to a small group of people who knew Frank Curtis and were members of the Mormon faith, and who invested time in helping me understand their religion and the events surrounding Curtis's movements within the church. Jay and Jack Eveland were especially helpful, as was Keith Webb, who also shared valuable artifacts. Also, I am grateful to Steve Benson, who patiently taught me about Mormon culture and theology.

I was helped through the process of writing this book by so many people it is impossible to name them all. Some, however, require special thanks. I am immeasurably grateful to my editor, Colin Harrison, whose wise counsel, huge talent, and cool demeanor improved both the book and the writer. Likewise, in the early days of the manuscript, I benefited from the brilliance of Richard Todd, who convinced me to write this book, and Tom French, who taught me the value of the details. Maria Turner and Pat Kossan read every word more than once and this book is significantly better for their considerable feedback. Karen Zuercher copyedited an early version of the manuscript and made it readable. I am indebted to all of them.

I benefited from the reporting of some fine journalists who came to the Scott case before me. I am particularly grateful for the work of Michael Wilson, whose reporting at the *Oregonian* helped me tell this story.

Julie Meyerle at the Michigan Archives in Lansing was extremely helpful in my research of Frank Curtis's history, and Patti Duncan at Wilhelm's Portland Memorial Mausoleum assisted me in tracking his postmortem movement. I am also thankful to Dr. Jack McAninch, chief of urology at San Francisco General Hospital/University of California, San Francisco School of Medicine, for educating me.

I am thankful to Ginger Goforth Simmons, who helped me to understand the early investigations in the case. Likewise, the staff of the Racine County Circuit Court and the Honorable Emmanuel "Butch" Vuvunas were tremendously helpful in my research of events there.

I wish to thank my agent, Judith Riven, who believed in me and this book from the very beginning, and who worked hard to make other people see its value. I am also grateful for the work of Emily Remes, Elisa Rivlin, Kelsey Smith, Laura Wise, Kate Lloyd, and Cynthia Merman at Simon & Schuster.

I am fortunate to commune with some fabulous writers who support and inspire me. Howard Bryant encouraged and shepherded me through this project, without regard to the demands of his own work. His unwavering support propelled me forward whenever I stalled. The gang from Goucher College's MFA program were helpful and generous in their support, particularly Emilie Surrusco, Cecily Weintraub, Leslie Miller, Erin Martin, Richard Gilbert, and Molly Walling. Jon Franklin and Patsy Sims helped me get going. Joe Mackall and Suzannah Lessard contributed valuable insight. From the old school, as always, Brad Dosland showed me the view through a different lens and made me do better. Donnell Alexander propped me up. Nora Wallace listened, probed, and made everything seem more clear. Judy Daniel helped to organize the chaos. Fred Miller provided valuable information technology services. Chris Fiscus made me presentable.

The ancestor of this book is another story I wrote back in 1994 for *Phoenix New Times*. I am tremendously grateful to Deborah Laake for starting me down that path, and to Michael Lacey and John Mecklin for helping me along there.

I offer inadequate thanks to Christina and Colin Holmes, who took great care of me in Portland so many times, which allowed me to get the job done. I am also thankful for my writing homes at the San Mateo, California, Public Library and the Sterling Room for Writers in the Multnomah County Library in Portland, and for the wonderful people who work there.

Much love and thanks to my husband and my children, who endured random bouts of disorder and my periodic absences without complaint. I am equally grateful to Barbara Davis, my mother and role model, who served as babysitter, copy editor, and head cheerleader.

NOTES

This book is informed by numerous interviews with more than twenty-five people involved in the lawsuits stemming from the crimes of Franklyn Richard Curtis. I discussed this case periodically with Tim Kosnoff, Joel Salmi, and Linda Walker over a span of nearly ten years. Likewise, I conducted multiple and lengthy interviews with James Hillas, Jeffrey Anderson, David Slader, and Dawn Krantz-Watts, all of whom worked on the plaintiff's side of the case. The Church of Jesus Christ of Latter-day Saints, and its attorneys, were unwilling to discuss the case under terms that were acceptable to me.

I benefited from direct access to documentary evidence used to build the plaintiff's case. I also relied heavily on court records, transcripts of court hearings, and deposition testimony.

Except where otherwise noted, descriptions of the locations where various scenes take place are based on my on-site reporting.

Additional sources are noted here where applicable.

PROLOGUE

The events described are drawn from interviews with Tim Kosnoff and Stanley Saban Jr., along with the deposition of Stanley Saban Jr.

CHAPTERS 1–3

Several locally produced histories of the Portland neighborhoods helped me tremendously: *Portland Names and Neighborhoods: Their Historic Origins* by Eugene E. Snyder (Binford & Mort, 1979) and *Portland Then and Now* by Linda Dodds and Carolyn Buan (Thunder Bay Press, 2001). I also relied on a 2005 *Portland Tribune* article by Jacob Quinn Sanders titled "The Taming of Felony Flats." These chapters were further informed by publications of the Johnson Creek Watershed Council, including its 2008 State of the Watershed Report.

The narrative account of the early years in the southeast Portland neighborhoods comes from interviews with Stanley Saban Jr., Raquel Saban, James Goodall, and Robert Goodall, along with deposition transcripts from two other of Frank Curtis's victims during the same era.

CHAPTER 4

The *Seattle Times* news coverage of the trial of Shawn Swenson was particularly helpful in this and subsequent references to that case. Shawn Swenson was convicted of first-degree murder, which would typically have earned him up to twenty-eight years in prison. But a King County, Washington, judge found that the case involved "deliberate cruelty" and sentenced Swenson to fifty-five years in prison. Swenson appealed both the murder conviction and the sentence. In 2005, the Washington State Supreme Court overturned Swenson's murder conviction because jurors were given ambiguous instructions on the law.

The account of the 1997 meeting between the Scott family and the lawyers comes from interviews with all parties who were present at the meeting.

CHAPTER 5

The story of Frank Curtis living in the Scott household comes from my interview with Sandra Scott in 2001, and my 2006 interview with Jeremiah Scott. I also relied on deposition testimony of the Scott family members.

CHAPTER 6

I relied on information from the civil complaint in *Jeremiah Scott v. Gregory Lee Foster, The Church of Jesus Christ of Latter-day Saints, et al.* filed in U.S. District Court for the District of Oregon.

As mentioned earlier, I used the court filings in *Jeremiah Scott v. Gregory Lee Foster, The Church of Jesus Christ of Latter-day Saints, et al.* filed in Multnomah County, Oregon, Circuit Court, extensively. Reports from investigators Bill Anton and Ginger Goforth Simmons are attached as evidence to numerous court filings in the Multnomah County case, including the August 3, 2000, Motion to Compel Plaintiff's Further Production of Documents.

Biographical information on Hon. Ann Aiken came from news accounts in the *Oregonian* and *Eugene Register-Guard*, along with information from the Oregon State Bar Association.

Information on the Mark O. Hatfield U.S. District Court building is from the U.S. General Services Administration, U.S. District Court of Oregon Historical Society, Boora Architects, and Emporis.com.

As noted in the chapter, I relied on *Mormon America: The Power and the Promise* by Richard N. Ostling and Joan K. Ostling (HarperCollins, 1999) for financial information on the Church of Jesus Christ of Latter-day Saints. The information in that book was drawn from reporting by Richard Ostling and S. C. Gwynne for *Time* magazine, which published a cover story on the Mormon church on August 4, 1997. The church responded to the article, protesting the reporting. The church argued that the figures are high.

CHAPTER 7

Background information on the Scott family came from the transcripts of the depositions of Revis K. Scott and Sandra Scott, as well as my interview with Sandra Scott.

For information on the Mormon religion in this and later chapters, I relied on numerous church publications, including The Book of Mormon and The Doctrine and Covenants of the Church of Jesus Christ of Latter-day Saints. I also benefited from *Mormon Doctrine* by Bruce R. McConkie (Deseret Book Co., 1966), *Jesus Christ and His Gospel: Selections from the Encyclopedia of Mormonism*, edited by Daniel Ludlow (Deseret Book Co., 1994), and *The Miracle of Forgiveness* by Spencer W. Kimball (Bookcraft, 1969).

Information on Mormon missionaries comes from "A Call to the Rising Generation," by Brent H. Nielson, *Ensign*, November 2009, and "Kingdom Come," by David Van Biema, S. C. Gwynne, and Richard Ostling, *Time*, August 4, 1997.

I wrote the 1994 magazine article that Tim Kosnoff read and noted cases from while I was a staff writer at *Phoenix New Times*. "Sins of the Temple" appeared in that publication on December 22, 1994.

For information on the relationship between the Mormon church and Boy Scouts of America, I turned to *Scout's Honor* by Patrick Boyle (Prima Publishing, 1994) and *Scouting in The Church of Jesus Christ of Latter-day Saints*, a handbook jointly published by the church and the Boy Scouts of America.

Additional information on the church is from "Mormons Inc.: The Secret of America's Most Prosperous Religion" by David Van Biema, S. C. Gwynne, and Richard N. Ostling, *Time* magazine, August 4, 1997.

I benefited from the news coverage of the civil lawsuit over Charles Blome's crimes reported by Paul McKay at the *Houston Chronicle*. I also relied on news coverage of the conviction of Ralph Neeley and the subsequent lawsuit against the church published in the *Beaumont Enterprise*, Beaumont, Texas.

CHAPTER 8

The account of the depositions of the Johnson and Penrose families comes primarily from the transcripts of those depositions, along with interviews with the plaintiff's lawyers and Lisa Thomas, a paralegal at Dunn, Carney, Allen, Higgins & Tongue who worked on the Scott case.

CHAPTER 9

I benefited from the reporting of the *Oregonian* and the *New York Times* in writing about the Timur Dykes cases.

The account of Ginger Goforth Simmons's investigation came from the transcript of her deposition, her affidavit filed in the Multnomah County Circuit Court case, and my interview with her. Additional information came from my interview with Raquel Saban.

I relied on the Oregon Department of Public Safety Standards and Training for information on the laws governing private investigators in Oregon. Chris Brodniak, a private investigation compliance investigator at the department, was particularly helpful.

The excommunication information is from Church Defendants' Reply Brief and a transcript of the May 6, 1999, court hearing.

CHAPTER 10

For biographical information on Hon. Joseph Ceniceros, I relied on Oregon State Bar Association and Multnomah County Bar Association publications.

The account of the courtroom hearing is based on the transcript of the December 7, 1999, court hearing, as well as interviews with the plaintiff's lawyers who participated.

The account of Dr. Lloyd Hale's deposition is based on transcripts of that deposition and my interviews with Joel Salmi and Tim Kosnoff.

My description of the defendant in federal appeals court is based on U.S. District Court of Appeals docket information and my interviews with Tim Kosnoff.

The explanation of discipline as the first step in the Mormon repentance process is based on information in the Church Defendants' Reply Brief and the transcript of the court hearing of May 6, 1999.

CHAPTER 11

The account of Jeremiah Scott's arrest and conviction, the revelation that Frank Curtis had molested him, and the investigation surrounding those events come from numerous filings in the Multnomah County Court case, reports from the Redmond, Washington, police department, and court records in *People v. Scott*, filed in King County, Washington, criminal court, as well as a subsequent civil case against Sandra Scott filed in that county.

I relied on transcripts of the depositions of Jeremiah Scott, Sandra Scott, and Revis Kent Scott in my account of those scenes. Additional information came from my interview with Sandra Scott.

My account of the telephone conversations between Stanley "Manny" Saban Jr. and Tim Kosnoff came from interviews with both of them.

In *Scott v. Hammock*, 870 P.2d 947, 956 (Utah 1994), the Utah Supreme Court held that "nonpenitential communications are privileged under Utah law if they are intended to be confidential and are made for the purpose of seeking spiritual counseling, guidance, or advice from a cleric acting in his or her professional role and pursuant to the discipline of his or her church." The case began in U.S. District Court for the District of Utah. It is cited frequently in civil lawsuits involving a clergy-penitent question.

The Church of Jesus Christ of Latter-day Saints argued in numerous court filings that rebaptized members were given a "clean slate" through the exercise of the Mormon faith, and to allow a legal examination of actions prior to rebaptism was a violation of the Free Exercise Clause of the First Amendment. The quotations are taken from the Defendant's Motion for Protective Order, March 29, 1999.

For much of the Mormon and constitutional history, I relied on *Latter-day Prophets and the United States Constitution*, edited by Donald Q. Cannon (Religious Studies Center, Brigham Young University, 1991). I also was informed by *The Book of Mormon and the Constitution* by H. Verlan Andersen (Sunrise Publishing, 1995).

In a well-known address in the Mormon Tabernacle on April 19, 1885, Apostle Orson F. Whitney, a delegate to the Constitutional Convention for the state of Utah, laid out the church's beliefs regarding the Founding Fathers. In another address, the Mormon historian Charles W. Penrose articulated the church's embrace of the Constitution. The statements of J. Reuben Clark Jr. come from his August 6, 1957, address at the General Conference of the Church of Jesus Christ of Latter-day Saints in Salt Lake City.

For information on the Mormon history with the Founding Fathers, I relied on *The Discources of Wilford Woodruff*, edited by G. Homer Durham (Bookcraft, 1946). Mormon history tells that former LDS president Wilson Woodruff was famously visited by the Founding Fathers in St. George, Utah.

The U.S. Supreme Court case regarding polygamy referred to and quoted from is *Reynolds v. United States*, 98 U.S. 145 (1878).

CHAPTER 12

Information on the Mormon baptism for the dead is drawn from the *Encyclopedia of Mormonism* (Macmillan, 1992).

Additional information on the baptism of the dead came from the following articles: Ian Urbina, "Again, Jews Fault Mormons Over Posthumous Baptisms," *New York Times*, December 21, 2003; Gustav Niebuhr, "Mormons to End Holocaust Victim Baptism," *New York Times*, April 29, 1995; and Nancy Hobbs, "Baptism for Dead Adds Lincoln, Tolstoy to LDS Ranks," *Salt Lake Tribune*, August 17, 1991.

I researched the background of Franklyn R. Curtis, beginning with information from Curtis's membership records and the Detroit, Michigan, court research that Tim Kosnoff did in preparing for the lawsuit. From there, the following were helpful sources: U.S. Census Records; Circuit Court of Cook

County, Illinois; Cook County Bureau of Vital Statistics; Illinois Department of Public Health, Bureau of Statistics; Holy Name Cathedral, Chicago; *Chicago Tribune* archives; Oklahoma Department of Corrections; and Archives of Michigan.

The St. Charles, Illinois, public library was particularly useful in providing information on the Illinois State Home for Delinquent Boys.

My account of the historical events in Chicago during the years Frank Curtis lived there was informed by the *Encyclopedia of Chicago* (University of Chicago Press, 2004). Additional history of Frank Curtis came from his taped narrative "conversion tape."

The information on the history of Jackson Prison is from the Michigan Department of Corrections.

CHAPTER 13

My account of the events before, during, and after Manny Saban's deposition in Humboldt, Arizona, are drawn from transcripts of the deposition, and from my interviews with Stanley Saban Jr. and Tim Kosnoff.

My account of the bishops' depositions was informed by the transcripts of those depositions, including those of Dennis Dalling and Gordon Checketts. Additional information came from my 2008 interview with Jack Eveland.

I also relied on transcripts of the depositions of Dwayne Liddell, director of risk management, Church of Jesus Christ of Latter-day Saints, and Harold Brown, the church's managing director of the Welfare Services department.

Joel Salmi was particularly helpful in educating me on Oregon law concerning the reporting of child sexual abuse. In addition, I relied on information from the Oregon Department of Human Services.

My account of Tim Kosnoff's interview with Raquel Saban and of Raquel Saban's personal history came from interviews with both of them.

CHAPTER 14

My account of the events surrounding and following Tim Kosnoff's phone conversation with Robert Goodall came from my 2008 interview with Robert Goodall.

For biographical information on Hon. Ellen Rosenblum, I relied on articles in the *Oregonian, Willamette Week,* and numerous Oregon State Bar and Multnomah County Bar Association publications.

The account of Ginger Goforth Simmons's deposition is drawn from the transcript of that deposition and my interviews with Joel Salmi. Additional information came from my interview with Ginger Goforth Simmons.

CHAPTER 15

The Multnomah County Court House in Portland is on the National Register of Historic Buildings. In addition to my on-site reporting there, I relied on information from the Oregon Historical Society.

My account of the August 1, 2000, court hearing is drawn primarily from the transcript of that hearing. Additional information is from my interviews with Joel Salmi and Tim Kosnoff.

For information on the events surrounding Donald Anderson's conviction for child sexual abuse, I relied on transcripts of his deposition and newspaper accounts from the *Oregonian*.

Information on sexual abuse perpetrators and victim recidivism is from the American Psychological Association. Additional information came from *A Profile of Pedophilia: Definition, Characteristics of Offenders, Recidivism, Treatment Outcomes, and Forensic Issues* by Ryan C. W. Hall and Richard C. W. Hall, Department of Psychiatry and Behavioral Sciences, The Johns Hopkins Hospital, Baltimore, Md., and *Pedophilia and Sexual Offending Against Children: Theory, Assessment, and Intervention* by Michael C. Seto (American Psychological Association, 2008).

My account of the mock jury trial was informed by my interviews with all of the participating lawyers, along with Bert Lybrand of Market Decisions Corp. in Portland.

CHAPTER 16

My account of the story of Pearly Hankins and Frank Curtis in Grand Rapids is drawn from the transcript of Pearly Hankins's deposition, along with my interviews with Tim Kosnoff.

For information on the circumstances surrounding the molestation of the Carter children, I relied on reports from the Wyoming, Michigan, police department and court records from *Jeremiah Scott v. Gregory Lee Foster, The Church of Jesus Christ of Latter-day Saints, et al.* filed in Racine County, Wisconsin, Circuit Court. Additional information came from my interviews with Jay Eveland and Jack Eveland.

Information on Frank Curtis's February 1992 attempt to turn himself in to the Detroit police appeared in the *National Enquirer*.

Telephone records showing that Wisconsin attorney Matt Flynn, who represented the Carter family, was appearing telephonically from the Salt Lake City offices of Kirton & McConkie are a part of the court record in the Racine, Wisconsin, Circuit Court case file.

Additional information on the Wisconsin legal events is memorialized in the related court case filed in the Wisconsin Court of Appeals.

Information on the court hearing and decisions in Michigan came from the court file in *Jeremiah Scott v. Gregory Lee Foster, The Church of Jesus Christ of Latter-day Saints, et al.* filed in Kent County Circuit Court, Grand Rapids.

CHAPTER 17

Information on the legal issues come from the case record in Multnomah County Circuit Court. The Writ of Mandamus was filed by the Church of Jesus Christ of Latter-day Saints in the Oregon Supreme Court on March 1, 2001. For the matter of disciplinary records involving other members of the church, I relied on defendant's Motion for Intervention and Points and Authorities in Support of Motion for Intervention, filed February 21, 2001.

Additional information came from my interviews with Jim Hillas and Lisa Thomas.

My account of the deposition of Mary Kay Carter, and the subsequent court hearing, in Racine, is drawn from the transcripts of those events. Additional information comes from my interviews with Hon. Emmanuel Vuvunas and with the court clerks and staff of the Racine County, Wisconsin, Circuit Court.

My account of the deposition scenes is based on the transcripts of those depositions, and from my interviews with Jay Eveland, Jack Eveland, and Tim Kosnoff. The Title IV federal lawsuit mentioned is *Communities for Equity v. Michigan High School Athletic Association*, 377 F.3d 504 (6th Cir. 2004). For additional information, I relied on news reports from the Associated Press.

CHAPTER 18

The Portland Memorial Mausoleum is listed in the National Register of Historic Places. Additional information on the site came from Wilhelm's Portland Memorial Funeral Home. The story of Frank Curtis's trip to Utah and conversion to Mormonism is from the conversion tape made by Frank Curtis. All quotes used in this chapter are from Frank Curtis. Additional information came from my 2009 interview with Keith Webb.

For diagnostic information on pedophilia, I relied on the *Diagnostic and Statistical Manual of Mental Disorders, DSM-IV-TR* (American Psychiatric Association, 2000).

Information on Mormon baptism is taken from *A Marvelous Work and a Wonder* by LeGrand Richards (Deseret Book Co., 1976), and *Mormon Doctrine* by Bruce R. McConkie (Deseret Book Co., 1966).

CHAPTER 19

The information on prostatectomy, orchiectomy, and penile implants is largely from my interview with Dr. Jack W. McAninch, chief of urology at San Francisco General Hospital and vice chair of the Department of Urology at the University of California, San Francisco, School of Medicine.

For the discussion on surgical castration and sex offender therapy, I relied upon information from the University of Texas Medical Branch, Institute for the Medical Humanities, Baylor College of Medicine's Menninger Department of Psychiatry, and a *Houston Chronicle* article titled "Drugs, Surgery May Temper Drive, but Sexual Interest Won't Normalize'" by Robert Crowe, May 10, 2005.

For information on the Multnomah County, Oregon, Circuit Court lawsuit against Manuel Ulibarri and the Church of Jesus Christ of Latter-day Saints, I relied on news accounts from the Associated Press.

The story of the meeting with Jeremiah Scott in Bellevue, Washington, comes from my interviews with Dawn Krantz-Watts and David Slader.

CHAPTER 20

For information on the Utah Supreme Court case, I relied on "Court Gives Utah Clergy Protection: Dismissal of Negligence Suit Against LDS Church Is Upheld," by Stephen Hunt, *Salt Lake Tribune*, March 10, 2001.

The plaintiff's team used the phrase "cloaking him in the garb of religious authority" in Plaintiff's Response in Support of Proffered Evidence Regarding Abuse Not Reported to the Church, filed August 3, 2001.

The lawsuits involving the Mormon doctor stem from the 1997 criminal conviction of John Parkinson in Solano County, California, Superior Court.

That conviction was overturned in 2003 by a U.S. District Court because of juror misconduct.

For information on the specific details of the church discipline records relating to Frank Curtis, which were later sealed by the court, I relied on news coverage by Michael Wilson of the *Oregonian*, who reported on the Jeremiah Scott case. The excommunication information is included in his article "$3 Million Settlement Ok'D in Mormon Sex-Abuse Case," September 5, 2001. Additional information came from my interview with Michael Wilson, now a reporter for the *New York Times*.

My account of the war room and trial preparation meetings in the Law Offices of David Slader are drawn from my interviews with all participants. Likewise, my account of the punitive damages hearing is drawn from interviews with the participants on the plaintiff's team. Additional information on the hearing is drawn from news accounts in the *Oregonian* and *Salt Lake Tribune*.

Information on the legal arguments comes from transcripts of the court hearings and from court records filed in the Multnomah County case, including Church Defendant's Memorandum in Opposition to Plaintiff's Motion to Amend, filed April 17, 2001.

CHAPTER 21

My account of the deposition of Robert "Bobby" Goodall is drawn from the transcript of that deposition and from my interviews with Robert Goodall and Tim Kosnoff.

CHAPTER 22

My account of the press conferences in Portland and Salt Lake City is drawn from news coverage of those events. Additional information came from interviews with everyone present on the plaintiff's team.

CHAPTER 23

The story of the encounter in the lobby of the law offices of David Slader is drawn from my interviews with Stanley Saban Jr.

My account of the meeting at the law offices is drawn from interviews with the lawyers present, Dawn Krantz-Watts, and Stanley Saban Jr.

For information on the Oregon State Bar complaint and investigation into the alleged professional misconduct of Tim Kosnoff, I relied on the October 12, 2001, complaint letter from Stephen English and David Ernst of Bullivant, Houser, Bailey to the Oregon State Bar discipline manager; the March 10, 2003, letter of results from the bar's discipline counsel; and accompanying evidence.

CHAPTER 24

The Curtis II lawsuit, known as *BB, CB, JG, RG, WCL, DL, WJL, DM, SS, RS, CS and SR v. Corporation of the President of the Church of Jesus Christ of Latter-day Saints and Successors* was filed in Multnomah County Circuit Court on January 9, 2002. The church filed a Notice of Removal of Civil Action to the U.S. District Court for the District of Oregon on January 18, 2002. The matter was remanded back to Multnomah County Circuit Court on September 4, 2002. My account of the legal issues involved in those lawsuits comes from court records and transcripts of court hearings and depositions taken in conjunction with those lawsuits.

My account of the events involving Manny Saban are drawn from my interviews with him. Additional information came from my interviews with attorneys Tim Kosnoff and David Slader, and paralegal Dawn Krantz-Watts.

My account of the search for lawyers in Utah is drawn from interviews with Jeff Anderson, Tim Kosnoff, and Linda Walker. For additional information, I relied on news accounts in the *Salt Lake Tribune*.

Press accounts of the lawsuit against the church filed in Utah's Third District Court in Salt Lake City include Adam Liptak, "Scandals in the Church: The Lawyers; Flush Times for Legal Vanguard in Priest Lawsuits," *New York Times*, April 27, 2002, and Angie Welling, "Lawyer Ready to Fight LDS," *Deseret News*, June 5, 2002.

CHAPTER 25

My account of the settlement is drawn from my interviews with David Slader, Dawn Krantz-Watts, Stanley Saban Jr., Robert Goodall, and James Goodall. Additional information came from Multnomah County Court records.

The story of Bobby Goodall's return to the apartment complex, and the events surrounding that, are drawn from my interviews with Robert Goodall. Additional information came from Multnomah County criminal records.